Praise for *Aesthetics of Discomfort*

"Discomfort, in all its forms, is what most effectively pulls us out of ourselves and forces us to see the world in a new light. In this ambitious and wide ranging study, Aldama and Lindenberger put under the heat lamp a vast array of material from music, film, painting, and other arts to show us that only work that rearranges our perceptions of reality, that questions the many assumptions we operate under, and challenges us to view things in an entirely different fashion—in short, to directly question what we think we know—has anything real to teach us. An essential read."

—Wheeler Winston Dixon, University of Nebraska's Ryan Professor of Film Studies and author of *A History of Horror* and *Black & White Cinema: A Short History*

"A stroll through the architecture of discomfort by two non-architects could be, well, uncomfortable. Instead Lindenberger and Aldama treat their readers to fresh perspectives on familiar, if disquieting, places. During an itinerant conversation that wanders from caves to cities, past mausoleums, dungeons, 1950s tract houses, zoos, museums, and mid-century modern masterpieces where shape disregards function, they identify the purposeful loss of conventions of beauty in the modern era. They all but prove that discomfort is in the eye of the beholder."

—Kay Bea Jones, Professor of Architecture, The Ohio State University

"This book opens up territory that is by its nature not just discomforting but downright repellent and, therefore, rarely addressed with any discipline, much less theorized. It is the book that scholars and layreaders have been waiting for."

—H. Porter Abbott, University of California, Santa Barbara, author of *Real Mysteries: Narrative and the Unknowable*

"Who knew a discussion about discomfort could be so enjoyable! The reader is a welcome eavesdropper to a genuine, insightful, and wide-ranging conversation between scholars and friends. Refreshingly, Aldama and Lindenberger shed traditional academic shackles and engage multiple scholarly disciplines in their quest to understand the power of discomfort across a wide aesthetic palate. As a philosopher I imagined their conversation most at home not in Plato's Academy but in Aristotle's Lyceum. As a working jazz pianist they changed how I listen to and play the works of Thelonius Monk, among others. Their book will be a wonderful addition to courses in aesthetics. As an alternative—shall I say antidote?—to the academic journal article, it should be required reading for all graduate students in the Humanities!"

—Bill Vitek, Professor of Philosophy, Clarkson University and Jazz pianist, on Facebook at "A Fine Line Jazz"

"Taking the form of a dialogue between Aldama and Lindenberger, two scholars coming from different fields of research, theoretical orientations, and generational biases, *Aesthetics of Discomfort* is a lively, well informed, and fearlessly wide-ranging conversation about the forms of literature, architecture, art, and music that evoke feelings of disgust, sensations of nausea, or more complex forms of disquietude. More authentic-seeming than any linear argument, the book operates like a series of personal and thoughtful inquiries that urge us to consider our own experiences and examples. In visual arts, for example, the authors explore their own responses to the disfigured portraiture of Goya, Picasso, De Kooning, and Bacon. But anyone interested in contemporary art extremes not covered, whether the abject sausages of Dieter Roth and obscene puppetry of Paul McCarthy or the raw-meat performances of Carolee Schneemann and Karen Finley, would also find plenty to chew on. The authors' conversation made me feel like I was along for the ride—or for one of their long walks along Crissy Field in San Francisco—and learning new things about my own tastes in art in the process."

—Jori Finkel, Correspondent for *The Art Newspaper* and regular contributor to *The New York Times*

AESTHETICS OF DISCOMFORT

Aesthetics of Discomfort

CONVERSATIONS ON DISQUIETING ART

Frederick Luis Aldama and
Herbert Lindenberger

UNIVERSITY OF MICHIGAN

Ann Arbor

Published in the United States of America by the
University of Michigan Press
Manufactured in the United States of America
⊗ Printed on acid-free paper

2019 2018 2017 2016 4 3 2 1

A CIP catalog record for this book is available from the British Library.

ISBN 978-0-472-07300-9 (hardcover : alk. paper)
ISBN 978-0-472-05300-1 (paperback : alk. paper)
ISBN 978-0-472-12163-2 (ebook)

To our children
Corina Villena-Aldama
Michael Lindenberger
Elizabeth Lindenberger,
whose early aesthetic discomforts have
helped feed these conversations

Ugliness exists only because of Beauty, which is its positive premise. If there were no Beauty, there would be no ugliness, because the latter exists only as the negation of the former. Beauty is the original divine idea and its negation, ugliness, as it is a negation, has only a secondary existence. Not in the sense that the beautiful, because it is beautiful, may be ugly at the same time, but in the sense that the very properties that constitute the necessity of Beauty are converted into its opposite.

—Karl Rosenkranz, *Aesthetik des Häßlichen* [*The Aesthetics of Ugliness*] (1853)

[Ugliness] has not completely vitalized and controlled the material which it has taken within its action; and . . . this inability to execute its plan, this stammering and falling short in the utterance of its message, gives pain.

—John Bascom, *Aesthetics; or The Science of Beauty* (1886)

The value of an aesthetic experience is determined today not by the way a crisis is resolved but rather the way in which, after propelling us into a sequence of known crises determined by improbability, it forces us to make a choice. Confronted by disorder, we are then free to establish temporary, hypothetical systems of probability that are complementary to those systems that we could also, eventually or simultaneously, assume.

—Umberto Eco, *The Open Work* (1989)

Disgust offers an entirely different set of aesthetic and critical possibilities from the one offered by desire. . . . In its intense and unambivalent negativity, disgust thus seems to represent an outer limit or threshold of what I have called ugly feelings, preparing us for more instrumental or politically efficacious emotions.

—Sianne Ngai, *Ugly Feelings* (2005)

"Downers are good for the soul."

—Overheard on the San Francisco Muni Railway (2015)

Contents

Preface xi

Prologue: Scratching at the Surface of Discomfort 1

ONE
Digging *Deeper* at a Possible Theory for an Aesthetics of Discomfort 16

TWO
Bottoms Up 43

THREE
Awkward Spaces 58

FOUR
Noise to the Ears 93

FIVE
Retchful Art 117

SIX
Revolting Reels 155

Epilogue: Now *That's* Disquieting! 179

Works Cited 189

Index 199

Preface

These conversations began on our frequent walks over the years along Crissy Field, San Francisco's first landing field—notable at once for its close-up view of the Golden Gate and the fact that many brave pilots, long before the age of smart planes, crashed there to their fiery deaths. It was during these walks that we first discovered our mutual fascination by that segment of art, music, film, and literature that purposefully sought out a reaction of displeasure. Cage, Rabelais, Schoenberg, Bosch, Sade, Mapplethorpe were among that band whom we invited along with us—and whom we discuss at frequent points in these pages. In the spirit of these initial conversations, we have written a book in a conversational format that covers a range of none-too-pleasant notions based on conspicuously discomforting examples. Because most consumers of the arts seek out experiences based on what they take to be the pleasing and the beautiful, the ideas we discuss here have all too often been sidelined from serious aesthetic discussion. We hope that our discussions will provoke others to develop these ideas in greater depth.

Our book sets out to consider on its own terms the presence of art (literature, music, film, visual arts, and architecture, for instance) that *discomforts*. This is not art that has discomforting moments built into its design so as to ultimately bring us to some sort of feeling of catharsis or satisfaction. This is art that in its aims and goals seeks as its raison d'être from alpha to omega to disturb, discomfort, disquiet, and repulse. Of course, we are not the first to take on the subject of disquieting art. Our conversation will be joined by the formulations of others such as Aristotle, Hegel, Hume, Descartes, and Kant along with more contemporary theorists. We hope to enlarge the discussion à la *conversación de sobremesa* (a tradition in Latino culture of discussing subjects in great detail and at great length after dinner) about how the disquieting in and of itself is an essential ingredient in formulating theories of aesthetics—just as the beautiful is. It is there and exists in itself and by itself.

In *Aesthetics of Discomfort* we explore everything centrally relevant to the use of aesthetic devices in the creation of new shapes aiming to disquiet in as many of the arts as possible—without, of course being exhaustive. We consider the map *not* to be the territory. We know well that our book can't cover all the ground in the various arts. Yet we aim to be thorough in our exploration of examples, illustrating our approach to aesthetics and to the categories we use in aesthetics. We will consider first and foremost how the shaping devices respective of each art medium create disquieting objects. And this *novelty* can itself be disquieting. Hence, Baudelaire and Rimbaud and others in the nineteenth century and early twentieth century considered it an imperative to *make it new*; knowing well that the shock value of the new didn't last long, they were in permanent search of new forms, new shape-giving instruments. Hence, the explosion in literature of tools that became a trademark of the modernists.

In order to allow for a free-flowing yet far-reaching exploration of our topic, we envisioned a dialogue where a great many related topics might be broached in an economy of space. Though we are both scholars accustomed to publishing in a variety of different formats, choosing to give this topic the shape of a conversation allowed us to maintain our separate voices—and with these our differing experiences and knowledges, and also our sometimes differing judgments. Our aim: to create a judicious contrapuntal interplay of two independent voices that move in and around one another to create the total composition that brings to light a whole bandwidth of themes built in and around the discomforting in art. As the book unfolds, we use the term *discomforting* alongside and in overlapping ways with the subtype, *disquieting*—all with the clear sense that the former is a capacious term used to identify a wide swath of phenomena and experience and the latter the experience of violation of one's own quiet and protected, say, space.

An ongoing concern of this book is how it is that consumers of art have been able to overcome earlier resistances to particular artists and works, whether to Góngora's knotty poem *Polifemo,* or to Beethoven's late quartets, or to Picasso's *Les Demoiselles d'Avignon*. And we shall frequently invoke cognitive-development psychology as well as recent experiments in neuroscience that begin to explain phenomena of this sort.

Although our mode of presentation remains the conversations that took place between us, readers will also, we hope, discern an ongoing argument—namely, that art that discomforts us, even though it did not become predominant until the modernist revolution over a century ago, has always been with us, for example, as we'll show later, in the disconcerting (literally!) dissonances in Claudio Monteverdi's music, dissonances, moreover, that did not merely displease the more traditional-minded music theorists of his time but, until the advent of modernism, were repeatedly criticized by music historians adventurous enough to examine old and long-forgotten scores.

We've organized our conversations according to the artistic medium—literature, architecture, music, visual art, and film. Each of these media poses its own, distinct forms of discomfort. Each addresses different senses within the human body. For instance, a temporal form such as music or film, as we'll show, provides ongoing discomforts that differ from the more temporary discomfort to which a consumer is subjected in visual art. And each form is characterized by a distinct authorial engagement: while writing, painting, and music remain largely the activities of autonomous individuals, architecture and filmmaking (and operatic composition, as well) demand group participation and external financial interventions, no matter how independent the architect or auteur seeks to present himself—with the frequent result that the effects to which the work's creator seeks to subject his audience become compromised.

Our ensemble of contrapuntal voices comes together in the careful orchestration of exposition (prologue), development (its interior six chapters), and denouement (epilogue). The chapters are composed as follows. Chapter 1, "Digging *Deeper* at a Possible Theory for an Aesthetics of Discomfort," begins to give shape to a possible history of the different approaches to the disquieting in art in order to begin to consider the presence of the repulsive across all the arts. Here we reflect on how nineteenth-century avant-garde movements sought to break with traditions (realism or otherwise) as well as how some twentieth-century artists sought to *make new*; we therefore also consider concepts related to the hypothesis of *enstrangement* (as in Benjamin Sher's chosen neologism in his translation of Shklovsky's *ostranenie*, also a neologism) as foundational ingredients in a theory of aesthetics (not just an adjunct to it) inclusive of objects that disgust. (See Shklovsky's *Theory of Prose* xvii–xix.) Chapter 2, "Bottoms Up," considers several significant works of literature that exist largely to *discomfort* by authors such as Rabelais, Sade, Kureishi—even Shakespeare. Chapter 3, "Awkward Spaces," turns its focus to architecture in both its everyday, mundane, ugly forms and those that willfully use the ingredient of disquietude to *make new* our perceptions, thoughts, and feelings. Here we consider Wright, Le Corbusier, Loos, and Gaudí, among others. Chapter 4, "Noise to the Ears," attends to composers such as Schoenberg and Cage as well as various important musical phenomena such as, during the mid-twentieth century, musique concrète and heavy metal as well as musicians such as Boulez, Tom Waits, and the more contemporary techno and rap. In Chapter 5, "Retchful Art," we take into account artists such as Bosch, Brueghel, and Arcimboldo as well as the frequently discomforting art of today, including asylum art and the photography of Arbus and Mapplethorpe. In chapter 6, "Revolting Reels," we explore the function of the "disquieting" in films such as *Salò, Audition, Titus, Psycho, Clockwork Orange, From Dusk Till Dawn, Funny Games, Happiness*, and *Antichrist*.

With *Aesthetics of Discomfort* we argue that the category of the discomforting and of its subtype the disquieting constitutes a great stake in any move to formulate an aesthetic theory. What better way to tell this story of the art that discomforts and that plays such a central role in our search for a comprehensive aesthetics than as a conversation that includes more than us but that reaches out to you as the reader to participate in this exploratory journey of aesthetics in its myriad of discomforting forms?

Finally, we hope to stimulate as well as to further delineate a territory of study that scholars and professors will feel inspired to continue to explore—and to study anew. We imagine this might be especially interesting to a young generation of teachers and students readily oriented toward cultural phenomena that discomfort. We imagine, too, that many might shake heads with skepticism. We hope that the exploratory journey offered by the conversational format will lead others to enter the discussion, adding examples and counterexamples to deepen and refine our understanding of the properties and mechanisms that underlie our experience of art that discomforts.

Prologue: Scratching at the Surface of Discomfort

FREDERICK LUIS ALDAMA: In our book-length conversation we spotlight a subject you and I have spent a lot of time thinking and talking about: objects that discomfort from literature to music to film to visual arts and architecture—as many areas as possible where there is a deliberate incursion into the aesthetic domain of the discomforting.

HERBERT LINDENBERGER: Not just an incursion, Frederick. I think we can show that the discomforting is part and parcel of the aesthetic domain, that, in fact, it is central to the way we experience art.

FLA: We focus our attention on art that we variously identify as that which disgusts, discomforts, unnerves, offends as well as art that triggers in us experiences of pain and shame. It's art that we also identify as gross, cringe-worthy, and grotesque.

HL: I agree. Some identify more a psychological response, others a physical, and yet others a combination of the two.

FLA: For instance, we can be disgusted by a smell but also by a work of visual art, a poem, or a film. However, we can also experience this same sensation and emotion when we witness a grave injustice done to another person.

HL: And it scarcely matters if it's an actual smell we react to or the detailed description of a visit to a public bathroom in some novel. What happens within our body in real life and in something we classify as "art" is much the same. But beyond disgust, I suspect there are not many reactions that are so strikingly similar in art and life.

FLA: This is a very tricky problem, Herbie. Even in a realistic approach or realistic mode where the author's or artist's will to style is based on the use of realism (realism, not as defined by many scholars as a mirror image of reality or imitation of real life or anything in the universe, but a creation and *re-creation* of the chosen slice of reality), the end result (even the most accomplished) is that it will trigger a series of reactions such as disgust, but it will do so in its own *artistic, aesthetic way*. It will do so, that is, based on an elaborate work that is willed as something designed to exercise an aesthetic effect. For instance, in *The Autobiography of the Brown Buffalo* the author, Oscar "Zeta" Acosta, has his character describe his feces as a Dalí painting; that is, he describes something that normally causes disgust (feces) in a realist way and with humor to create an aesthetic effect that is at once gratifying (humor and style) and repulsive (the feces). As readers we experience the aesthetic attraction by obeying the dictum established by the author to appreciate the way he creates and re-creates the scene. We are taken to the domain of the aesthetic, but the content is repulsive, so we take a step back and find the description disquieting. But this disquieting (as with the grotesque in Rabelais, for instance, that we will discuss later) produces this aesthetic appreciation—this *awe*—in how the author's will to style gives shape to the repulsive, and that creates an aesthetic effect. That is, we have to consider the whole aesthetic effect, which thus includes the repulsion concerning the content *and* the admiration concerning the way this content is given shape. These are inseparable.

HL: When readers and viewers get roused up at what they see as disgusting, they usually lack the patience or the will to consider that the artist was transforming this content into something new.

FLA: In this consideration of the content and the shape given to this content in the total aesthetic effect we experience many other emotions, including shame. These are real emotions that are based on reality, but a reality that is *re-created* in specific ways by the authors and artists that include also our appreciation of just how well they have given shape to this content.

HL: Just as it takes some training for somebody to understand a difficult poem, so it demands training for people to see that what elicits unpleasant reactions may be something other than what they think it to be—that a disgusting object, whether visually or verbally transmitted, may have become a different object altogether by dint of its aesthetic transformation.

FLA: In our artful encounters negative feelings such as disgust and shame may seem to be most qualitatively like our everyday encounters in their degree of intensity. Perhaps this likeness, however, is more the result of academic formulation and not actual practice. Much momentum was gained after Freud (in "Three Essays on the Theory of Sexuality," for instance) identified shame and disgust as the primary psychic resistances against the libido. Both shame and especially disgust have been the subject of subsequent scholarship that seeks to identify our everyday protective responses. (I'm thinking of two otherwise unrelated Millers who use the word *disgust* in their book titles—Susan B. Miller in *Disgust: The Gatekeeper Emotion* and William Miller, *The Anatomy of Disgust.*) But perhaps we have been too quick to conflate the everyday response of disgust with the aesthetic effect that can trigger both the emotion of disgust and the emotion of appreciation and awe—simultaneously.

HL: It's harder for an artist to elicit feelings of shame than disgust even when shame is being overtly depicted, as in the many paintings of the naked Susannah being ogled by her grotesque elders. But a visual depiction of blood, as in Francis Bacon's picture of blood on the sidewalk, or of feces in whatever setting, makes us react with exclamations such as "That's *gross*!" And then there's the scandal perpetrated by that fraternal team, the two Chapmans, Jake and Dinos, whose sculpture, entitled *Piggyback,* depicting a teenage girl with a dismembered male member sticking out of her mouth had to be withdrawn from Rome's museum of twenty-first-century art after a complaint from a group representing the rights of minors (Povoledo). (Those Brits keep upping the ante in the shock effects they concoct for us!)

FLA: Repulsion for the sake of protection—as when we withdraw from the blood-dried, putrid smell of rancid meat. At the same time, we are oddly drawn to the rancid meat. We plug the nose but look through fanned fingers to see what could possibly cause such a stink, and if there might be something crawling out of the meat. Carolyn Korsmeyer considers this component of desire in things that disgust us as "the presence of allure packaged with aversion" (6). For Korsmeyer there would be a difference between, say, rancid meat and art that disgusts us. Such art, she writes, "commutes the disgusting properties of the object portrayed and achieves a more acceptable aesthetic emotive quality: tragic, grotesque, or comic, perhaps. The objects portrayed that would be disgusting in nature may be rendered so as to arouse pity, compassion, amusement, and so forth, but they lose their capacity to disgust" (40). Accordingly, art that discomforts would trigger reflection more than vomit. Again, however, I turn us back to the need for us to consider the *total aesthetic effect* whereby we experience all sorts of negative and positive emotions, including the emotion of admiration—if, of course, the artist's and author's will to style is such that the shape given to the aesthetic object triggers such a reaction.

HL: Korsmeyer's distinction here between "reality" and "art" is something that many contemporary artists have worked hard to break down. Bacon, not only with his pool of blood but with his innumerable grotesque faces; Damien Hirst, with his pickled animal parts; Pasolini, with his actors supposedly consuming turd sausages in *Salò*—all go to great lengths to make their viewers feel the reality of the awful things they see so that they will surely want to throw up. And it may well be that some of these viewers even rushed to the nearest restroom. But this sort of "reality" usually occurs only when something is new. The early audiences of Strauss's *Salome* evidently had a tough time dealing with the heroine kissing John's freshly bleeding head—to the point that the Metropolitan Opera halted its first production in 1907 after only a single performance. Nowadays *Salome* draws large crowds who, though recognizing the shocking subject matter, find themselves excited by the work's great music.

FLA: Is it that artists (contemporary or otherwise) have tried to break down the distinction between "reality" and "art"? As human beings we are part of the universe; whatever we call reality is this universe. No matter what we do (from tilling the soil to going to the bathroom), we are always dealing with reality—something out there. The difference is that we work with this reality out there in a special way when applying aesthetic goals. Moved by aesthetic goals, don't we add something to that reality out there by re-creating that thing out there? Given that all prime matter is taken from reality, do artists really want to break down the distinction between art and reality, or is it more that artists strip down and then reconstruct any and all aspects that make up our world? Put otherwise, don't they purposefully ingest, digest, and then release into the world a newly constituted matter that adds something to the universe?

I know we will talk more about this later, but if there is something clear in *Salò*, it is precisely that Pasolini proceeds on two levels: (1) to denounce fascism; (2) to present a critique of fascism in the most artificial way imaginable; the film proceeds according to a very choreographed series of scenes. He attacks the most brutal reality—fascism—through the most *art*ificial, highly stylized means. He wants to bring something *new* into the world. The film's content is a critique of fascism, but the shape of the film is almost balletic in its careful, high degree of choreography.

HL: Sade's novel, *The 120 Days of Sodom*, on which Pasolini's film is based, had also attempted to convert its characters' gross doings into elegant rituals. Yet there's a limit to the variations an author can work on who is doing what to whom—eating one another's feces, positioning oneself for sex, flatulating into the mouths of others—and having to fill up

120 days inevitably led to boredom, at least for the reader if not necessarily for the participants. (To be sure, Sade can work up more variations in acts of violence [sadism, no less!] than with feces and sex.) Through the novel's repetitiveness our disgust wanes; disgust, one might speculate, cannot survive repetition. Pasolini, by contrast, in his less than two hours playing time, allows us to experience the gross and the elegant at once without the slightest boredom. And all of this is subsumed under the director's powerful antifascist message.

FLA: Disgust doesn't survive repetition, indeed. Hence, the seeking to make new by artists of discomfort. Let us return to this concept and to that of the juxtaposition of the disparate in the making of new, discomforting art later in our conversation.

For now, we can say that this can take place visually, verbally, and aurally and in any combination thereof. We see this clearly in the example Colin McGinn gives in his recounting of this joke: "How do you know your sister has her period? Because your dad's cock tastes funny" (210). The effect: the juxtaposition of unpleasant images make new each of the images taken on their own. However, I'm pretty certain that most of us would twist up our minds in disgust more than we would laugh.

HL: I'm not sure about the intent of the joke—to make us laugh or cringe—but it is certainly the case that many contemporary artists refuse to be funny about these juxtapositions in their art-making, with the result that they can really manage to gross us out.

FLA: Interestingly, we rarely hear the use of the term *gross* when it comes to aesthetic theory. Perhaps it's too base a term for high-minded scholarship—even if the latter's focus is on the base. Or perhaps it's that gross art is art that does not have as its main purpose the aim of discomforting audiences, but rather to flaunt its coarseness, its vulgarity, and its bad taste.

HL: Vulgar, you'll recall, is from the Latin *vulgaris* of the mob.

FLA: Yes, and so we might even interrogate an expression like "in bad taste" as this carries with it a certain snobbery—an implicit hierarchy in art where none in actuality is to be found—that an aesthetics of discomfort seeks to dash to the ground. Of course, we would not be the first to see this. In *Anatomy of Disgust* William Miller considers how the ideological use of disgust creates artificial hierarchies of difference between the bourgeoisie and proletariat. For Miller, the way one uses disgust can act as a distancing mechanism: to increase or diminish the distance felt between social classes.

HL: One of the classic authors whom Miller most often quotes is, not surprisingly, Jonathan Swift. When, for instance, he cites the line from "The Lady's Dressing Room," "Oh! Celia, Celia, Celia shits" (69), much of the horror comes from the poet's discovery that a classy female can engage in such unbecomingly offensive behavior. The poem exercises a special discomfort for me since both my mother and one of my granddaughters bear the lady's name.

FLA: "All shit stinks the same," as they say in today's common parlance. We know well from common sense and the formulations of others that have come before that ideology often sticks to objects of disgust. In 1993 I visited a friend in New York and went to the Whitney Museum's exhibition titled "Abject Art: Repulsion and Desire in American Art." The exhibit aimed to bring me to that place where disgust, ethics, and ideology seem to want to mishmash—an area traveled by others, including Julia Kristeva. (With "abject" in the title of the exhibit, the connection to her 1980-published book, *Horror: An Essay in Abjection*, was made clear.) Kristeva formulated how art and ethics are connected through the practice of desire, recognition, and misrecognition in the way we construct a sense of ourselves vis-à-vis that which is not ourselves—objects or otherwise. Perhaps her idea of misrecognition (formulated within her theory of abjection as that which is removed from the body and made Other) can be more commonsensically understood as our experience of that which makes us cringe.

HL: Cringing is one of the most common varieties of aesthetic discomfort, including, surely, such emotional reactions as shame and embarrassment. Imagine one of those monologue plays that have become the fashion in recent years. The actor is demonstrating the functions of the various apertures characterizing the human body, together with the fluids emanating from each. Even if he is able to elicit a laugh here and there, you—and presumably your fellow audience members—stare straight ahead, for it would prove too embarrassing to share your (at best, mild) amusement with your neighbor. The cringing I'd experience in this sort of situation is really a form of pain.

FLA: Yes, I think of this often when I teach film. My students often mention how the viewing of such and such a film pains them. Does it *really*, I wonder. I mean, I don't experience physical pain the way I do when, for instance, my seven-year-old pinches me—even if in the spirit of play.

HL: Although direct physical pain such as a child's pinching may tap a different part of the brain from cringing, the pinch you describe, Frederick, is far less unpleasant than most instances of cringing when watching an uncomfortable movie or the monologue play I just imagined.

FLA: Yes, pinching causes pain as a neurophysiological reaction to an immediately physical cause. There's no appraisal or any other cognitive mediation. When Corina was a baby and would arbitrarily pinch me to get a reaction, it would cause me immediate pain, but it was a pain that disappeared immediately. The cognitive faculties are not involved in any way. Whereas when we watch a discomforting film or a theater production or view a piece of art and cringe, this is always a mediated response. It can be a much more long-lasting effect—and this precisely because it involves both the cognitive and emotional systems.

HL: Even when we complain of having a negative emotional response to a work, the cognitive element in this experience has also caused us to think about our response and also, perhaps, about how precisely the work went about eliciting this effect on us. I consider this sort of discomfort a way of contributing to our intellectual growth.

FLA: Perhaps we can add some nuance, too, to how artists build into and give shape to discomfort in their art. I feel uneasy when I view a vegetable painting by Giuseppe Arcimboldo, but not to the point of nausea as I do when listening to a Cage composition.

HL: Can music, even music that, like Cage's, often irritates, actually set off nausea? For me, at least, nausea needs one of the representational arts such as painting or film, to be ignited properly. Like when I saw a wedge of well-holed Swiss cheese covered with black human hair in a recent retrospective at MoMA of that great master of discomfort, the installation artist Robert Gober. The nausea welled powerfully up in my esophagus until I read the label, which explained that Gober, though using real hair (his own, perhaps?), had made the cheese wedge out of beeswax. Once I could accept it as make-believe, my digestive system calmed down.

FLA: For me it is less a question of the type of art—that is, the medium or the genre—than it is the artist who willfully creates an object that disgusts. Perhaps Aurel Kolnai can shed light on this topic. Kolnai has written much on the topic of disgust, including a succinct piece titled "The Standard Modes of Aversion: Fear, Disgust and Hatred," wherein he writes how "disgust adheres to and penetrates its object rather than merely signaling and portending their disquieting presence or proximity; it is inseparable from an intrinsic interest in the object" (586–87). While Kolnai delineates the experience of disgust at the physical (olfactory/gustatory) and moral levels (among others), for my purposes here it is his identification of it as an "eminently aesthetic emotion" (587) that is important to keep in mind. That is, he considers it as resulting from the relationship created between the object and the subject.

HL: Kolnai's powerful phenomenological analysis of disgust suggests what a special place this feeling occupies in our reactions to art: the object-relatedness that Kolnai claims can be tied to the objects that, say, a painter or filmmaker presents to us in all their obnoxious detail. Kolnai also argues for the special power of hatred among the emotions (590–93), but the emotional effects of hatred in art can't compare to those for disgust: we may hate the villain in a romance, but this hatred is no more than an instrument that the writer uses in order ultimately to resolve a complicated plot. I suspect that a brain scan of us in the process of reading would show starkly different results between disgust and hate. After finishing a novel about some hateful character, we don't usually brood about the character, but our feelings of nausea can easily be reawakened when we think of disgusting images we recently experienced in some work of art. Disgust can be so excruciating an emotion (perhaps because of the acute discomfort and even embarrassment you feel when throwing up) that it's had a special attraction for people writing on aesthetics: just think of such recent full-length philosophical books on the topic by the likes of Menninghaus, Korsmeyer, William Miller, Susan Miller. Whereas literary and visual works featuring feces readily give me twinges of nausea, a poem so full of hate as Sylvia Plath's "Daddy" does not awaken analogous feelings against the author's object of hate but, at least in my case, it makes me empathize with the poem's emotionally damaged speaker.

FLA: I fear I empathize more with the villain who is disquieting—ugly, even—in physical form more than the one who is pretty but morally suspect: Richard III more than Shakespeare's Aaron in *Titus Andronicus*. Keep in mind that both create discomfort in their choice of actions. That is, their actions trigger an emotional reaction that is tied to codes of behavior—and in this case, an ugly moral outlook. Let us not forget, too, its etymology in Old Norse: *uggligr* as derived from *uggr* fear.

HL: In the course of our conversations the various things that we and other people deem to be moral will never be distant from our discussion of the discomforting emotions central to our arguments.

FLA: Artists, directors, architects, novelists, and so on use devices to give shape to discomforting art; they look for shapes that will unsettle us and take us away from our comfort zone. As mentioned already in our Preface, Victor Shklovsky used the neologism, *ostranenie* (translated by Sher with his neologism *enstrangement*) to describe how authors, artists, and the like, reorient our sense of an object not by distancing us from it, but by drawing us ever more deeply into it. To put it simply and in Shklovsky's words, creators "make a stone feel stony" (*Theory of Prose* 6). In distilling, then reconstructing those objects that fill up the world and that we've become habituated to, they create something new that in its turn creates a new kind of relationship with the subject, a new aesthetic relation with the subject

Like any other aesthetic effect, then, the sense of discomfort is to be located not in the object nor in the subject but in the relation between the object and the subject. We can already say in advance, therefore, that this relationality is flexible and changeable in time and place. We'll talk more at length on this issue, but what is discomforting yesterday might not be today or even a few years after its appearance (rock and roll and comic books, for instance). And artists modify their discomforting shapes depending on their political, social, ideological environment, and this determines how they make it new.

To this I should add that neuroscience (fMRI images, for instance) can give us snapshots of aesthetic effects (reception) on the brain, and these will vary according to the modifications: the shape-giving of the brain as we encounter a given art object will vary according to the time and place that we perceive and consume it.

HL: And we are still early in our understanding of what happens in the brain when we are experiencing art. It remains to be seen if we'll ever be able to see what happens inside the brains of artists while in the process of creating something new.

FLA: In all artists we have this will to style—this impulse to use devices to make their art new and to elicit the interest of readers, audiences, viewers, and so on. This will to style for those like Rabelais, Joyce, Borges, Cage, Pasolini, and Picasso is not only accepted, but applied—and applied within a sharp awareness of the fact that newness in and of itself is neither an aesthetic value nor a long-lasting value. It can be very ephemeral. This making new takes place with the preservation of certain grammatical rules; we read Joyce's discomforting work all while appreciating how he deforms classic patterns of grammar and generic forms. When Borges was a young author, he made new by creating surprising syntactic moments in his early short stories. However, he realized quite quickly that these artificial means put an expiration date on his text. In his later work he *made new* all while allowing the reader to appreciate the extraordinary way he used classic syntax.

Discomforting art is valuable in general because of its enstranging effect—the willfulness of the artist to make it new. However, as we've said, discomforting art can also be very ephemeral and marked with an expiration date.

HL: We can't expect what was initially shocking to retain its strong effect over time, though a few works come close to doing so. But something of that shock remains a factor in our experience of, say, *Ulysses*, of both Wilde's and Strauss's *Salomes*, and of *Les Demoiselles d'Avignon*. And for some works, Schoenberg's *Erwartung*, for example, or, to go back to the Baroque period, Gesualdo's madrigals or Góngora's poems, time does little to mitigate this strong effect. I still have no satisfactory explanation for why the discomfort that's set off by certain works lessens over time, while other works pretty much retain their disconcerting power. Recently I spent a few weeks going line by line through Góngora's two major poems, the *Polifemo* and *Soledades*; at best I could finish 200 to 250 lines a day. It was pure agony but it's some of the most dazzling poetry I know. This was the sweetest discomfort imaginable.

FLA: During our conversations we will, of course, be exploring in more detail such terms as the horrible, distasteful, and repulsive as well as others like the grotesque. And we will be able to give some of these categories substance by turning to the cognitive and neurobiological sciences as well as to aesthetic theory—especially attending to those respective formal devices that give music, art, film, architecture, and literature their discomforting shapes.

Let me amplify on what I mean here by aesthetic shaping devices. I consider the category of *shape* as the main tool for any understanding of aesthetics generally as well as all the subdivisions of all the art we consider in this book. Furthermore, in addition to this formal shaping device (or shaping device that gives form) operating to create subdivisions within artistic activities (music, architecture, film, and the like) it is also the creator of all the subdivisions within aesthetics such as comic, tragic, heroic—and, of course, the grotesque.

HL: As we'll see when we take up literature, a seemingly innocuous technical device such as free indirect discourse—in which a narrator in fiction, while still using the third person, goes inside the mind of a character—can dramatize the latter's anxieties and distress with greater immediacy than either a first-person or a conventional third-person account. And the reader shares in the character's world to a degree that he or she wouldn't without this powerful device.

FLA: The use of formal shaping devices such as the intermixing of a narrator's omniscience with a character's limited point of view in literature can and does create new phenomena. Other arts, of course, deploy other devices. On a more basic level, we see how architecture and painting are separate activities, yet architects and painters constantly mix these: we have murals painted on walls of buildings and architects who incorporate sculptures into facades on their buildings. We see all kinds of mixtures of the big divisions we consider in our book, from literature to music to architecture to visual arts to filmmaking—arguably, the most monumental and now most common form of this mixture.

HL: The violation of the boundaries between genres and art forms that people at any particular time took to be normative often creates considerable distress for art consumers regardless of the content of the works they are trying to deal with. What was once a mixture of genres or a mixture of art forms can eventually become a new genre or art form. The process by which this happens has occasioned great aesthetic wars, especially in the more classicizing cultures such as France and Italy. Today some of the most radical mixing goes on within what we call conceptual art, which often distresses museumgoers to the point that, as often happened with earlier movements, above all, at the beginning of modernism, they keep asking whether "this is really art."

FLA: Indeed, Herbie, the discomforting in art can and does function to take us out of the art—to create a disruption in the reality effect; it can and does expose the artifice or constructedness of the art. However, there are those like Winfried Menninghaus (in the tradition of Kant) who considers the fact of our tremendous physical and psychological reaction to discomforting art as leading to the collapse of any distinction between us (the subject) and the art (the object). I'm not sure I've had the experience of being so disturbed that I've lost sight of the boundaries between myself and the object, yet there might be something to his formulation.

HL: As Menninghaus shows, disgust has played a role in German aesthetics from Lessing and Kant to the present day. The very word *Ekel*, which is actually the German title of his book, exercises a visceral effect that the Latinate terms *dégout* and *disgust*, which refer to taste, do not have. Having been raised by German-speaking parents, I get twinges of nausea at the very sound of the word *Ekel*.

FLA: No matter the degree of presence and use of disquieting devices in giving shape to aesthetic forms, they work within and against (sometimes to the point of destruction) rules, restrictions, and self-imposed restraints. The device of perspective that became the norm in painting from the Renaissance to the end of the nineteenth century was used, abused, and made new by Picasso when he created objects that we could see simultaneously from multiple angles.

HL: That of course was the purported theory behind cubism. It could provide a new way of seeing things as they "really" were. But that's not how viewers actually have seen them. For early viewers Picasso and Braque were willfully distorting what several centuries of painters had painstakingly taught us to see as "real." As time went on, the disquieting shock of cubism became absorbed and even routinized, and Picasso had to go on to a succession of new period styles that he kept inventing, and these could now disquiet us in new and different ways.

FLA: Picasso and Braque mentioned that there was nothing new in cubism, that they were simply reflecting reality more accurately and that cubism stuck more closely to the realistic genre in painting. By dashing perspective to the floor, they were returning to pre-Renaissance techniques (not entirely of course). I'm thinking of the shift from pre-Renaissance uses of flat, two-dimensional representation to the time of the Renaissance when artists developed the tool of perspective—the geometric trick of giving the illusion to a third dimension. This allowed these artists to geometrize stories in a more textured way with more characters and scenes, filling out a more layered representation of time and space. It's quite possible that the introduction of perspective discomforted many a Renaissance viewer.

By the early twentieth century it seemed as if there was nothing that could not be re-created by artists. The new generation of artists who sought *to make new* sought other ways to make art. Picasso and Braque, as we know, were huge admirers of African masks; they incorporated into their art the way of geometrizing of stories used in Africa. They returned to the flat, two-dimensional painting of the pre-Renaissance; they also began to use protean versions of the readymade with their painted collages that mixed paint with found objects. In Kandinsky's work we see the discarding of story altogether and simply the conversion of art into pure form.

Following on the tail of all these artists were the monochromatic works à la Ad Reinhardt. They don't trigger disgust in the subject matter they represent, but rather as a result of repetition and monotony. When I walked from one room to another in Florence's Uffizi viewing so many (ad nauseam) iterations of the Virgin Mary, boredom led to the feeling of wanting to vomit. That is all to say, both perspective and the lack of perspective are *shape-giving* devices that can and do lead to discomfort.

HL: Not for me! I lived in Florence for about a year and got to the Uffizi regularly (this was in the days before those long lines). The differences between artists rendering the same mother-and-child often in the same pose was of the greatest interest.

FLA: *Suum cuique pulchrum est*—right, Herbie? We will necessarily also need to consider how the use of the disquieting as the dominant shaping device in a given art object can be destroyed by its opposites: boredom and laughter. For all its aims to discomfort, the blank canvas in the museum can be boring. For me, it's not disturbing like Picasso's *Guernica* or *Les Demoiselles d'Avignon*.

HL: Not necessarily, Frederick. In the mid-twentieth century there was a lot of experimenting with monochrome paintings—like the black paintings of Reinhardt or the white, or off-white, ones of Robert Ryman, which teased you into looking hard for subtleties in texture underneath the paint surface (looking for subtle differences among black or white paintings has the same interest for me as looking for differences between Renaissance Madonna-and-child pictures). But I realize a lot of people simply get bored by these seemingly monochrome paintings, or, even worse, they think the painter is pulling their legs.

FLA: Clearly, you are the intended, ideal audience of the Reinhardt and Ryman paintings, Herbie. You've had more experience with this art and in this way, I would say, it has educated you more than me to step into the shoes of the ideal audience. Artists create with the intention of triggering certain responses in us—and their blueprints, say, can educate us to know how to experience it—but the artists can't control how their flesh-and-blood consumers will experience the art.

HL: These so-called flesh-and-blood consumers can all be taught how to view works of art—for instance, to see the subtlety in the textures and even find bits of other colors in the seemingly monochrome paintings I just mentioned. But an audience's reaction can only be controlled up to a point.

FLA: We've all had the experience in the cinema when an audience laughs instead of shrieks while watching a horror film. Often, this is a consequence of the audience's distinguishing between what is old hat and something innovative as well as its understanding that which is blatantly bad and that which is well made. No matter the reason, when an audience of an art object that aims to horrify or repulse reacts in the opposite way with laugher and glee, we see in action how something like laughter can be the greatest dissolvent of the aesthetic category of the discomforting—and all others, for that matter.

HL: Shock effects within a particular work do not last forever. As we've said, the horrendous doings in ancient castles that once sent shudders through readers of early Gothic novels now elicit easy laughter. Could it be that the shower scene in that great horror film *Psycho* will eventually seem pretty funny?

FLA: This is a great and very relevant question, Herbie. Yes, over time cultural phenomena can change from triggering disgust to something that's even laughable. The reception can and does run counter to the aims (explicit or implicit) of the artist, director, composer, and author. There is undoubtedly an erosion that takes place over time of the *aesthetic shape* of the object.

Changes in society (social, economic, political) also produce changes in the reception of art. The making and consuming of art is a social activity. It changes in time as our knowledge and technology of making change—and all this, of course, takes place within and between people. Likely sometime in the future *Psycho* as well as some other great horror movies will appear funny to audiences.

To this, however, there is the added phenomenon of the expiration date. Some products are made with a short expiration date—this happens with a lot of gore films, for instance. They rely on singular ingredients that shock, and then it's over. The shape of the genre is very limited—like pornography as a genre. What makes it *new* is not its willful use of various shape-giving devices, but the presentation of something we have not seen in the genre before. So some products aim exclusively at producing disquieting reactions and thus have a short expiration date.

The change in the reception of a film, novel, music, and so on, over time and the quick degree of obsolescence of certain artistic products such as gore or pornographic films are more likely to take place when the artistic product is not thickly layered and thus is not prone either to subtle interpretations or to many repeat visits. You listen to or view it once and you don't feel compelled to return for a recapitulation of the experience. This might be the difference between a *Walking Dead* TV show and a novel such as *Gargantua and Pantagruel*.

That is, if the artist (director, author, musician, architect) builds such a sturdy design that we feel compelled for repeat visits, the art *does* indeed stand up against any and all pressures of shifts in social, political, and economic contexts. This has consequences in terms of the permanency and longevity of the genres. For instance, in the creating of *Tales of the Kolyma* Russian author Varlam Shalamov uses such a tight integration of form with content that we can't help but react with both a kind of sublime awe and deep disgust. The turns of phrase are so well sculpted and the observation of the narrator so attentive to details, and the use of synecdoche so powerful that we experience an odd mixture of emotion toward the Siberian labor-camp guards and torturers. We feel simultaneously a gut-wrenching discomfort and a deep admiration for Shalamov's extraordinary skill at giving shape to these tales.

HL: If a work can make people feel comfortable about their *discomfort*, the more the merrier!

FLA: Herbie, as we will continue to explore, we will note that the aesthetic (discomforting or otherwise) exists *not* in the *object* (Reinhardt's monochromatic works) *nor* in the *subject* (in the way we look at things), but in the relationship created by the artist between the subject and the object—and this relationship changes historically (as we've seen in the compressed history of painting in Europe given above) and also changes as we in the role of subjects have come to see ourselves over time. An aesthetic phenomenon doesn't have a permanent hold in the object or the subject. It has a fluctuating, flexible, always evolving home in the relationship between the subject and the object.

HL: And as I look back at myself as an individual subject, this relationship has changed steadily over time—for example, in the new art I'm experiencing, in the way that this experience with new art has changed the way I reexperience earlier art, in the way that changes within myself and in the world around me have made me rethink what I believe art should say and be. Nothing remains the same, and certainly not the forms in which my discomfort can manifest itself.

FLA: Perhaps our book will help answer this question and many others for us as well as our readers. Are we overreaching in our hope that this book might provide a framework—a model, a seedbed—for our readers in their analysis of just how we experience real, discomforting emotions in our encounter with aesthetic objects that also include emotions of admiration?

ONE | Digging *Deeper* at a Possible Theory for an Aesthetics of Discomfort

FREDERICK LUIS ALDAMA: Herbie, we are so used to teaching and writing about art that ultimately pleases, I wonder if our focus on art that discomforts will in fact be a possible mapping out of an anti-Western art tradition?

HERBERT LINDENBERGER: I don't find it in the least "anti-Western." It's part and parcel of the Western tradition. To be sure, "uncomfortable" stuff became a mainstay of the arts during the twentieth century, but if you look back in time—at Greek satyr plays as nasty comments upon lofty tragedies, or at what Erich Auerbach called "creatural realism" in a writer such as Rabelais (276–77) you realize that it's always been around, as we can show in more detail in the section on literature.

FLA: It's certainly centrally present, but I for one have shied away from teaching (and writing on) art that discomforts. When I have crossed into the forbidden territory, it has largely been via art and theories that consider aesthetics from the point of view of how we move through moments of discomfort to experience pleasure.

HL: Throughout Western tradition, as we know, theorists of art have advocated the need of viewers to move from negative to positive feelings. It's already there in Aristotle's theory of catharsis (22), however we may debate the exact physical nature of the process he refers to. Although a tragedy, according to the theory, excites feelings of fear and pity in us (feelings, moreover, that we may already have brought with us to the theater, like the germs we carry in our bodies), the plot mechanism that the dramatist has concocted sets off the catharsis that allows us to leave the theater feeling good. Similarly, Kant, in describing the sublime, stresses the "purposiveness" in the process by means of which we reach "a pleasure that is possible only by means of a displeasure" (117).

FLA: But why should it have to be this way? Why can't the unpleasantness simply be *there*?

HL: It certainly shouldn't have to be that way, and, at least since the advent of modernism a century ago, a lot of practitioners in all the arts have demonstrated that "displeasure" can be central to a work without leading its viewers to pleasure—at least in any traditional sense of that word.

FLA: What we seem to be getting at is how creators make objects whose design serves the purpose of creating discomfort in the reader, onlooker—the subject; that is, this discomfort grows from a specific relation created by the artist between the object and subject.

HL: I hear echoes here of Wolfgang Iser and the various reader-response theorists of a generation ago.

FLA: Absolutely, Herbie. Iser had much to offer in terms of understanding how this relationality is constructed within the minds of readers. However, the scale is tipped so far in the direction of the receiving subject that such reader-response formulations forget about the presence of the creator in creating an object that establishes a relationship with the subject.

HL: Reception theory, which hit big during the 1970s, now looks like an extreme attempt to undo the stress that earlier theories had put on the role of the artist-creator, especially during the nineteenth century. And it also sought to undo the stress that others, like the New Critics, had placed on the so-called work itself. You seem here to be trying a strike a better balance between the artist or the work, on the one hand, and the consumers, whom the reception-minded concentrated on.

FLA: It is certainly the case that in all my work, Herbie, I've tried to keep this tripartite model centrally in mind: creator-work-audience. I'd like us to turn the clock back a bit to earlier formulations on aesthetics more generally. We don't need to rehearse the long history of thinkers who considered aesthetics *grosso modo*, but it is useful to turn for a moment to philosopher Alexander Baumgarten's *Aesthetics* (1750), written during a time when "aesthetics" became a conceptual category in and of itself. Baumgarten could write a book on aesthetics only at the moment when human activity had created a separate domain for objects and their *relationships* with humans—what we might identity as the *aesthetic relation*.

HL: Creating this separate domain satisfied the need that many thinkers during the eighteenth century—much more in France and Germany than in England, to be sure—felt to classify areas of thought. If people went out into nature to observe plants for the purpose of classification, why not treat art so that it, like botany, could function as an autonomous realm with its own particular species (genres)?

FLA: Categories delineate and give order to objects we seek to study; they helped define aesthetics as that which exists within the totality of reality, but as a subsystem with its own interrelating systems. Mario Bunge's formulation of a *systematism* is useful in this regard. He writes, "Systematism postulates that *every concrete thing and every idea is a system or a component of some system*. Therefore, every inquiry into an object (or an idea) ought to include a study of its environment, which in turn requires embedding the study in the system of human knowledge" (286). A scientist *discovers* (or unveils) a previously unknown existing feature of reality and determines its place within a system of knowledge, a science. An artist *creates* (conceptually or materially) a previously nonexisting item, and this item is a system that becomes a new addition to reality, even though its ingredients are always necessarily taken from reality.

HL: A scientist *finds*; an artist *makes* (or at least he pretends to).

FLA: Yes, we can and must distinguish between discovery (the realm of science) and creation (the realm of art). Since the seventeenth century philosophers have put human beings at center stage. Therefore, the concept of beauty and other aesthetic concepts were also centered on human beings. In René Descartes's *Passions of the Soul*, for instance, we find these words: "When the first encounter with some object surprises us, and we judge it to be new, or very different from what we knew in the past or what we supposed it was going to be, this makes us wonder and be astonished at it" (52).

HL: His language certainly anticipates that of the eighteenth-century sublime. The words *wonder* and *astonish* are central to its vocabulary. Though not of course to the concept of the beautiful, which did not depend on discomfort and in fact defined itself through its distance from disquieting emotions. The wonder and astonishment that Descartes describes here when we encounter something unanticipated represent the kind of jolt that often results in discomfort—as readers of this book may have felt when they first noted the Robert Arneson self-portrait on the cover.

FLA: I detect a strong odor of philosophical idealism wafting through the air with Descartes. We of course find this as well in Plato's formulations. According to Plato, all aesthetic objects as well as all aesthetic concepts find their true reality or their truest nature not in this world but in the world identified as the *topos uranus* where all that pertains to this world has its ideal counterpart.

Perhaps Aristotle's materialist worldview sheds more light on how the discomforting fits within a comprehensive theory of aesthetics. Yet he still considered all artistic creation as *an imitation*—as a mimesis of the real world. Like its many other variants through history, this view posits that we have reflectors or mirrors that simulate the real world, so the world is in effect split in two. It is more naturalistic in explanation than Plato's theory, but it is still dualistic.

Plato and Aristotle attempt to get at a unified aesthetics but come up short because they don't see how music, art, literature, architecture, and so on, are products of human activity that are identified and acquire a signification, a meaning (a sense) only in what I have been calling an aesthetic relation.

HL: So exactly where do things happen in art—in the "work itself," in us, or in some "neutral" realm?

FLA: As briefly mentioned earlier, I would say that the aesthetic is not to be found in the object nor in the subject but in the relation between the two. If this is the case, and I'm pretty certain it is, then we can understand how the aesthetic is built into *any* creative activity. The ugly and discomforting is not *in* the object, it is *in* the relation between the subject and object. To break it down, in all aesthetic relations, we have (1) a subject—the individual who creates the work of art; (2) the work of art itself that we can call the blueprint (ugly or otherwise); and (3) the consumer who completes the blueprint.

HL: And we also have the whole tradition that stands behind the author and the work—the various conventions that the work utilizes, the earlier works it echoes and that are also awakened in the reader. So there is a whole bunch of relationships actually taking place in the making and consumption of art. And evaluation doesn't mean just deciding whether something is good or bad (though it does that too), but above all it means deciding what earlier materials you're finding it appropriate to select for your work, and, from the consumer's point of view, how you're going to react to it, what mental resources and personal experiences (including earlier aesthetic experiences) you want to bring to it and to the whole tradition standing behind the work.

FLA: Nicely stated, Herbie. There are of course other aesthetic relations that are created not of our creation (utilitarian, artisanal, or artifacts built for the sake of aesthetic response) that we find in nature. Some of these naturally made objects are quite discomforting—like that species of fruit we call quince (figure 1).

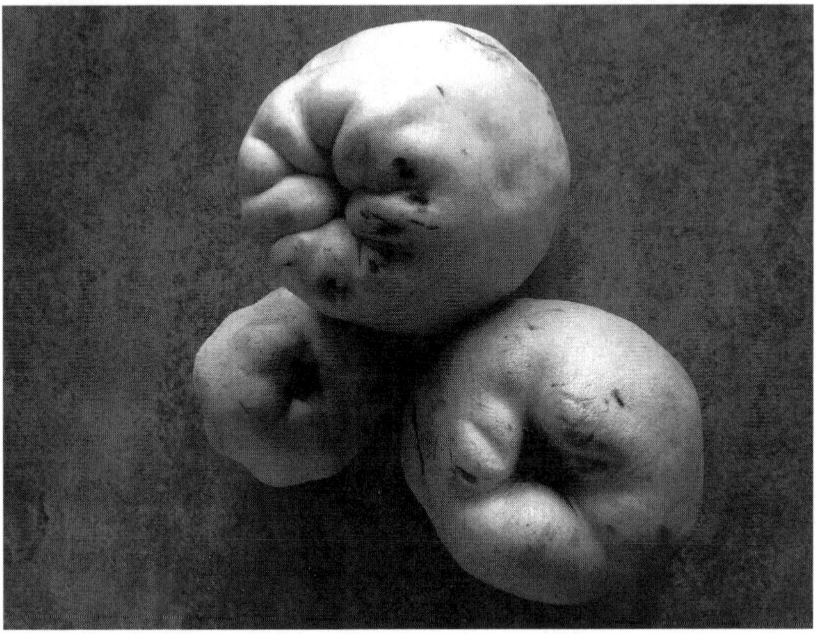

Figure 1. Trio of quince. Photo by Herbert Lindenberger.

Its bulbous shape is off-putting in the extreme. The discomfort of viewing it is matched by its taste, which is coarse and insipid. Bite into it, and it's also likely to break any loose teeth in your mouth.

HL: You present some of nature's uglier side (though I might add that quince can be made into quite comforting jam), but there are beautiful things in nature that can create considerable discomfort—like the large rattlesnake I passed on a trail last week as I was walking up the Santa Cruz Mountains (figure 2).

It was at once scary and beautiful—nicely coiled up in such a way that it looked potentially ready to strike. Two frightened young women passing me by warned me to keep my distance. A guy behind me on the trail started looking for a rock so he could kill it, but there were no big-enough rocks in sight, and I felt relieved since I hated to see a beautiful creature like that wiped out. And I suspect that its scariness added to my aesthetic experience—an experience perhaps not so much of the beautiful but of the sublime as it was defined in the late eighteenth century. (To be honest, I wasn't quite as scared as the

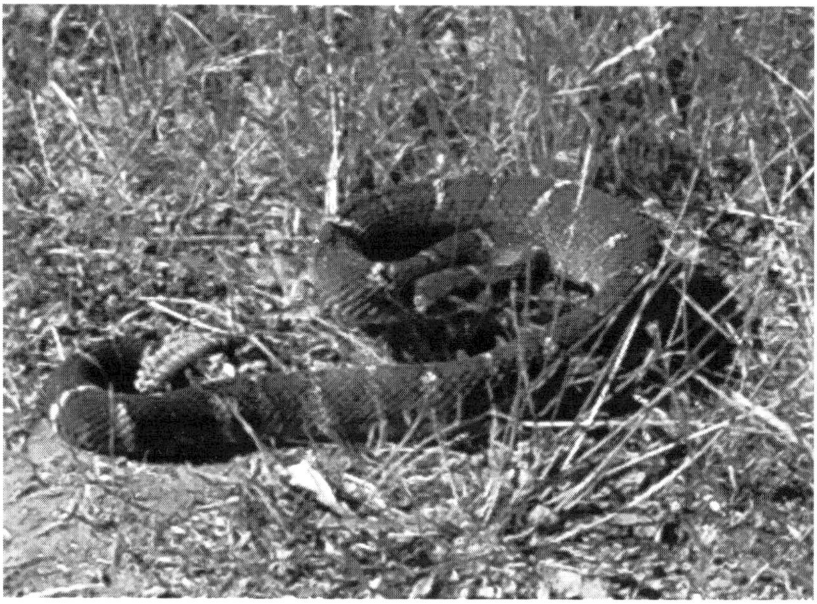

Figure 2. Rattlesnake on trail, Santa Cruz Mountains, California. Photo by Herbert Lindenberger.

viewer might think, for I was using my zoom, which meant I could keep a distance of four feet!) But your point is well taken: objects in the natural world can be quite discomforting, but, as with this snake, we can also find some of the same power (including scariness) in them that we do in certain uncomfortable works of art.

FLA: We often hear people say that there is beauty in nature or that nature is beautiful. They often also say that a car is beautiful. This language might risk an essentialist outlook. Perhaps it would be more accurate to say that we *find* beauty in nature, cars, and so on. But even this formulation is not entirely accurate. Whether we use the word *is* or the word *find* we don't escape the risk of essentialism entirely. We adopt an aesthetic relation toward nature and the other objects such as a car when our attitude is one of "disinterestedness"—to use Kant's concept. But are we disinterested or rather highly interested in the object we're observing and judging as beautiful—snake or otherwise? I think the concept of disinterest also falls short. This is so because what's involved in our ascription of beauty to nature, a car, or even an Apple product such as an iPhone is the establishment of a specific relationship of the observer with the object. We've been calling this the aesthetic relation.

Human-made aesthetic relations involve the exercise in a specific and directed way of all the mechanisms involved in our everyday relational activities. Those activities that allow us to (*a*) create knowledge and transform nature, society, and ourselves as humans and (*b*) to create aesthetic artifacts that obey their own laws in terms of their creation (author, director, composer, etc.) and reception (the audience's reasoning, feeling, and affective activity).

HL: Perhaps in our delimiting the contours of an aesthetics of discomfort we should also consider its opposite: "feeling good"? Much of the most significant lyric poetry since the late eighteenth century—at least until the advent of modernism—has assumed the task of making its readers feel good. This goes back at least as far as Rousseau's "prose-poem" meditations called *Reveries of a Solitary Walker*, in which the writer's own sufferings, above all, his excruciating feelings of persecution (both real and imagined) are transformed, in the course of each walk, into something altogether benign; and I assume that in these posthumously published pieces he intended his huge reading public to go through the same process.

This process became the basis for a major lyric genre starting in English with Coleridge's "Frost at Midnight" and Wordsworth's "Tintern Abbey" (1798), in which each poet recounts some of his personal woes and then, usually through the contemplation of nature (or his memory of earlier such contemplations) gradually eradicates his disquieting thoughts and achieves some sort of peace and serenity. There's no generally acknowledged name for this genre—though M. H. Abrams dubbed it "the greater romantic lyric." Whenever I want to be facetious about this genre—which is living a continued afterlife in many typical *New Yorker* poems—I call it simply feel-good verse. What's important from the point of view of our conversations is that the poet's ruminations are supposed to infect the reader, who, after coming to share the poet's troubles through some sort of reader-empathy, ends up, like the poet, shedding her discomfort and feeling pretty good about herself.

FLA: *Reveries of a Solitary Walker* is certainly one of the most beautiful works that Rousseau ever wrote. Its syntax and vocabulary capture well the state of being in deep reverie; his prose poetry works wonderfully to immerse us deeply in the experience of daydreaming. In the process, I wonder if it's Rousseau's sufferings that are turned into something benign, or if it is nature that he transforms into the benign. His walks seem to meditate on how the whole of nature is turned into something of an English garden in contrast to the well-sculpted, geometric, and deliberate French garden. In his time, the transformation of nature by industry and technology was making it less and less raw and rugged; it was a time of the increased taming of nature by human intervention. His carefully designed prose poetry invites us to feel good (your "feel-good verse" effect) in its daydreamy shape—all while commenting on the willful transformation and taming of the natural environment.

HL: The benign feeling that Rousseau conveys to the reader in the *Reveries* is pretty hard-earned, for he creates considerable discomfort in us by forcing us to share the feelings of persecution that caused him to seek refuge on the island of St. Pierre. When I note him moving from what are obviously real persecutions to those he seems to be fantasizing, I cringe with a feeling of pity and embarrassment for him.

FLA: Yes, Rousseau is careful to balance the fantasy of daydream with the nightmare of persecution. When we daydream we experience comfort—a pleasurable feeling—and this in opposition to a nightmare. This has me wondering if our brain's automatic reflex when it encounters objects that discomfort (untamed nature, a nightmare, or otherwise) is to search for this feel-good life vest; to grasp for something in the art object (prose-poetry or otherwise) that *does* comfort.

HL: It may be that a certain hedonistic impulse is built into our evolutionary development. But there are times I like to buck this trend and seek out uncomfortable forms of art—Schoenberg's *Erwartung*, for instance, or a nasty film such as Michael Haneke's *The Piano Teacher* (or the equally nasty Elfriede Jelinek novel on which it is based).

FLA: I too seek out artist-made objects of discomfort, knowing of course that I have ultimate control over how (time and place) I interface with these objects. However, let's leave our conversation of the specifics of Schoenberg and Haneke to a later moment in our discussion.

HL: Agreed. But I must make the more general point that, for most of Western tradition, works have culminated in feelings of comfort (even if viewers need to fall back on Aristotelian catharsis to make themselves feel good at the end of a grueling tragedy). This movement from discomfort to a happy resolution is something endemic to such temporally based arts as literature and music. In music the sonata form (developed during the late eighteenth century and dominating musical form until the atonalists undid the whole thing) thrives on moving from dramatizations of struggle, especially in first movements, to a happy resolution.

But the tonal system, long before sonata form was developed, cultivated the movement from distinctly unpleasant chords to their resolution. At the turn of the seventeenth century the great Claudio Monteverdi was severely reprimanded by the tradition-bound theorist G. M. Artusi for the unresolved dissonant chords in some of his madrigals (Strunk, 393–412); and the unresolved dissonance in the first two bars of Monteverdi's renowned *Lamento d'Arianna* kept being attacked for at least a century and a half (Lindenberger, *Opera in History* 15–21). There's no question that the resolution of dissonance has always been the norm against which the occasional iconoclast has sought to make his mark.

FLA: Herbie, each work we enjoy and analyze is a source of an aesthetic experience, including discomfort. It would appear that the work is the independent cause of the aesthetic experience. Its effect in the consumer would appear as its consequences; that is, between the work and its consumer it would appear that there is a causal relation. I believe that we have been identifying a more complex phenomenon. That which seems a cause and effect is actually a relation between the object and subject. This said, it would be interesting to continue the analysis of the consumer.

HL: From the consumer's point of view, then, we might ask, in sonata form do we actually experience much discomfort during the times of musical struggle? After all, we know from our earlier musical experiences that everything will eventually be resolved and the piece—both the first movement and the last—will end with a triumphant return to the tonic chord.

FLA: Perhaps this could be considered in light of a theory of aesthetic relationality; that is, the sonata form creates a relationship with the audience that triggers negative, then positive emotions.

HL: Experienced listeners of course know this in advance, so composers had to find new ways to internalize the struggle that goes on, especially in first movements. Haydn, composing when sonata form was still something new, found constant ways of surprising his audiences (as in the aptly named *"Surprise"* Symphony), but by far the most radical step came when Beethoven composed his *Eroica* Symphony (1803), far louder and longer than anything that had come before, and now the audience underwent a number of painful struggles before the work made its way slowly to its ultimately triumphant conclusion.

Since this final triumph is built into the sonata form, every succeeding composer had to find a way of keeping the audience in suspense till the end.

FLA: We've been talking about the sonata form as a classificatory concept linked to the feelings of satisfaction, surprise, pain, and suspense. Perhaps we should consider how emotional responses to crafted moments of satisfaction and pain (beauty and ugliness *grosso modo*) crystalize as essentially genres: comedy, tragedy, and the grotesque (the simultaneous presence or combination of the ugly and beautiful), and any number of combinations thereof.

Might it be useful to map these aesthetic genres onto positive and negative emotions? And if so, would the grotesque and tragic be characterized by negative emotions only?

HL: Grotesque surely, but in a temporal form such as the symphony, grotesque sections such as some of Mahler's scherzo movements are only one segment of a larger whole that usually culminates in triumph—but that's not wholly true of Mahler since after the grotesquerie that characterizes the third movement of his Ninth Symphony, we undergo a final movement that feels like the most hopeless despair. To be sure, Mahler, as we look back now, represents the culmination of the symphonic tradition. Where else could you go after that? I'm about to hear his Ninth done once again by what I consider to be today's premier Mahler conductor, Michael Tilson Thomas, and I know in advance I won't leave the symphony hall feeling good. Still, this symphony is the exception that proves the rule: the mainstream within the symphonic tradition up to the triumph of modernism (of which Mahler was clearly an avatar) insists on a triumphantly happy end. (To be sure, Tchaikovsky had pioneered the letdown ending a decade and a half before in his *Pathéthique* Symphony, but the effect he created now pales for us in comparison with that of the Mahler.)

FLA: This triumphantly happy end is a form of catharsis, indeed. In an essay of yours that I teach a lot ("Arts in the Brain; or, What Might Neuroscience Tell Us?"), you talk about Aristotle's theory of catharsis as at once the goal and the pleasure of tragedy. We might here consider the possibility that we also feel discomfort in order to feel *comfort*.

HL: Absolutely! Aristotle, at least most of us assume, teaches us how fear and pity are removed from our body and then we feel good again. So in tragedy the discomfort leads us viewers to a postcathartic space of comfort. But the letdown we feel at the end of the Mahler Ninth doesn't much feel like an Aristotelian catharsis. Mahler, at least in his later work, portrayed the gloom that a budding modernist composer such as Schoenberg exploited more fully.

FLA: Perhaps you're right in this particular case. I think we can make a more general statement with regard to the nontemporal visual arts. Contrary to all time-dependent arts such as music and literature, in the visual arts you can't have the same form of movement from discomfort to catharsis.

Catharsis is a result and thus it is an event that takes place in time; it's something that builds up and is the consequence of a series of things that come before. It's a temporal phenomenon by definition and thus can only exist in temporal phenomena. I walk in the wind and rain up to the top of a mountain and the sun shines and I feel suddenly well throughout my being; the same experience takes place when sitting through a play or a Mahler Ninth when we have to follow the note in a time dimension. All these take place in time. However, when it comes to viewing a disturbing Frida Kahlo painting we don't have temporal movement. I ingest the painting in one blow—an immediate gestalt recognition of the painting and its subject matter—and each time I view the painting it is again in one gulp. And this gestaltic experience happens even if we focus inch by inch on the analysis of a given painting's style, geometry, and texture.

You look at a painting or sculpture, and that's it. There's no movement from discomfort to comfort at all, so if a painting is clearly unpleasant, you are left feeling disquieted, with no postcathartic place to go. In this sense, the concept of catharsis doesn't take place either when we view an atemporal Frida Kahlo painting or a beheaded Medusa in one of Benvenuto Cellini's sculptures. With both Kahlo and Cellini we perceive beauty and horror simultaneously. In these artists there is no evolution from horror to catharsis. We perceive and experience their works as a gestaltic whole out of time. But let's pick up once again where we left off in our discussion of how composers (authors, artists, architects, directors, and the like) create "blueprints" that trigger these discomforting reflex responses in our encounter with their art.

HL: We will hit on this later in the book when we talk about films (thrillers, horror, and so on in such films as Haneke's *Funny Games*), but we need to consider how fear operates in the aesthetics of discomfort. For Burke and Kant the discomfort of fear, whether in contemplating nature or a work of art, was central to the pleasure one would ultimately feel. After bringing up such threatening natural phenomena as "threatening rocks," "volcanoes with all their destructive power," "hurricanes with all the devastation they leave behind," Kant tells us that "the sight of them becomes all the more attractive the more fearful it is." But then Kant adds an important qualifying phrase: "provided we are in a safe place" (120). With the snake pictured earlier, my possession of a zoom lens gave me a certain safety.

Having been through a recent hurricane in New York, as well as a number of California earthquakes, I might add that, limited as he was to the benign natural conditions that Königsberg offered, Kant overestimated the safety one feels on either coast of the United States. But I basically agree with his point as far as art is concerned. While experiencing even the most gruesome horror movie, you always know (even after if you temporarily forget this!) that you're inside a theater and that, once it's all over, you'll step out into the street and have nothing any more to fear. As it happens, I went through one of the Bay Area's worst earthquakes—the one in 1989—more as a spectator than as a sufferer, for when the quake hit I was lying in a hammock attached to two springy birch trees—with the result that I hardly felt a thing, though I heard the kids next door screaming bloody murder. Like several million other people at that moment these kids were going through a real-life horror movie, while I observed the whole thing like somebody (for a moment at least, until I figured out intellectually what was happening) thinking it all to be a fiction.

FLA: The discomfort of fear has certain similarities with the discomfort of disgust in that they are both connected very directly with physiological reactions. Again, we will return to this in later chapters of our dialogue (for instance, the scene in Pasolini's *Salò* where the guests are made to eat a stew of feces), but what can we say today with the way we cope with scenes—whole texts—that disgust us?

HL: Disgust is a particularly disconcerting feeling. As we suggested earlier, it seems to be different in kind, or at least in intensity, from other negative feelings—if only because the physical act of vomiting, or at least the fear of vomiting, adds shame and embarrassment to one's discomfort. It hardly matters whether it's a so-called work of art or something in everyday life that's disgusting you. When I see (and smell) some badly spoiled food or even some fresh food for which I never got over my childhood disgust (chicken for me), I am aware that something awful has been tapped in a particular area of the brain different from areas associated with other negative feelings. And unlike, say, with fear, one's memory of disgust reactions keeps lingering in one's mind for days after the experience.

FLA: For you it's chicken and for me it's tequila—but I'll save us the details of that long night I spent with my cousins in Mexico City. We know from advances in the neurosciences that negative emotions (dislike and disgust) are just as much aesthetic emotions as, say, awe or ecstasy. That is, our sensing, emoting, and evaluating of aesthetic objects follows the same processes we use in object-appraisal generally. So it's not surprising that aesthetic objects can trigger a range of emotions along a spectrum from the sublime to repulsion.

HL: Not only is it not surprising—but it's also a good thing we have this large range of responses handy in our brains. (May I be facetious enough to speculate that our brains may have evolved as they have in order to facilitate our responsiveness to art?) And that way art can constantly surprise us.

FLA: This range also allows the creator to build aesthetic objects that make us angry as consumers.

HL: Of course, there's art (a considerable amount of modernist art, for instance) that arouses anger in us. I often ask myself: what really motivates this anger? Are we as consumers worried that the artist is making a fool out of us? Or are we simply angry that the artist hasn't made it easy for us ("easy listening")? Perhaps the most notorious instance of art that arouses anger is John Cage's *4′33″*, "composed" in 1952 and performed by Cage's favored pianist, David Tudor, who came to the piano to play the announced work but instead simply sat on his stool for the four minutes and thirty-three seconds prescribed in the title. At the end of this time he got up without having played a single note. Although one could call Cage's act an affront to his concert audience, the composer countered by reminding us that one *did* hear sounds during the performance—mumblings and coughs from the audience as well as weather and traffic noise from outside.

Whatever anger this first performance aroused would have come from the feeling that the composer was mocking his listeners—far worse, I suspect, than the anger aroused at the premiere of *The Rite of Spring*, which at least gave its irate listeners some "real" music, cacophonous though they may have found it. In retrospect, *4′33″* now counts as a canonical moment in the history of the various arts: in late 2013 the Museum of Modern Art devoted a whole show to the event, not simply displaying the composer's written instructions but also exhibiting a number of works (mainly visual, for example, Rauschenberg's *White Painting* [1951], consisting of panels done with nothing but white paint that sought to eliminate all signs of brush-marks) that fed into Cage's creation and others (again mainly visual) that derived from it. One could speak of this "tradition" as that of the "affronted audience."

FLA: Unlike the experience of disgust, in which we appraise an event as inherently aversive, anger involves appraising the affront as deliberate as Cage's "composition" indeed was. Our response: we're motivated to deal with the threat to our goals; but when our goal to apprehend an object or when an activity that goes against our taste and values (possibly) is blocked, we might well become angry. However, it's unlikely that we will act on this impulse and, say, tear up a piece of art—or physically assault the unplayed piano or Cage himself, for that matter.

HL: You're giving me the inspiration to create a piece of installation art that stages a confrontation between artist and viewer: the artist draws something provocative in front of a group of museumgoers, then hands it to the viewer, who has the right to tear it up, or stomp on it, or even to use it as toilet paper. This is not as improbable a museum script nowadays as one might think.

FLA: I reviewed many such performances while moonlighting during my graduate school days as a theater critic for the *SF Weekly*. Especially memorable was Guillermo Gómez-Peña's *Mexterminator* show. Part of the show included holding the audience captive behind barbed-wire fencing with border-patrol guards (*la migra*) taunting us with foul language. Yet, once you experience the show once and know its tricks, you don't feel all that compelled to return. At what point, we might ask, does our experience of disquieting art turn us off (boredom) or become part of our habituated experience?

HL: Boredom is a possible by-product of all art, comforting and discomforting alike. If *4′33″* had been much longer than it was, it would doubtless have turned anger into boredom as its "listeners" twiddled their thumbs. But there's some major art that moves so slowly—I think of Beckett's novel trilogy and Debussy's *Pelléas et Mélisande*—that many otherwise savvy readers and operagoers complain of excruciating boredom. I happen to love Debussy's opera—the slowness for me is hypnotic—but every time I've attended a performance I've heard people during the two intermissions complaining of how bored they feel. Being bored and being under hypnosis are states of mind quite close to one another.

FLA: Yes, this is the boredom that *can* and *does* destroy art. We turn off. In a sense the art no longer exists. Our brain has evolved the capacity to reward itself with the release of oxytocin and dopamine, for instance. Discomforting art must somehow reward us, no?

HL: If it's the discomfort from hearing a dissonant chord that's resolved soon after, obviously we're being rewarded—or at least if we know the conventions of tonal music that dictate eventual pleasant chords, we know we can expect an ultimate reward. But feeling hypnotized, as with *Pelléas* for me (or, even more so, by Debussy's disciple Olivier Messiaen in the five-hour-long *Saint François d'Assise*), is very pleasurable indeed, and it certainly does not "destroy" this art even if you and most people refuse to feel the hypnotic spell. Moreover, when Schoenberg, say, in *Erwartung*, refuses to reward us after the dissonances he has unleashed, the "reward" we get is a certain distraughtness, even disorientation, not to speak of anger or boredom on the part of some listeners. But I consider the disorientation that much modernist art gives us a reward of sorts.

FLA: But don't audiences eventually get used to things that once upset their predecessors? In our prologue, we talked about how when audiences became accustomed to cubism and other modernist art they no longer responded with discomfort—Picasso's many raw (brutal even) depictions of women, for instance.

HL: You're right about Picasso and, for that matter, most of his contemporaries in all the major art forms. But it was a slow process. When I started my museumgoing in Seattle during the 1930s—the local art museum was only a few blocks from where my family lived—there wasn't a single Picasso on display. Once I got to Chicago and New York during my college years in the late 1940s, I'd invariably hear somebody next to me angrily declare something like "My five year-old can do this just as well"—not, to be sure, at the Museum of Modern Art, which you wouldn't visit if you weren't prepared to like Picasso. I don't think you'd hear that statement any more, even in museums out in the provinces. But people's ability to accustom their eyes to modernist art does not work nearly as well, I think, with the temporally organized arts. Although Stravinsky's *Rite of Spring* has become as easy to take as cubist art, this is not the case with *Erwartung*, which still manages to disorient most listeners. And, to turn to literature, *Finnegans Wake* (1939), even though one can get some help from guidebooks, is not much easier to deal with than it was when new.

FLA: We seem to eventually acclimate to certain once seemingly impossible works.

HL: Some people may never get used to art that outraged or baffled them. But their children might find this art very pleasing indeed. Still, a few people do become converted to things they earlier rejected—usually through the mediation of a docent at a museum or some adult-education course they take, maybe even finding that friends they like and respect are enjoying the things they themselves reject. Also, abstract art has influenced commercial design, and one's exposure, say, to Miró-like shapes in one's everyday visual life or Mondrian designs on fabric may soften one's negative feelings toward the artist's work itself. Still, some artists seem to resist getting used to. I recently presented Gertrude Stein's short prose poem "Susie Asado" and Schoenberg's *Erwartung* to two different groups, both of whom rejected what I hoped they'd be able to appreciate (if not necessarily "like"). But one person, though despairing of "understanding" "Susie Asado," admitted that the words had a "pleasant lilt" to them, and then I realized that this might be a way of getting people engaged: forget all about meaning and just listen passively to the succession of sounds—and maybe this would work with *Erwartung* as well.

FLA: Is this what we can call the process of *distortion* or what we mentioned earlier as enstrangement? That is, the shape-giving procedure whereby the artist makes the "stone stony" by reorienting our perspective, thought, and feeling toward the object.

HL: You can keep the experience of reorientation (or disorientation) going for a certain amount of time, and then you become habituated to it. Still, there is *Erwartung* (and lots of other Schoenberg and Webern pieces) and there is *Finnegans Wake*, which never habituate their listeners. And actually many more works, including, as I mentioned earlier, some premodernist ones like seventeenth-century Luis de Góngora's poems and Gesualdo's madrigals. This idea of habituation (of becoming "automatized" to what once seemed disconcerting) was of course central to the Formalist understanding of literary history.

FLA: Like Joyce's *Finnegans Wake*, in his day Góngora's poetry was considered impenetrable. This is what made it disquieting. Readers of the exceptionally skilled Góngora admired the execution of his work as well as his knowledge of poetic form, yet few *actually* read and understood his work. It's disquieting precisely because line by line the poems put this impenetrability front and center in the reader's mind.

This tends to turn readers away from the work. As you say, with certain works habituation never takes place. Góngora's poems and *Finnegans Wake* will likely always make us feel discomfort. On the other hand, more often than not we *do* habituate ourselves to discomforting aesthetic artifacts, and sometimes we even find that we enjoy them.

HL: For years now I've assumed the fact of our habituation without being able to figure out the "how." It may be that we need to develop tools to watch the brain in action over multiple exposures to difficult, discomforting works. Sometimes ways can be found to ease our way into these works. To cite *The Rite of Spring* once more: although it caused a riot in Paris in 1913, by 1940 it pleased vast audiences when it appeared as one of the eight pieces making up Walt Disney's *Fantasia*.

But a number of things tamed down this once-upsetting piece: for one thing, it was shortened; second, the conductor, Leopold Stokowski, chose not to make the dissonances and the fortissimi as earsplitting as more recent conductors regularly (and correctly) do; and, most important, one's attention was aimed at the gorgeous animation, above all, the fishes and dinosaurs. I saw it at eleven when it was new and wasn't bothered a bit though I knew nothing about modernist music. This taming of the *Rite* is, I think, paradigmatic of how audiences have become habituated to high-powered modernist works: college teachers present paraphrases of *The Waste Land* to fill in the uncomfortable gaps in the poem; museum docents explain the biographical facts behind *Les Demoiselles d'Avignon* and show you, despite the women's repulsive faces, how well composed the painting really is; and preconcert lecturers in the symphony hall play tidbits of difficult passages, which, they assure you, are necessary to achieve the powerful effect on an audience that the composer sought and that you're about to experience yourselves. In other words, good rhetoric can disarm viewers—at least to a point.

FLA: Much of this can be lost to the inattentive, Herbie. Many critics forgot to attend to Robert Mapplethorpe's balanced, elegant compositions and his careful use of light and shadow in his photography. Instead, they focused on the content: men (black and white) fisting one another among other seemingly extraordinary and *outrageous* activities.

HL: I agree that Mapplethorpe's elegance, at least at first glance, helps mitigate the shocking effect of the subject matter. Still, if you look closely, you realize that the "beauty" can really exacerbate the shock.

If we had been shown Mapplethorpe's more confrontational images in a more straightforward way, they would likely have had nothing more than a conventionally pornographic effect, one that we can choose either to dismiss or to enjoy for its ability to arouse a person sexually. But to present these images in a form ordinarily associated with "beautiful" objects and people is to complicate the whole matter: don't these two realms—one of frank and blatant sexuality, the other of rarefied "high art"—belong to entirely different orders? To bring these realms together, as Mapplethorpe does, is to create something close to cognitive dissonance.

FLA: For all its critical controversy that grew from images that made its onlookers feel disgust, Mapplethorpe's deft ability at creating this cognitive dissonance seemed to pleasure his viewers. The exhibit attracted huge crowds.

HL: I went the first day the show opened in Berkeley in 1989. We took our eighteen-year-old daughter, fresh from her first term in college. She wasn't in the least shocked, nor did the Berkeley crowd look at all shocked. I admit that Berkeley is usually an exception to everything.

FLA: We might have brushed elbows, Herbie. I too was at the opening—but still a rather green undergraduate at UC Berkeley. I think I can speak for those of my generation in attendance when I say that we were not as shocked as some of the other audience members. Perhaps the differing responses to discomforting art could be generalized across generational lines. Twenty-somethings today seem to have a bigger capacity to absorb and even enjoy art that discomforts.

HL: Absolutely true! This was certainly the case in the nineteenth century when Beethoven and Wagner, much of whose work was difficult for their first listeners, became absorbed by the following generations. But there's something else one can say about young people today: the popular music they hear, unlike popular music of earlier generations, is loud and intrusive, and even though rock is still largely tonal music, their experience of popular music since the 1960s has probably made it easier to be adventurous with disturbing classical music.

FLA: Perhaps it might be better to understand us, audiences, who become used to art that discomforts and who therefore no longer alter the initial or original aesthetic relation. When the lights go out at the museum, we no longer perceive the art. To our senses, the work no longer exists. However, this doesn't change the object—the Picasso, the Mapplethorpe, and so on. It doesn't even change us, in the strict sense of the term. We still go about our everyday activities as always. What has changed is our relationship to the discomforting art. What has changed, in short, is our aesthetic relation.

HL: Or perhaps modernism has extended the realm of what we take to be aesthetic experience. With each new innovation in the course of the twentieth century—cubism, total abstraction, pop art, minimalism, conceptual art—people have exclaimed, "But *this* isn't art!" and then somehow the artist or the style has become absorbed and people are willing to call it art after all. In museums nowadays you see all sorts of installations—like the one about the artist's drawings being torn up that I fantasized above—that challenge the visitor's conception of what constitute the limits of art. Arthur Danto, the best theoretician of late twentieth-century art, has shown, by means of subtle philosophical argument, how a controversial work such as Andy Warhol's *Brillo-Box*, which has long provided an example of how so-called nonart has been canonized by its advocates, performs many of the functions that art has always performed—in the case of this Warhol piece, as Danto puts it, "externalizing a way of viewing the world, expressing the interior of a cultural period, offering itself as a mirror to catch the conscience of our kings" (208).

FLA: We can identify this appreciation (or lack thereof) in twentieth-century art as part of the phenomenon of blindness: we might simply reject the art object because it does not correspond to our expectations or because we don't have adequate knowledge of the shaping devices used in the making of the art object.

HL: That's where the museum docent, or the literature professor, or the preconcert lecturer comes in. But to obtain the knowledge that will widen our range of expectations, we need to be *willing* to have this happen to us, to show a little humility, moreover, about the things we don't understand. One can't get to everybody: there are engineering students who wouldn't have been caught dead in the course I used to give on Yeats and Eliot; and even though museums, above all museums of modern art, are crowded these days as they never were when I was young, they still gather only a small segment of the population, even of the educated population.

FLA: I wonder, Herbie, what the neurosciences might tell us about *how* the art of discomfort *educates* people to deal with their uncomfortable states?

HL: As you know I've become increasingly interested in what the neurosciences has to tell us about our neurobiology, especially as it affects the making of art. Scholars like Semir Zeki and V. S. Ramachandran were pioneers in this regard and today there's the whole field of neuroaesthetics—you published a pioneering edited volume that helped push the field in this regard. Your coedited series now with the University of Nebraska Press has been actively shaping this field, publishing books such as Sue J. Kim's *On Anger* and Irving Massey's *The Neural Imagination: Aesthetic and Neuroscientific Approaches to the Arts*.

FLA: Our work (along with those we mentioned above) variously considers both how our sensory input moves from the limbic to the cortex (bottom up) and also how higher-order expectations and appraisal influence our perception (viewing or listening) processes (top down). The idea is that if we can understand the mechanisms involved in our perception of color, detection of motion, hearing of sound, recognition of faces, experience of rhythm, we might be able to see more clearly how we stitch all this together in the apprehension of an aesthetic object, including those that cause us to revolt, turn away. Simultaneous with our sense-making activities in the stitching together of all the processes above there's the emotional response: fear (the amygdala) and disgust (insula) as set in opposition to pleasure (nucleus accumbens), problem solving (prefrontal cortex).

HL: When we've studied these reactions with real subjects in the fMRI, as many researchers are doing today, we can tell, as you put it, which parts of the brain are experiencing particular reactions. I might add, though, that one scientist who has worked closely with groups using the fMRI told me that in most instances if you ask the subject how he or she is reacting, you'll get as good an answer as you would tracing that reaction to, say, the amygdala or nucleus accumbens. If you say that a particular photograph disgusts you, it's predictable that an fMRI picture would show the anterior insula involved.

FLA: Yes, I suppose on some level we don't need such advanced technology to tell us what we know well: we've evolved biological mechanisms for survival, including our rejection of harmful things (disease and contagion) like vomit, feces, rotting meat, and, to a certain extent, insects. Yet advances in technology go hand in hand with advances in our knowledge of the world—and advances in our creativity. The fMRI technology along with the neuroscience is not the same technology and "science" used by our Paleolithic ancestors when they chipped away at rocks to create arrowheads.

HL: Another neuroscientist I know, though she agreed with the earlier one that subjects can reveal their feelings about art as readily as machines can in their present state, predicted that eventually these machines may be able to know what's going on in our minds better than we consciously do. Whether or not we need technological proof that a work of art really affects us, in a tech-biased society such as ours concrete proof about how the work precisely gets into and through our bodies can surely enhance the role that this society grants to art.

FLA: Certainly, and I see among the undergraduate students a waning interest in the study of the humanities—something that has been confirmed during recent months in newspaper articles. However, courses that wed the neurosciences with the humanities draw huge numbers; the same appeal can be seen with the huge number of applicants to the Humanities & Cognitive Sciences High School Summer Institute that I codirect at OSU. Like my students, I want to know more deeply about the cognitive and emotive mechanisms involved in the creating and consuming of art. I want to know more about how, for instance, our evolved reflex response to that which harms us along with those evolved mechanisms of attraction are used to create art and are active in our engagement with it.

HL: Here again we see how neurobiological confirmation has the extra benefit of taking aesthetic objects, reactions, and relations away from the impressionistic babble that has often surrounded them.

FLA: Our knowledge of the functioning of the brain has made huge advances in the last several decades. This research is leaving less and less room for the "impressionistic babble," as you put it, that surrounded aesthetics and that was so much in vogue not so long ago in the work, for instance, of Heidegger. Of course, we don't have to know anything about neurobiology to be repelled by certain art exhibits such as Piero Manzoni's canned feces in his *Artist's Shit* (*Merda d'artista*). Certainly, excrement by itself causes disgust.

In less extreme cases, and we know this from firsthand experience, we tend to avoid stinky people—and those more generally who violate the social conventions linked to disgust. That is, we begin to grow from childhood a taste for good-smelling people versus bad-smelling ones, who thus evince health. I'm so worried that I might have bad breath after lecturing that I always pop a mint before students come up to ask questions after class. I do this precisely because I don't want to be one of those stinky people. I don't want to be avoided or to appear as a walking health hazard!

Actually, I want to be liked and to have students gather around after lectures. That is, here as in other of my daily activities, I want to be thought of as a guy you want to hang out with—and who in turn wants to hang out with others. This is perhaps a long way of getting at how, for instance, our reaction to smells can lead to our desire to be with people or not; that perhaps it is this good smell versus bad smell that orients our altruistic impulse and possibly affects somewhat our ethics system.

This line of thinking leads me to ask, how might artists play on this in terms of orienting us toward objects of disgust and acts of transgressive ethics? An author like Rabelais seems to present situations that disgust—Gargantua's birth is filled up more by feces than placenta—and at the same time lead us to reorient our ethical compass.

HL: It's been an axiom for most of us teaching literature that examining the unpleasant content of literary works has ethical implications: we believe, or at least we hope, we can make better, more responsible people out of our students by encouraging them to examine and think about the darker sides of art. And of course those of us dealing with modernist texts and art don't have much opportunity to examine the "lighter" aspects of art.

FLA: Earlier, we touched briefly on how ideology has been tied (artificially) to reflex emotions—smell and class, for instance. Ideologues have used propaganda to identify people as dirty and to be shunned and to solidify out-group and in-group boundaries. There's the Nazi portrayal of Jewish people as filthy rats. Perhaps we should consider whether bad smells, or the mention thereof, leads to xenophobia, or if this is the result of ideology. More to the point of our discussion, we might ask how authors turn such ideological uses of smell (good smell = included vs. bad smell = excluded) upside down. I think of Art Spiegelman's choice in *Maus* to portray Jewish people as rodents.

HL: Long before the Nazis, as Sander Gilman has shown in his studies of anti-Semitism, Jews—especially the so-called Eastern Jews who had emigrated to Germany from Poland and Russia—were associated with such repulsive traits as disconcertingly high voices, filth, and bad smells. Spiegelman's turning this upside down, as you put it, was a brilliant artistic move. It's fascinating, as well, that *Maus* is now presented in the schools to teach the young about the Holocaust. But as you read the narrative you think of these folks as human beings, and you forget all your usual feelings about rodents.

FLA: Might authors and artists generally create blueprints that teach us to override knee-jerk emotions of disgust together with any sense of an ethics built on in-group versus out-group? After all, don't we learn to do this in other contexts (such as a lack of revulsion when a caretaker is changing a child's soiled diapers)? We might ask, then, if we have social and biological limits to the making and consuming of art that triggers base, negative emotions.

HL: The social limits keep changing as artists—and their interpreters—push these limits further. Whereas Joyce's use of the word *fuck*, as well as a few other "indiscretions," did not allow *Ulysses* to be published in the United States until after a court action in 1933, today we hear this word spoken constantly in plays and films. I recently attended a Scottish play, Gregory Burke's *Black Watch*, whose soldier characters used the word in virtually every sentence—as soldiers, the audience was to assume, actually do in real life. It's getting increasingly hard to find limits that artists can push against.

FLA: Perhaps we should consider how artists can push thresholds by eliciting a whole range of other negative feelings.

HL: Yes, we've talked about anger, fear, and disgust, among other unpleasant feelings that art can awaken. But there are a number of others, hate, for example, which you mention above in the disgust toward Jews that the Nazis sought to awaken. But this disgust was closely related to hate, which German literature, art, and film strove hard to fan up through the negative images of Jews that peopled all their forms of art. But there are also more "respectable" ways of creating hate—not toward members of a particular group like the Jews but the hate we have traditionally felt toward obvious villains such as Iago and also toward characters who aren't exactly villainous, for example, Mr. Casaubon or Rosamond Vincy in *Middlemarch*, but who block the aspirations of the novelistic heroes and heroines we identify with.

FLA: We do this with films all the time, Herbie. I feel a certain positive emotion for the actor Javier Bardem—yet as the villain in the last Bond film, *Skyfall* (2012), he not only made me feel deeply uncomfortable, but I came to dislike him to the core. I can say the same of his role in Alejandro González Iñárritu's *Biutiful* (2010) where he most certainly plays a despicable character.

There are of course other characters (antagonists) that I feel less anger and disgust toward and rather something like embarrassment. I don't mean embarrassed for the actor for doing a bad job, but embarrassed for the character because he reveals too much of himself to the audience.

HL: I agree. There are more complicated situations where a strong emotion that artists think they're communicating to us turns into a feeling of embarrassment on our part. Rousseau's *Confessions*, which I've done many times with students, is full of passages that end up embarrassing us—teacher and students alike. Rousseau's intention was to be as honest and frank about himself as possible, as in the passage in Book II where he tells how he ruined the life of his fellow servant Marion by falsely accusing her of stealing their mistress's ribbon (86–89). He feels shame, and I think he wants us to share this feeling—as well as to praise him for his honesty—but the way he tells it, you feel embarrassment above all. Similarly with his story in Book IV about the grotesque male making a pass at him: Rousseau wants us to share his disgust, but instead we feel embarrassment at the way he chooses to be intimate with his readers (161–62). It's not all that different from the embarrassment I described earlier in the monologue play whose actor concentrates on his or her body's various openings.

FLA: And painting can have the same effect. I think of Courbet's *L'Origine du monde*.

HL: Yes, Courbet's depiction of female genitalia commissioned by Khalil-Bey (the Turkish ambassador to Greece and Russia) and painted with Courbet's characteristic realism, triggers similar feelings of embarrassment. If you see it alone, as I did in an empty room at the Louvre, it communicates the erotic message that the ambassador evidently craved. But when I next saw it at a crowded Courbet show in New York, I found myself thoroughly embarrassed passing by it, and I looked at it only through the corner of my eye. If I had stared at it the way I had at the Louvre, the other museum visitors might have branded me a dirty old man. Before this painting went to the Louvre it was owned by the psychoanalytic theorist Jacques Lacan, who tacitly acknowledged its potential for embarrassment by keeping it in a small cabinet that he opened only for selected guests (was he delicate enough to leave the room so that they could view it alone?). I remember being embarrassed in a museum for a somewhat different reason when I took my eleven-year-old daughter to see Judy Chicago's early-feminist installation *The Dinner Party*. Chicago has set a group of banquet tables with ceramic plates on which all manner of vaginas have been painted and fired. I had not originally intended to take Elizabeth there, but we were on our way to the ballet, and, having some time to kill before it began, we walked into the museum that was then next door to the opera house. Whatever she may have thought privately, Elizabeth retained her composure throughout, but I suffered considerable embarrassment wondering what the other visitors thought about a father who would expose his young daughter to an exhibit of this sort.

FLA: It seems we've moved onto how art can instill feelings of discomfort in more complex ways than the triggering of base reflex emotions. Those feelings you describe in your encounters with Rousseau's *Confessions* (1782) and with Courbet's semiclandestine painting *L'Origine du monde* (1866) such as embarrassment and shame are more self-conscious emotions. They result from having a sense of self and being able to reflect on what this self has done.

In other words, emotions such as embarrassment are unusually complex and require our higher-order appraisal function, appraising events as congruent or incongruent with one's goals, values, and moral perception of oneself; they are emotions triggered more often than not by one's appraisal of an action as having been caused by oneself instead of by someone else; and as consistent or inconsistent with personal and social rules of moral behavior.

HL: When we get into these complex situations—embarrassment at one's own acts, appraisal of blame, one's inability to live up to moral norms—one wonders to what degree neuroscience, with limited means it commands today, can tell us about these matters.

FLA: The discovery of the mirror-neuron system can tell us much not only about our mechanisms for empathizing with other people's emotions (experiential and conceptual knowledge of others' emotions), but also about our shared neural basis for seeing and feeling the various negative emotions such as anger, disgust, hate that we've brought up. Indeed, there was an experiment conducted in 2003 (Wicker et al.) whereby subjects hooked up to an fMRI first inhaled repulsive odors, then observed video clips of others portraying facial expressions of disgust. Perhaps not so surprisingly, the same sites in the anterior insula (the area of the brain involved in emotional regulation and physiological homeostasis) were activated during the olfactory and the visual experiments.

Turning to another question, do we sometimes empathize with a character or feel for a tune or engage with a work of art that irritates us?

HL: I think we often do so involuntarily—for instance with tunes that we find banal, irritating, or disgusting, or all of these at once. The musical "brainworms" that Oliver Sacks talks about (41–48) keep plaguing us no matter how much we try to rid ourselves of them. Similarly, disgusting images from horror movies reenter our minds against our will.

FLA: Perhaps we can end this chapter by talking about how artists create aesthetic relations of discomfort that suggest hierarchies of value.

HL: Dare we say its name: judgment! I'm all for this, even if it has not been in fashion for some time to identify bad versus good art.

FLA: How can we do otherwise than evaluate a work of art, right, Herbie? This is necessarily integral to the aesthetic relation of discomfort, because the aesthetic experience is all about contemplation, shape, and meaning. The work of art is contemplated and experienced as an aesthetic object on account of its shape and its meaning—the shape and the meaning conferred on it by the artist and perceived and contemplated by the viewer, listener, or reader, who is engaged in the act of contemplation by perceiving and appreciating shape and in their turn ascribing meaning to the object and its shape.

HL: Yes, we evaluate as well done or not well done on the basis of our past experiences with art—and also, I might add, of our particular temperament, which varies among us in the tolerance with which we can deal with discomfort.

FLA: As we both already confessed, we happen to be drawn to objects created (paintings, literature, films, music, etc.) that do a *good job* at making us feel uncomfortable. While drawn to them, I don't necessarily, however, fill my environments with these objects. John Cage is not on replay on my CD player, nor does my house have poster reproductions of Serrano's *Piss Christ* up on the wall. However, the encounter with discomforting art can shed light on the deep evolutionary basis of our sense-emotion-interpretation mechanisms as they intersect with the universal making and consuming of the arts.

When the first hunter-gatherers of the Paleolithic found delight in both the arrowheads they had made *and* in their capacity to produce them, there was something certainly new appearing in the world: an aesthetic relation toward the object produced *and* with respect to the maker of the object who takes pride in the making of this new object. These aesthetic relations acquired more and more an independent status with respect to the object *and* the subject. The pride in the work well done was no longer, say, inside the maker; that pride became independent of the maker *and* became the property of the viewers of the arrowhead. What was once a private experience became a public experience. More and more, aesthetic relations became independent of the object, taking place in the experience of a sunset or an animal running at a distance. That is, the aesthetic experience was no longer immediately dependent on the man-made object; the pleasure could be triggered by nonhuman made phenomena such as a sunset, an animal running, and much more.

HL: From your argument, Frederick, I can see that Damien Hirst, as I speculated earlier, could never have kept his pickled animal parts confined to the privacy of his home.

FLA: In our evolution, the aesthetic relation becomes more varied *and* more complex; it emancipates itself from the direct attachment to object and the creator, and becomes more and more a specific relation—the aesthetic relation. As it becomes more varied and complex, it has come to include phenomena such as discomfort. There can be and there is an aesthetic of discomfort—or an aesthetic relation of discomfort.

HL: Like you, I don't play uncomfortable music like Schoenberg's *Erwartung* as often as I do, say, a Bach Passion or a Mahler symphony. But something still draws me to hear this sort of music on occasion—it's as though I feel the need to be drawn into, and to cope with, the disquieting world into which the composer has invited (or, to be more accurate, has confronted) us. Often having more knowledge about works and their place in history helps mitigate some of the discomfort. It helps, for instance, to know that changes in style and subject matter have always—and not just with the advent of twentieth-century modernism—created discomfort for consumers. To know that the vaunted Beethoven caused discomfort for his early listeners may help people understand the discomfort they feel with Stravinsky, though it may not help with Schoenberg or Cage, who instituted changes more radical than Beethoven (or Stravinsky, for that matter). But knowing that Schoenberg's *Erwartung* deliberately avoids tapping the pleasure centers of our brain by refusing to give us any melody that can lurk in our mind or that Cage determined the pitch changes of his *Music of Changes* by means of chance operations at least allows us to see that there was method in their supposed madness, that they were trying out something that nobody had done before; and knowing this may not make their art less disquieting, but it might lessen the anger that listeners often vent toward them.

FLA: To sum up, then, our formulation thus far of an aesthetics of discomfort does well to take into consideration how artists create objects to establish a specific relationality with its subjects that generates new perceptions, thoughts, feelings—and meaning. In the art we focus on herein, this relationality is shaped by the creator's willful use of devices to create art that discomforts.

On the basis of this preliminary discussion, we can now continue in each one of the following chapters to examine with a certain amount of detail specific art forms, beginning with literature.

TWO | Bottoms Up

FREDERICK LUIS ALDAMA: In this chapter we're interested in traveling across and through some of those literary artifacts created with the aim of discomforting readers.

HERBERT LINDENBERGER: As we've begun to show, it's not just modernist works that are particularly discomforting. When we look back we'll find the disturbing element all over the place, though in the literature of past centuries it's not always as in-your-face as it became in twentieth-century writing.

FLA: Earlier in our conversation, we brought up Shklovsky's concept of *ostranenie* that identifies how an artist writ large gives shape to her prime matter to reorient our perspective, thought, and feeling toward the object. Shklovsky was part of that brain trust in early twentieth-century Russia known as the Formalists. I think their identification of the two categories of *story* and *discourse* to be very productive.

In the case of story they include the prime matter—understood as transformed matter, first worked upon by the imagination. Once transformed (operated upon) this image becomes a story or plot, even if only the beginning of a story. Story contains the prime, and still unformed, matter upon which the mind shaping the discourse will do its work.

HL: Which means that, from the point of view we're pursuing here, some extremely discomforting story material can be transformed into something almost benign, while, to take it in the other direction, some seemingly harmless material can be plotted in such a way that it can become dangerously uncomfortable.

FLA: Absolutely! The shaper of discourse, using the totality of available devices, can indeed be used to give shape to a story that will turn the most benign idea and plot into something quite horrifying. I think of how film directors taking a simple, relatively harmless story like *Little Red Riding Hood* (though the Brothers Grimm were never entirely gentle with their readers) and turning this prime matter into horror films such as Shawn Jennings's short slasher film, *"Red" Red Riding Hood* (2008), Giacomo Cimini's horror flick *Red Riding Hood* (2003), and David Slade's more re-creative *Hard Candy* (2005), which leaves us guessing as to which one is the bad wolf—the fourteen-year-old who entraps and tortures a pedophile, or the pedophile himself.

This is to say, the discourse comprises the full apparatus of generative devices that will give the aesthetic shape to the aesthetic object that the artist wishes to create. A device such as free indirect discourse—a device you mentioned earlier and whose history you sketch in your edition of Leo Spitzer's essays (41–42, 454)—is simply a specific operation of this discourse shaper. This and many other devices serve a shape-giving function and exist within the umbrella category of the discourse.

HL: Indeed, free indirect discourse—or FID, as some analysts have come to dub it—has turned out to be one of the most powerful mechanisms an author can use—as powerful and transformative as, say, perspective once was after Renaissance painters had discovered its possibilities. FID allows the narrator to pretend to stay out of the picture while she (and I say "she" advisedly since its first major practitioner in English was Jane Austen) allows her characters to reveal themselves through their own characteristic (and often self-damning) thought processes.

Let's look at a novel still little known, though written in the late 1940s—H. G. Adler's *The Journey*. This book, set mainly in the Nazi camp Theresienstadt, to which the Czech-born author and his family had been deported, tells the thinly disguised story of the family's stay in this camp and their further deportation to the death camp Auschwitz. The mind of an elderly doctor, Leopold Lustig, based on the author's father-in-law, is captured via FID as he contemplates the death trip he has been assigned to take—without of course knowing for sure where he'll be headed. To convey this point adequately, let me quote from the novel at some length:

> Onward a little farther. Maybe even backward. Leopold had always wished for that. After the war . . . that's what he always said. That is not necessary, for even during the war one can travel. It does one good and enriches oneself to experience the wide world, for it nourishes life. You all can see for the first time how many towns there are in the countryside. There's plenty of room for you, for you don't need much. The horizons of travelers are broadened,

> and you always valued education so much. Can you appreciate the fact that we're doing all of this for you for free? All we ask in return is your life, thus the price is cheap, for what is your life worth? Used up and worth nothing! No one would think of buying it, and so it belongs to us, and we're shipping you off. You have nothing to lose, and only something to gain. Whoever doesn't know how to help himself otherwise, just go with the flow! Get yourselves ready and don't be late, because in three days we'll be picking you up. The song is over. (144; ellipsis Adler's)

The narrator zeroes in on Leopold's thought process as he moves from fantasizing a pleasure trip to his realization that this is really a forced journey to his death. As is typical in FID, the language we hear, despite its being in the third person, consists of the clichés that one imagines emanating from the character's mind, in this case that of a cultivated European bourgeois: "[Travel] does one good and enriches oneself"; "the horizons of travelers are broadened." But quickly the fantasy stops, and Leopold hears the voices (in the second person) of the Nazis—not to be sure their real voices, which never directly addressed their killing operations but rather what he imagines is really on their minds: "What is your life worth? Used up and worth nothing."

The genius of FID is that the writer can dramatize what goes on in a character's mind far more powerfully than if these thoughts were described directly by the narrator himself (for example: "Leopold tried to cover up his fears by imagining a benign pleasure, but soon after he realized that he faced a trip culminating in his death") or in the first person by the character (for example: "I'd like to think of my impending trip as something I'm doing for pleasure and self-education, but now I realize that I am fooling myself, for they are transporting me to my death"). And the result, given the fact that we share the mind of somebody facing his imminent and ghastly end in the Holocaust, would be deeply upsetting to any reader, and considerably more so by means of FID than in the other versions I have suggested here.

FLA: So FID is a shaping device that allows an author to create more discomfort than with other means of presentation. It diminishes the distance between the mind of the character and that of the reader.

HL: The more we get inside a character's mind—and FID, more often than not, does so more effectively than letting the character just speak in the first person—the more discomfort the reader is likely to feel (or even the more comfort if the character is presented in a happy light). It's through FID, moreover, that we experience the self-centeredness afflicting Austen's Emma as well as the lurid, cliché-ridden fantasies emanating from that other Emma, namely Flaubert's.

FLA: I'm more partial to the second Emma, Herbie. But Flaubert's *Madame Bovary* is mere child's play when it comes to discomforting the reader if compared to those third-person accounts of the Marquis de Sade in *120 Days of Sodom*. And yet, for all Sade's discomforting aims, their endless repetition turns discomfort into boredom. He wrote important work inasmuch as he deliberately set out to create works that would discomfort through and through. However, he's not a great writer.

HL: A single act of violence such as Emma's suicide is more readable—and certainly more memorable—than the repetitive acts presented by Sade.

FLA: Therein lies the difference between Sade and others interested in creating discomforting works. I think of Edgar Allan Poe, who also sought to discomfort through and through, but with a greater will to style. To pick up and revise Hemingway's expression that all modern literature came out of Huckleberry's cap, in many ways we can say that all modern disquieting literature came out of Edgar Allan Poe's short stories and some poems such as "The Raven."

HL: Especially when we note how Baudelaire, so smitten by Poe (and he was his French translator to boot!) funneled some of Poe's discomfort into later writers!

FLA: Like Poe and unlike Sade, Flaubert's use of a greater palette of shaping devices (including FID) gives *Madame Bovary* much more of a layered and satisfactory feeling of discomfort than Sade. Indeed, there are many tools that can be used in giving shape to the disquieting in literature. Let's not forget the fact that Roth's disquieting (and funny) and much-decried novel *Portnoy's Complaint* is a first-person narrative—a monologue, actually. The only intervention of another character comes in the form of the last line of the novel—a line delivered by the psychologist: "So. Now vee may perhaps to begin. Yes?" In spite of this, it comes off as a very polyphonic novel. Roth's skillful use of the monologue never leads to the kind of monotony of a monovocal or univocal narrative we experience with Sade, for instance.

Yet others employ the first person to great disquieting effect, including the aforementioned Oscar "Zeta" Acosta as well as the so-identified postcolonial author Hanif Kureishi. Kureishi wrote a marvelous first-person narrative about a forty-something invited over to his eighteen-year-old girlfriend's house for dinner—with her parents.

The forty-something narrator-protagonist suddenly has to "have a crap" (*Love in a Blue Time* 132). He gives nuanced detail about the defecating process itself—"I can feel the soft motion through my gut, in one piece. It's been awaiting this moment the way things do, like love" (133)—only then to detail the "bobbing turd" that refuses to flush: "The brown bomber must have an aversion to the open sea. The monstrous turd is going nowhere and nor am I while it remains an eternal recurrence" (135). Rather than try to flush again and risk its not disappearing down the sewer, he decides that it's better to "fish around until my fingers sink into the turd, get a muddy grip and yank it from the water" (136). Before wrapping it in toilet paper and throwing it out the window, he remarks: "I glance at the turd and notice little teeth in its velvet head, and a little mouth opening. It's smiling at me, oh no, it's smiling and what's that, it's winking, yes, the piece of shit is winking up at me, and what's that at the other end, a sort of tail, it's moving, and oh Jesus, it's trying to say something, to speak, no, no, I think it wants to sing" (136).

This moment with his turd is discomforting, to say the least. But it teeters into the humorous. Incongruous combinations of the profane and the existential not only disturb, but they do so with a wink and a smile. The tale of the turd is his own tale—one where his life seems to go on "despite everything, not knowing why or how" (137). There are other similarly discomforting moments that combine with existential musings. I mentioned already the moment in *The Autobiography of the Brown Buffalo* (1972) when Acosta stands up from the toilet to compare the different colors, the mucus coating, and the overall shape of his poop with a Dalí painting. It is both disgusting and humorously satisfying.

HL: The moment in *The Autobiography* along with the opening pages of "The Tale of the Turd" that you quote certainly awaken the usual feelings of disgust that hit you when you confront feces in literature. Joyce opened up this world when he showed Leopold Bloom defecating in his outhouse in the Calypso episode. When I first read *Ulysses* at college age (it was still rarely taught formally in classes!), I remember feeling thoroughly nauseated by the phrase "above his own rising smell" (56), and thinking about it over the years I can still recapture a bit of that nausea. But Kureishi's turd ceases to nauseate the reader once it starts being analyzed. At that point you read the story more as allegory than as realism—and possibly with a smile as you do so.

FLA: I'm glad you brought up Bloom in the outhouse. I've only taught

Ulysses once to undergraduates. I thought that if I picked the chapters that were most discomforting that I might catch their attention. Maybe it's a question of generation, but they seemed to be nonplussed by the outhouse passage. To be honest, I ended up feeling rather uncomfortable. I couldn't help myself laughing at the incongruity built into this chapter: Bloom on the toilet contemplating his bowel movements *and* questions of ontology.

HL: Yes, being that intimate with someone other than ourselves in a latrine certainly triggers a sense of discomfort. And of course the careful orchestration of the incongruity here—bowels and mind—is above all funny.

FLA: A focus on the nether parts seems to be an obvious area for authors to create at once sensations of pleasure (laughter) and deep discomfort in the reader. Some seem particularly gendered, too.

In another of Kureishi's stories (a story I've taught in postcolonial literature courses precisely to complicate students' ideas of what counts as "postcolonial") that comes to mind, "The Penis," the character Alfie realizes that he's got a penis "complete with balls and pubic hair" in his pocket (*Midnight All Day* 207). After he puts it on the table it begins to wriggle, and his wife, worried that her mother will see it when she comes for lunch, remarks: "Get that thing off my kitchen table!" (207). He manages to get rid of the penis and then we discover the owner, the porn star Doug. After visiting several pubs and clubs he'd been at the night before—"Someone had left behind a shoe, a shotgun, a pair of false eyelashes, and a map of China. No penis had been handed in" (211)—he spots his penis coming out of a coffee shop "accompanied by a couple of young women" (211). The penis smiles as he stands "tall, erect" and wears "dark glasses and a fine black jacket" (211). When he finally confronts his penis, the penis tells him: "I'm going solo. I've been exploited for years. I want my own career. I'm going to make more serious films" (214). The story ends with Doug being "rejoined" with his "love" (217) and not much more. The story in itself is rather disturbing . . . yet can it be that I enjoy it?

HL: Again, as with "The Tale of the Turd," it's the opening pages, when the protagonist finds the penis in his pocket, that have the strongest emotional effect. It's not disgust here, as with the turd, but rather a certain cringing that affects males when they are treated to a graphic description of a severed sexual organ (I suspect female readers would cringe in a similar way if they read about a hot poker being slammed into a character's vagina). But again, as with "The Tale of the Turd," Kureishi moves from realism to allegory for most of the story, and even though the penis is treated as graphically as ever, we experience it more on an intellectual rather than an emotional level.

FLA: Yes, I feel the discomfort as a tightness in my groin, and at the same time a sense of pleasure (*awe!*) in my appreciation of Kureishi's gift as a storyteller. Of course, as you mention before, we experience instances of discomfort that result less in a direct base reflex response and more from a frontal-cortex operation.

HL: Certainly, I think our discomfort in our encounter with, say, *Othello* is a result of our higher brain-function operation. It arises in our discovery of the sheer unpleasantness in Iago's manipulation of the Moor.

FLA: Yes, the discomfort springs from our privileged access to the deep manipulation that Othello is blind to.

HL: *Othello* is pretty hard to take when you read it with care. Think of the way that Iago makes a murderer out of Othello by means of sheer brainwashing. I used to go through those manipulation passages in detail with undergraduate students, and I believe we all ultimately realized we too could be talked into doing terrifying things, or, in some cases, we might become the manipulators ourselves.

FLA: Oh, the joy of traveling with our students into the most discomforting of territories.

HL: At one point, in fact, I feared that my pedagogical method would cost me my job. I refer to an incident that occurred in 1956, when I was an assistant professor at the University of California, Riverside, a position I felt lucky to have got a couple of years before in what seemed an impossible job market. We had a new chancellor at the time, Herman Spieth, and a party was given for us to get to know him. He was a distinguished biologist—did pioneering work with fruit flies that still garners respect from geneticists—whom I'd known a bit during the preceding couple of years before he'd entered the administration. And I always found him quite likable—even in the years after this incident.

During the party he made the rounds among my humanities colleagues to ask them how their teaching was going. When he got to me, I told him I'd been doing *Othello* with a freshman class. He encouraged me to tell him more about it. I said I was trying to get under the play's skin, which meant that as a group we were discovering the sheer unpleasantness in Iago's manipulation of the Moor—after all, during the first act we'd all been rooting for this improbable marriage to succeed, and now it was being destroyed in the most devastating way. By the end, moreover, after Othello's cruel choking of Desdemona, we never quite feel, as I think we do with *Hamlet*, that some sort of order has been restored. It's a very unpleasant play, indeed, and I could see that the students were feeling distinctly uncomfortable.

"You should never make students feel uncomfortable," the chancellor suddenly—and angrily—turned on me. There was nothing I was prepared to answer: all I could think of was that now, even though I knew I was doing the right thing getting down to the bare bones of a literary work with students, I'd probably never achieve tenure and that I needed again to think about law school, which had been my career alternative until I landed that job. But I fully understood how a scientist who'd likely had no exposure to the humanities would react the way he did: if you're working your lab with fruit flies, it's only the latter who experience any discomfort.

FLA: There's of course an additional layer of discomfort, Herbie. After all Othello is identified as the black Moor. His character is certainly not stupid, but very gullible. Either way we take it, Iago's manipulation to tragic ends can take place because he's never under suspicion, whereas Othello's default as a racialized subject falls *automatically* under suspicion. As twenty-first-century readers or audiences we would certainly experience the discomforts of racial prejudice as an ingredient in this tragedy.

HL: I'm glad you brought up the issue of race. In 1956 race was only starting to become part of a public debate, and I don't remember making it an issue in discussing *Othello*—there were enough other things in the play to provoke discomfort. But today of course we can't avoid the racial issue. In her book on *Merchant of Venice* Janet Adelman writes, "Insofar as the figure of the Jew with the knife draws on the ancient image of Jews as Christ-killers and ritual murderers, it will be anti-Semitic in effect, no matter how 'humanized' Shylock is at certain moments—just as *Othello*'s final invocation of a violent sexualized act between a black man and a white woman will be racist in effect" (111). Adelman's statement points to the fact that works of art can offend long after their initial audiences, who were not likely offended by racist biases, have been replaced by audiences who share a different set of values. In fact, when Othello at the end displays his loyalty to the Venetian by exulting at how,

> in Aleppo once,
> Where a malignant and a turban'd Turk
> Beat a Venetian, and traduc'd the state,

I took by the throat the circumcised dog,
And smote him thus. (5.2.353–57)

And then, of course, Othello smites himself in a similar way. I for one always cringe a bit at this seemingly noble death-speech, for the ethnical strands—Moors, Turks, Muslims, Christians, circumcised Jews like me—have become hopelessly entangled.

FLA: I'm glad that we've been discussing literature that might not seem at first glance to be *discomforting*.

HL: Yes, most of the texts we've singled out for the discomfort they offer have been modernist, and there's no question that for at least the last century consumers of the various arts have complained of their discomfort more than people did in earlier centuries. But when we look at a number of classic texts, we often find them discomforting, though perhaps in different ways from more recent ones. Remember that for over a century and a half, from 1681 until well into the nineteenth century, *King Lear* was ordinarily performed with the happy ending that Nahum Tate gave the play to save Cordelia from death. Samuel Johnson complained of the distress he felt reading this play: "I was many years ago so shocked by Cordelia's death, that I know not whether I ever endured to read again the last scenes of the play till I undertook to revise them as editor" (*King Lear*, xliv). In our own, post-Holocaust time, perhaps needing to prove how capriciously the gods treat us, we gladly reenact Shakespeare's original ending.

FLA: Marquis de Sade's first major work, the 1785-published *The 120 Days of Sodom* that you brought up earlier, has long been considered one of the most perverse and discomforting of novels. So much so, that its publication led to Sade's imprisonment. In spite of the violence (forcing young maidens to swallow plucked out eyeballs, breasts torn from women's chests, and sodomizing young girls, for instance) and psychopathology, the novel is repetitive and boring, as we already pointed out.

HL: Boredom, as we said earlier, is a source of discomfort, and in Sade our feelings of boredom are likely stronger than our reactions to the repeated violence. I earlier tried to put a positive spin on some works, like Beckett's novels or Debussy's *Pelléas et Mélisande,* that may seem long and boring but that, for at least some of us, get you hooked through the hypnotic effect they have on you. But I've never had that reaction to Sade.

FLA: Sade was very familiar with Hobbes, accepting as doctrine Hobbes's formulation *Homo homini lupus* or Man is a Wolf to Fellow Man. He did so to perhaps to justify his codes of behavior that went against social decorum and that aligned more with "nature" regarding pleasure and the erotic.

HL: A Hobbesian view of the world, powerful though it may be when you read *Leviathan,* is so monolithic that when somebody like Sade adopts it, it feels just as monolithic. It's all so earnest.

FLA: Perhaps it's the attitude toward solemnity that is the difference that *makes the difference* in the way an author such as Rabelais creates pleasure in readers all while conveying rather discomforting scenes. I think of the birth of Gargantua in Rabelais's *Gargantua and Pantagruel* (circa 1532), which is hardly comforting. The midwives arrive to help the mother Gargamelle: "Groping underneath, they found some flesh excrescences, which stank, and they were sure this was the baby. But in fact it was her asshole, which was falling off, because the right intestine (which people call the ass gut) had gone slack, from too much guzzling of tripe" (21). He's finally born from her ear, and rather than cry he shouts, "Drink! Drink!" (21). As a baby, he never cried, "But he did shit himself all the time" (23) and would be calmed only by wine. As a teen in Paris he decides to unbutton "his handsome codpiece and, sticking his tool right out in the air, bepissed them so violently that he drowned two hundred sixty thousand, four hundred and eighteen people, not counting women and small children" (42). This is all rather gross. However, there's movement, energy—and pleasure in the last instance.

HL: Yes, unlike with Sade, reading Rabelais is pleasurable, discomfort and all. The reason is that Rabelais has a superb sense of comedy. He makes what we would ordinarily find gross a genuinely funny experience. Discomfort is an effect of much comedy—certainly of the sort you hear in popular venues. The image of Gargantua "bepissing" and drowning the crowd is so outrageous that it ceases to discomfort. I think the same can be said about the passage listing the ways of wiping one's ass (Book I, chapter 16).

FLA: Some authors (and I might include the Sade here) seem to have more of a reputation for creating discomforting art than they actually produced. The foul-mouthed brawler Charles Bukowski is one such author. He sold many of his more disturbing stories to porno magazines that the readers of his poetry would likely not have seen. Yet he became famous for writing free verse poetry that wallowed in self-pity. They don't really disgust. I think of "numb your ass and your brain and your heart." It opens: "I was coming off an affair that had gone badly. / Frankly, I was sliding down into a pit / really feeling shitty and low / when I lucked into this lady with a large bed" (24). And there are those like "the night I fucked my alarm clock" that at best shock more than disturb. Critics have applauded Bukowski's relishing in discomfort—his Epicurean approach to life. They seem to enjoy *the idea* of encountering an author who creates sensations of discomfort in their display (poetic?) of a life lived that is radically outside the bounds of the normal.

HL: For me the problem is that, unlike Rabelais, Bukowski is not a great comic writer. The discourse in these passages comes off for me as silly rather than as funny. The effect is that form of discomfort we've tagged as embarrassment—the embarrassment we feel when somebody makes a fool of himself in our presence. And this is particularly true if we hear a poet like Bukowski in a public reading—it's like the effect of the embarrassment-generating monologist I described earlier.

FLA: Certain creators of comic books (*comical* or not) also choose to take us to disquieting spaces. The Latino graphic novelist Wilfred Santiago chooses to use the device of the splash page to take us even more deeply into the disquieted mind of his protagonist, Omar. As the story unfolds in his graphic novel, *In My Darkest Hour,* we turn a page and suddenly a deeply disturbing image of a bound female figure appears (figure 3).

HL: It's fascinating to me how a beautiful woman instead of the grotesque one that Santiago pictures here would have a decidedly different effect—an erotic effect, no less. But I also suspect that a grotesque rendering of a nude whom one would wish to see as erotic is more upsetting than a grotesque reproduction of a clothed person.

FLA: I don't recall other details that fill out the pages of *In My Darkest Hour,* but I certainly remember this one—the one that creates the greatest degree of discomfort. What might this say about the sensation-memory-meaning processes that we bring to our experience of literature generally?

HL: And how is it that bad tastes linger in the mouth longer than the most delicious ones, ugly sights crowd out the memory of handsome ones, nauseating smells pester the nose more powerfully than sweet ones? As in so many instances regarding aesthetics, we keep hoping that neuroscience can supply us with the answers we crave.

FLA: We rounded up the usual suspects like Joyce and Sade, but there's a whole bunch of novels that have since the twentieth century become a

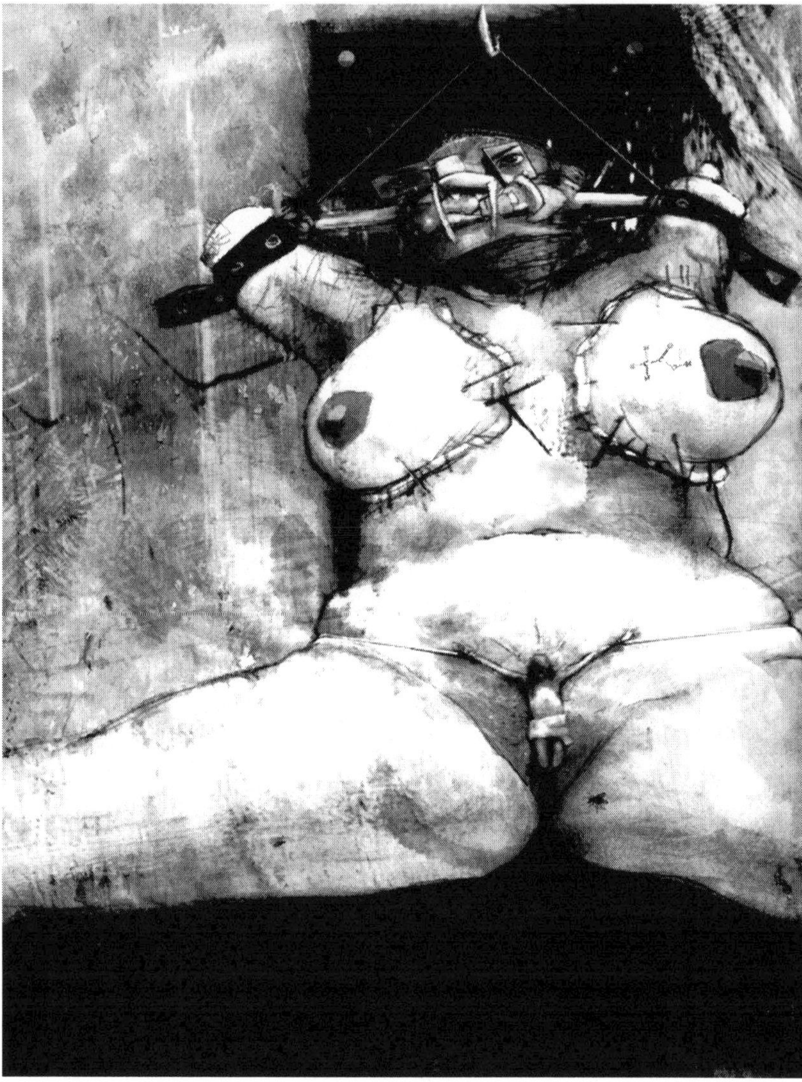

Figure 3. Splash page from Wilfred Santiago's *In My Darkest Hour* (2004).

genre in and of themselves. Some have become the great pillars of literature in the twentieth century.

You mentioned briefly Adler's *The Journey* as an example of FID, but there is also the literature that grew out of the two world wars generally. Of course there's the literature writ large of the Holocaust as well as the war camps in Russia; I mentioned earlier Shalamov's *Kolyma Tales*. In addition, there are the novels (and poetry) focusing on World War II that are extremely disquieting. Take one of the foremost Italian novelists, Curzio Merced Malaparte, who wrote two novels, *The Skin* and *Caput*. The former novel takes place during the occupation of Naples by the U.S. army that depicts such poverty and starvation; there's a scene with a young girl exhibited as a virgin and upon paying a fee one could verify her virginity. In *Caput* there are other very disturbing scenes of violence against women, including disquieting scenes of gang rape. This is not to mention the abundance of literature (poems and novels) written on World War I; some of these poems and novels are extraordinarily disquieting, such as Erich Maria Remarque's *All Quiet on the Western Front* as well as Henri Barbusse's *Le Feu: journal d'une escouade* (*Under Fire: The Story of a Squad*).

There's a whole range of post-Rabelaisian and post-Cervantean literature that combines humor with disquieting scenes. I think of the novels of Henry Miller and those of Anaïs Nin, including her well-crafted diaries about her father who was her lover while she was a teenager. I think of Roth's *Portnoy's Complaint* where Alexander Portnoy masturbates with a liver, among other things. There's also Roth's *Sabbath's Theatre* where his character Morris Mickey Sabbath (the self-proclaimed Monk of Fucking) jerks off on the grave of his dead mistress, Drenka. I think also of Chuck Palahniuk's short story "Guts" (first published in *Playboy* magazine) that recounts some of the most discomforting scenes of masturbation I've read. They involve accidental eating of a lubricated carrot inserted into a rectum, a bloodied penis from inserting candle wax into the urethra, and a sucking out of the narrator's lower intestines while the protagonist masturbates sitting over the water intake of a swimming pool filter.

Many other authors of world literature seek to discomfort their readers, including some of my favorites like Gabriel García Márquez and William Faulkner. I recall with vivid detail reading García Márquez's novella *The Incredible Sad Story of Innocent Eréndira and Her Heartless Grandmother* as a teenager; I recall those discomforting scenes where the grandmother forces her fourteen-year-old granddaughter to have sex with hundreds of men in the most disquieting (even horrifying) of situations. I recall too reading during this same period William Faulkner's controversial *Sanctuary*, especially the scene where Popeye uses a corncob to rape Temple Drake. This not to mention others of my literary diet at the time such as the work of Yasunari Kawabata, Carlos Fuentes, and Julio Cortázar—and of course their literary forefather, Edgar Allan Poe. And *Lolita* is one of the most disturbing pieces of literature—and one of the greatest modernist works of art. There's the extraordinary Brazilian poet Hilda Hilst, who couldn't earn a living as a poet and so began to write pornography out of classic children's stories, the experience of which is at once extremely discomforting—and awe-inspiring. The list is legion and the genres used expansive. Such authors were pioneers and stylistic innovators in giving shape to the disquieting.

There are many other authors who wrote disquieting novels throughout the history of world literature—and especially in the twentieth century. In fact, it's hard to talk about the great books of world literature in the twentieth century without including the vast number of these that are extremely disquieting.

HL: What you're reminding us is that the discomforts in much modernist literature result not only from the stylistic distortions that have upset readers but, at least as important, from the subject matter, which forced readers directly to confront unpleasant things that, during earlier centuries, were either taboo or, as with *Othello*, lurked under the surface.

FLA: Can you believe that in several colleges across the country there are students demanding a "trigger warning" to be placed on texts that might create discomfort? Not only does one have to ask, who decides what is disturbing or not, but also with this kind of censorship in place most of twentieth-century literature would be wiped from the face of the earth.

HL: I was subjected to this form of censorship about twenty years ago after I'd assigned a paper to an undergraduate class on Yeats's great sonnet "Leda and the Swan." The assignment asked students to analyze the poem by way of the revisions that Yeats had made. There are few poems of such consequence for which so much early material is available (Yeats's widow had retrieved the early versions from her husband's waste basket). And I'd done this assignment in classes over many years—with some memorable papers coming out of it. But now I was threatened with having to stop doing it: a delegation of quite solemn women graduate students, who'd heard about my assignment from my teaching assistant, marched into my office and demanded that I not only stop doing this assignment but that I also stop teaching the poem itself: since the subject was rape, they said, the poem could have a deleterious effect on women students. There was no way of arguing with them, so I took their advice under advisement and thanked them for their concern (and of course I continued to teach the poem and assign it for papers, though to honor gender diversity I know I should also have sought out a companion poem about some guy who got his penis lopped off!). This experience, together with that earlier run-in with my chancellor over *Othello*, provided the motivation for me to suggest discomfort to you, Frederick, as a promising subject for a book.

THREE | Awkward Spaces

FREDERICK LUIS ALDAMA: In what we call architecture rather than just the construction of buildings there is a fusion of the aesthetic appeal and function. Whether a residence or a skyscraper, buildings are disquieting to the extent that they are seen as uninhabitable, unlivable. That is, they disquiet when there is a rupture between purpose (function) and any kind of aesthetic criteria of ugliness (and beauty) that we want to apply.

HERBERT LINDENBERGER: Unlike the other art forms—music, literature, the visual arts—that we are discussing, architecture inhabits two, often incompatible realms: the aesthetic and the practical. We can have an aesthetically pleasing building that's dreadfully uncomfortable to live or work in, and we can also have a conspicuously ugly building that's been fixed up with sufficient amenities to render its inhabitants oblivious to the ungainly space they occupy. And of course one can cite countless buildings that are thoroughly unpleasant both to look at and live or work in.

FLA: There are, for example, the medieval dungeons, Bentham's Panopticon, and modern-day prisons—all are spaces deliberately designed to discomfort rather than comfort, to eject us rather than invite for habitation. Even in a beautiful structure like the Château de Chillon (made famous by Byron) we see how its "basement" is transformed into a space that triggers fear. These are all spaces built to dispossess us—to make us feel literally disposable.

HL: My single visit to Byron's dungeon coincided with a memorably awful intestinal upset triggered, I believe, by gorging myself on chocolate while touring the Nestlé factory the preceding day—with the result that the negative responses you list here were grossly compounded for me.

FLA: Thank goodness you weren't shackled during such an upset. What do we make of another such foreboding space—the cemetery? Even in the Protestant tradition, where graves are often only marked by white crosses (as in military cemeteries like Arlington) there is no habitable purpose created in the cemetery. If allowed, you can walk on the lawns, and so on. In many Catholic cemeteries, you find the opposite: graves are literally built upon; you build something on top of the grave, sometimes even big structures—mausoleums where in theory a family could live inside. And in the Latino community we have *Día de los muertos* every year—a festival that we celebrate in actual cemeteries. However, no matter how much drink and music and celebration generally, the cemetery remains a place we don't inhabit while there's still breath in us. Likewise, no matter the size of the mausoleum, they are not made to be inhabited by the *living*.

What's disquieting about these buildings is that there is no relationship between habitation as non-living quarters with the shape and form; there is no longer a uniform whole between function and form—its shape and thus its aesthetics.

HL: But Frederick, please don't forget the memorializing function of cemetery art, which occasionally is very good. Even though the living don't inhabit these places, they can visit them the way they do visual works of art, and those who feel some connection to the deceased, whether by religion or personal relationship, can experience a functional pleasure together with the aesthetic. There's a gorgeous monument in a St. Louis cemetery, Bellefontaine, that Louis Sullivan created for a local family, the Wainwrights, for whom he had designed one of the first great high-rises. Or the Stanford family tomb on the Stanford campus—severely neoclassical but with a spicy touch in front with those sphinxes, which embody the late nineteenth-century neo-Egyptian craze (figure 4).

And, speaking of Egyptian, there are the pyramids, not to speak of the Taj Mahal. These have their multiple functions, aesthetic and practical at once. You and I are so secular-minded, Frederick, that we forget what functions tombs like these have for the more religious. Although the remains of the deceased may be inside, their souls (or however these may be designated in various religions) reside in some nonearthly realm—or, to use computer terminology, in the cloud. These remains remain firmly placed within the earthly structure, and that itself must provide some comfort to the mourners, themselves still bound to earth. And one might remember that some of the most important domestic artifacts we possess from ancient Chinese, Egyptian, and Etruscan culture, to mention only three, were found in tombs, where the dead supposedly continued their ordinary lives.

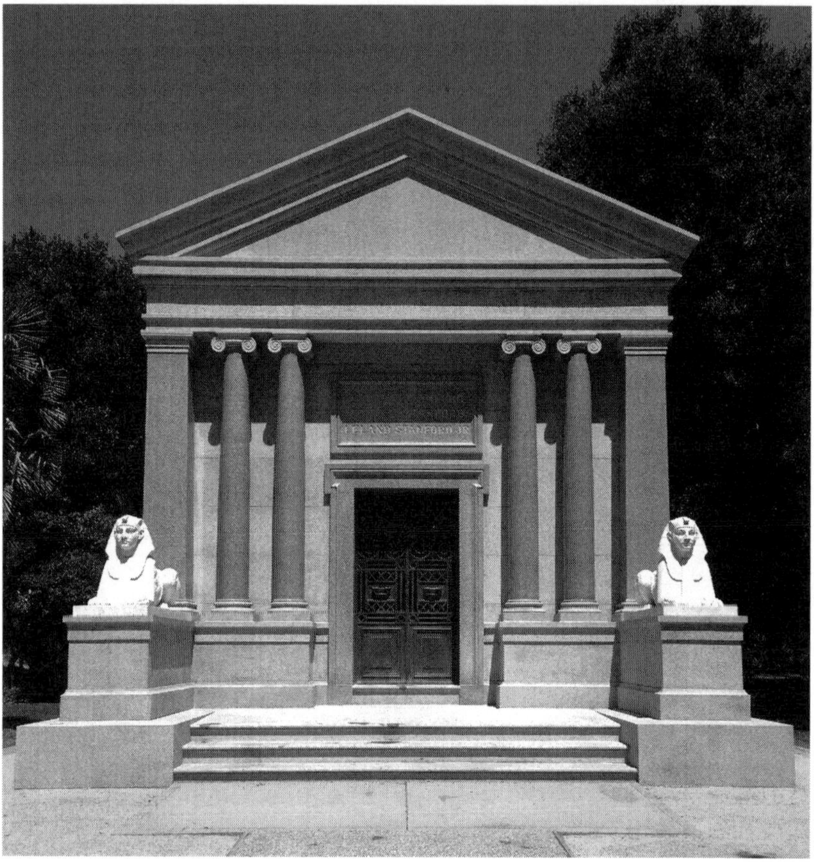

Figure 4. Stanford Family Mausoleum, Stanford University, designed by Caterson and Clark, architects (1888). Photo by Herbert Lindenberger.

FLA: Material habitats for the non-tellurian-bound—what a paradox, Herbie! For the record, I'm not upholding *functionalism* in architecture—or art in general. When I speak about function (and maybe "role" is better, given that "functionalism" carries other baggage in other disciplines) I refer to the fact that the buildings (whether an office or house) are to be *inhabited*. We might consider this the content (in the Formalists' view of literature it would be the *story*) and that this can be given many different shapes (in the Formalists' view of literature it would be the *discourse*); there is no limit to architectural creativity in this sense. Inhabiting can be done in a myriad of different shapes.

As we've been discussing, each art has its own specificity; its own content (matter) and shape (form); I cannot inhabit a sculpture or piece of music or painting or novel. In this sense, and only in this sense, each art form has its *own function*.

Architecture as an art form—as a branch of aesthetics—is the unity of shape and function. Not all buildings matter to aesthetics. Not all buildings have to do with aesthetics. The cave has nothing to do with aesthetics; it functioned to shelter our ancestors. The same with those cages that are called tenements and that are built to house working-class people in cities all over the world. They are disquieting to the extent that they embody this rupture between shape and function. They disquiet to the extent that they expel the aesthetic (viewpoint or consideration). Whatever their size, these buildings are eternally disquieting because they have *expelled* the aesthetic. They are irredeemably disquieting.

HL: Again, Frederick, I'd like revise or at least augment what you're saying. The lack of a builder to exercise his will to style does not necessarily condemn a habitation to aesthetic insignificance. At least some cave dwellers learned to make the dwellings that nature had designed for them remarkably pleasing aesthetically. Think of the paintings at Altamira (whatever "meanings" they may have had for their creators in that prehistoric time), which show a superb way of adapting art to the particular configurations that nature gave to the inside of these caves. Though the inhabitants likely resided only in the anterooms, they had their own communal "museum," or, perhaps more likely, their own set of chapels, at hand every day.

FLA: I tend to gravitate toward extremes, Herbie, to make my points crystal clear. I would argue that the paintings ornament the cave, but don't function to unify shape with function. In this sense, there's the expulsion of the aesthetic; there is no aesthetic aim or ambition in the shaping of the nature-given cave. There is nothing that unites shape with function with the cave, and thus there's no aesthetic relation. And this can go for more modern habitations, too, such as tenements—and tract houses. Both the cave and the tract house disallow an aesthetic relation.

In architecture there are a whole series of schools—of ways, or methods to approach and deal with the aesthetic relation with respect to building. There is a will to style—an aesthetic relation between that which is built and the procedure used for its construction, from engineering calculations through the choice of materials and the decision to inscribe the building within an aesthetic context.

HL: You're letting bad architecture off the hook too easily by refusing to apply aesthetic categories to buildings like tract houses that make no pretense to artistic distinction (though sometimes the ads that are used to market them may fall back on traditional aesthetic vocabulary). When I first noted those ungainly tract houses that sprouted all over after World War II (at a time the U.S. government gave cheap loans to veterans, who after all desperately needed housing for their families), I felt aesthetically violated—especially when I saw the gorgeous wooded landscapes around Seattle, where I grew up, suddenly covered with designs seeking to attract the lowest common denominator of taste. But then it's only fair to remember a great exception: Joseph Eichler, who had once lived briefly in a Wright house and, as a result, hired a Wright disciple to design thousands of inexpensive tract houses throughout the Bay Area from the 1950s to the early 1970s. These were wonderfully livable and aesthetically pleasing houses. But they are the exception that, alas, proves the rule.

FLA: What of the introduction of disquieting spaces in earlier epochs? I think of Roman architecture, of course a facsimile (and, at its best, an adaptation) of ancient Greek architecture. Apart from the underground of the Coliseum, where slaves and animals were kept, I don't think I can put a finger on buildings that disquiet coming out of these periods when architecture seemed exclusively predicated on the guiding principles of balance and sobriety.

HL: The same can be said of Italian Renaissance architecture, which adapted Roman styles just as the Romans had gone back to the Greeks, whose buildings were still standing when the Romans visited them.

FLA: Since the nineteenth century—and especially the twentieth century—architecture has become a part of treatises on aesthetics. When those, from Baumgarten to the present, discuss aesthetics, they talk about architecture as a discipline.

HL: And it's fascinating how these treatises, which I studied some years ago to see how they variously classify the arts ("Literature and the Other Arts," 367–77), often placed architecture at the bottom of the hierarchy—and all because those aestheticians were unable to view architecture, which necessarily possesses practical uses, as "pure" art. Hegel, in his *Aesthetics*, allowed architecture top place during prehistoric times when mankind had not achieved what he called "self-consciousness," but by his own, self-conscious time, the highest laurels go to poetic drama. Unlike these treatises, which tend to praise aesthetic "purity"—what Kant called "purposelessness"—your remarks praise architecture for its very purposefulness in creating habitation.

FLA: Hence, the importance of understanding how each art disquiets on its own terms. As mentioned already, no matter the theory formulated—no matter how monumental the sculpture, we don't inhabit the sculpture. We cannot inhabit any other art product. The only art form that I can install myself and choose as a dwelling is a product of architecture; that is, all products of architecture play the same role of allowing *in*habitation, and this whether a Paleolithic cave or a tenement in the Parisian suburbs. Buildings are made to be lived in and worked in; they are made to be *inhabited*. But the cave that has a function—a role—does not have an aesthetic relation with the cave dweller.

Today's apartment buildings operate on a dollar-per-cubic-feet basis, thus the ripping in two of the possible unity of shape and function. Frank O. Gehry captures my thinking on the subject best in his oft-stated belief that innovations and responding to social needs are not mutually exclusive.

HL: Unlike me, Frederick, who cannot hammer a nail without missing its head and crushing my finger instead, you have designed, built, and remodeled houses with your own hands. When you build or modify a house, how conscious are you of this aesthetic relation?

FLA: In the will to style that I bring to the designing, then building of a structure, I constantly toggle back and forth in my mind between shape and function—a process ultimately modified by cost and materials. This said, while the latter modifies the realization of the final built space, I always try to maintain a unity of shape with function.

In sharp contrast to those structures that I build to please, we have those panopticon structures constructed to cage humans. I think of the famous one in Mexico—El Palacio de Lecumberri, which was made with a will to style intended to dehumanize. What you realize once you enter is that it is not an ordinary building that would serve to allow you to live or work, but a place where people are stationed like cattle; the role of these buildings is not a human and humanistic role, it's an antihuman role that at once seeks to pack human beings into small space and at the same time to isolate them from one another; you realize that this is a place where people are tortured and punished. All the inhuman forms in the usage of these buildings are extremely disquieting. (In Pinochet's Chile they used schools to store women until they gave birth, then massacred them en masse.) No matter how ornate or how much will to style used in their construction, there is a rupture between the role (function) and the shape (everything that goes into the making of the building according to aesthetic goals).

HL: If I'm being tortured, I suspect I won't have the presence of mind to realize how disconnected my dreadful experience is from the environment in which it is taking place.

FLA: In this violent dissociation of function and shape with prisons or with mausoleums we experience something that is abruptly and deeply disquieting.

HL: I still insist on those exceptional mausoleums like the Taj Mahal or Louis Sullivan's design in Bellefontaine Cemetery as having a function for the families of those interred there.

FLA: The first habitable dualities were the caves our Paleolithic ancestors inhabited. They served the function of shelter but did not as such have an aesthetic quality about them. There was no union between function and aesthetic categories such as ugliness and beauty.

HL: Unless, that is, you have paintings in these caves of the quality of Lascaux and Altamira. I was going to see Lascaux for myself, but they closed it to tourists just before my scheduled visit—the breathing of visitors, it turned out, endangered the paintings. But I made it to Altamira several times before it too had to be closed, and I can testify that I felt a strong aesthetic relation between the paintings and the total ambiance of the cave.

FLA: Certainly, the adornments made the caves more inviting as habitats. And caves by themselves can inspire awe in us. Today we can enter some of those great big caves in Mexico and experience what Kant called the sublime, but we recognize the cave as a nature-made phenomenon or structure.

With architecture as art we have the work of humans—humans construct buildings—and as products of human activity, we can apply aesthetic categories to these products. But what's disquieting about certain buildings is that they have destroyed, taken apart the unity between form (shape) and the function of the product; from the point of view of function in the abstract, with the rare exception there's no difference between my house and the Paleolithic cave; these tens of thousands of years make no historical difference: both protect from cold, rain, animals. The function is the same as a dwelling place. But the cave is made by nature and my house is human-made—myself, usually as the builder. A Paleolithic ancestor chooses a cave according to how well it will fulfill his or her needs; the same happens when we choose our homes. Most of the time all we care about is the function—

and this from a prison to a home or apartment or favela. We make choices that follow functional criteria that are no different from those of our Paleolithic forefathers.

Today, however, we have the additional possibility of following aesthetic criteria. And it is the latter that make the difference in this fusion of shape and function. So when there's a radical break of the possible unity of shape and function we react with discomfort—even repulsion.

HL: The proverbial 1950s tract house was highly functional, with all the conveniences its inhabitants yearned for, but, with the rare exception of those built by Eichler, it was usually aesthetically off the map. But how many of these inhabitants even thought about aesthetics? They felt lucky to have a shelter that, thanks to government lending policies, they could afford.

FLA: The disquieting in architecture, then, is not just a rupture between function (or role) and shape; it also includes buildings constructed with the aim of being inscribed within an aesthetic relation but which are extremely disquieting in certain circumstances. Beautiful buildings can be made to imprison, torture, maim, and kill people. Thus, in a different way we experience a rupture between the role (function) given to these dwellings and the shape. No matter how much of an aesthete you are, you can no longer establish an aesthetic relation with the object; the object's role totally changes when it becomes uninhabitable. This is where the disquieting enters the picture.

Those beautiful castles that pepper the European landscape also contain those antihumanistic spaces—the dungeons. This creates a rupture in us when we visit such castles. I recall a trip to Lacoste, France, with my father's wife at the time (French). I explored all of the nooks and crannies of the castle there, including the dungeon. It would send chills down my spine—and not those of the sublime. I later discovered that this was the Marquis de Sade's castle.

HL: I feel chills like that when I see ordinary people cramped into the smallest of spaces in ugly urban buildings.

FLA: We feel uncomfortable when we encounter a tenement in the same way we do when visiting a prison, even the ghost of one we might visit at Sade's castle or as a tourist at Alcatraz.

HL: And speaking of Alcatraz, this now decayed prison in late 2014 became the setting for an installation by Chinese dissident artist Ai Wei Wei, who, though not allowed to leave China to see the prison itself, created a scary reminder of what oppression means with an exhibit of

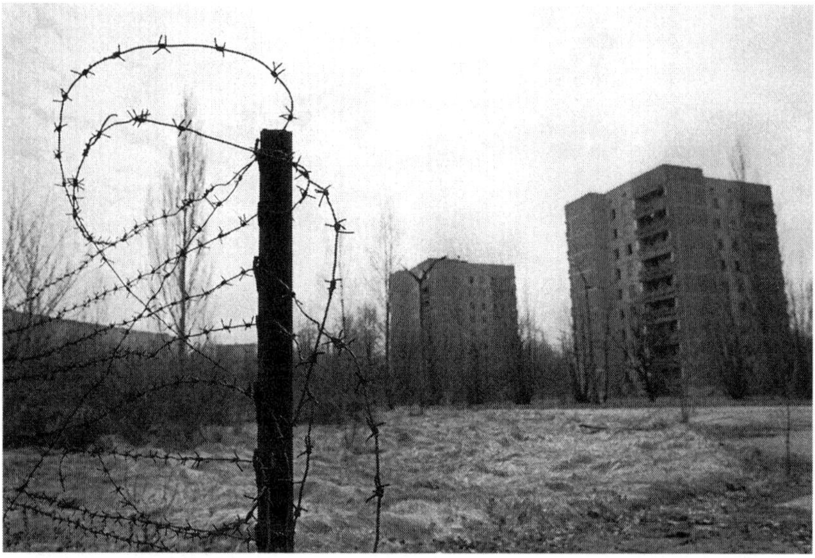

Figure 5. Katya Tolamacheva, *Barbed Wire and Building* (2013). Photo with permission from the artist.

some powerful visual and aural artifacts, the latter, for instance, including recordings of Martin Luther King and participants in the Russian feminist activist band Pussy Riot, piped into individual prison cells. The tourists I observed there seemed quite unnerved, for Ai Weh Weh's exhibit was exacerbating the discomfort they would ordinarily have felt during a visit to Alcatraz.

FLA: Ai Wei Wei aims to trigger in us what we feel inside those spaces built to eject humanity. We see this, too, in the work of the photographer Katya Tolamacheva. Her exhibitions gravitate around such disinhibiting spaces in Ukraine. She captures just how structures are built to be *inhuman* toward humans (figure 5). The images show well how they are built spaces that turn against humans.

The role of shelter and covered, protected environment to relax and enjoy and grow physically and mentally is annihilated, destroyed, and changed into its opposite: a hostile environment disconnected from essential human needs and threatening the ingredients we desire for a happy life. Such architecture triggers uneasiness, disquiet, and even anxiety.

I experience this same disquietude when taking Corina to the zoo;

there's this rupture between the aesthetic (the shape) and the function (the habitability) of the built environment. Zoos break this unity to such a degree that they can even trigger a sense of horror.

HL: Zoos are prisons, after all. And when the animal poses dangers, the spectator accepts this rupture between shape and function much as one would when viewing a murderer in jail.

FLA: Horror films use this rupture between shape and habitability in the turning of the plots in the house of horror. In *Amityville Horror* or in *Psycho* the houses become disquieting because of this rupture between the aesthetic and the habitability; the houses look menacing—not to mention its inhabitants—and there's no way to turn these houses into an aesthetics of pleasure like the one we experience, for instance, with Wright's Fallingwater house.

HL: And Fallingwater, remember, was just a weekend home, a pied-à-terre, so to speak, to which the Kaufmann family retreated from their doubtless sumptuous Pittsburgh house.

FLA: We also have some famous examples of architects and everyday builders who have built inhabitable, repulsive spaces. Again, what we see is a lack (deliberate or not) of a unity of function and shape. I think of those like Le Corbusier, Adolf Loos, and even Ferdinand "Le Facteur" Cheval, French postman-cum-builder who thought of his ugly structure as something beautiful.

HL: I see we must disagree here: as someone who refuses to see Le Corbusier's or Loos's work as ugly (perhaps not "beautiful" in the Burke/Kantian sense, but certainly "impressive"), I don't like seeing them linked to that comically eccentric Le Facteur.

FLA: Certainly, there's greater skill and knowledge patent in the will to style they bring that's not seen with Le Facteur. The minimalism we see in the work of those such as Frank Lloyd Wright, Le Corbusier, and Mies van der Rohe was a response to the excessive ornament used in architecture from the Baroque and rococo to the Victorian that leads paradoxically, I think, to states of discomfort.

HL: Only, I think, when it's overdone.

FLA: This Baroque ornamentation transcends historical period. We have it in the seventeenth century just as we have it in the modern, twentieth century with Gaudí—and, a little earlier, with Le Facteur Cheval.

HL: I think we'll need to take these strange figures up in more detail later.

FLA: Today we see these boxes with ornament pasted on that have nothing to do with the building; the ornament exists as an afterthought, and not as integrated into the whole.

HL: Nonfunctional ornament does not necessarily bother me. I happen to love Baroque ornament: functionality, after all, is a modernist bias. Living in San Francisco, I relish many of the wooden Victorian houses designed and built by ordinary carpenters who often went to other craftsmen for the ornaments that they then simply nailed onto these structures. But I agree that we feel uncomfortable when an architect today adds ornament that doesn't feel functional to us.

FLA: There are contemporary buildings the world over that discomfort. I think of Kunsthaus Graz art museum in Austria, Frank Gehry's EMP rock museum building in Seattle, and the Selfridge store in the larger Bullring Shopping Center in Birmingham, among many others.

HL: When a serious architect such as Gehry gives us what we perceive to be an ugly building, it's often a product of his or her iconoclasm: to be daring enough to design the Bilbao Guggenheim means you are also taking chances that something will turn out wrong—or perhaps your client, in this case EMP Museum Paul Allen, pushed you in this direction. And with computer-generated architecture all sorts of shapes—plantlike, animal-like, bulbous, bloated, severely angular—have become possible, so there's a far greater chance that ungodly looking buildings will emerge. Still, many buildings that first strike us as ugly or outrageous eventually come to seem appropriate, even beautiful. I'm thinking here of Loos's initially shocking 1910 building on the Michaelerplatz in Vienna, which caused many subsequent architects to move in his modernist direction and to get us accustomed to the daringly simple style that he had introduced.

But this is no different from what goes on in other arts: many of the pioneers of modern painting, literature, and music all went through the process of being labeled ugly before they came to seem beautiful (or at least powerful, since the term *beauty* rarely seems applicable even to the best modernist art). This is no guarantee, of course, that the buildings mentioned above will ever cease seeming ugly.

FLA: And this calls attention to that tension we identified earlier between the purpose of the art and the actual practices of its consumption. The latter can and does include ideological baggage. Like stinky people, some also deem certain buildings to be of a certain socioeconomic class—and this from their very inception. I think of Loos and the designing of the first huge tenements: gigantic rabbit cages that stood in sharp contrast to the nineteenth-century houses in working-class neighborhoods in places like Vienna for workers.

HL: Not only do we see a famous architect designing rabbit warrens stacked to the sky for the working poor, Frederick, but we are also reminded that architecture goes hand in hand with city planning. I recall the days in midcentury when it was common practice—and blatantly so—for city planners to "redline" areas of a city. They would get out their red marker pens and decide where to build the tenements, usually as far as possible from central business districts, middle-class denizens, and basic sustenance infrastructures (grocery store, banks, post office, and so on).

FLA: The consequences of which continue to feed the horrors that plague the urban African American and Latino populations living in areas like East and West Oakland, California. Favelas as makeshift houses are the result of forcing people to live in such degraded everyday circumstances; they pull whatever scrap available to create a shelter from the elements. Is there much of a difference here between the favelas and tract homes in the suburbs, however?

There's certainly a will, a project, and a plan in tract home development. There's science involved in determining the size of a house, the pattern of streets, parks, lighting, and so on. These are all deliberate decisions made by builders, bankers, city-planning commissions, and whoever else needs to be brought in. In the favelas all is built in an improvised way; and little by little one might add the comforts of more permanent settlements. This said, from the point of view of aesthetics there is no difference between a favela and a planned, suburban residential development. Even though there's a big difference in the planning and the profiteering, what they have in common is the rupture between the function and the aesthetic.

HL: In both these instances—favela or planned community—aesthetics is not on the mind of the agents. But let's face it, much of the space within most urban areas, with some few exceptions such as Venice, Paris, Prague, San Francisco, is depressing to see. Occasionally an exciting new building with architectural integrity gets placed in an otherwise dreary neighborhood, like Manhattan's New Museum (designed by the Japanese firm SANAA), which boldly enlivens the Bowery in the most conspicuous possible way (figure 6).

Much as I like the building (though the small space to which it was confined allowed galleries too narrow for curators to display their shows adequately), its surroundings also remind the viewer how discomforting urban landscapes usually are.

FLA: When we're talking about urban planning and built environments—recall Oscar Niemeyer's deliberately planned-out city that became the

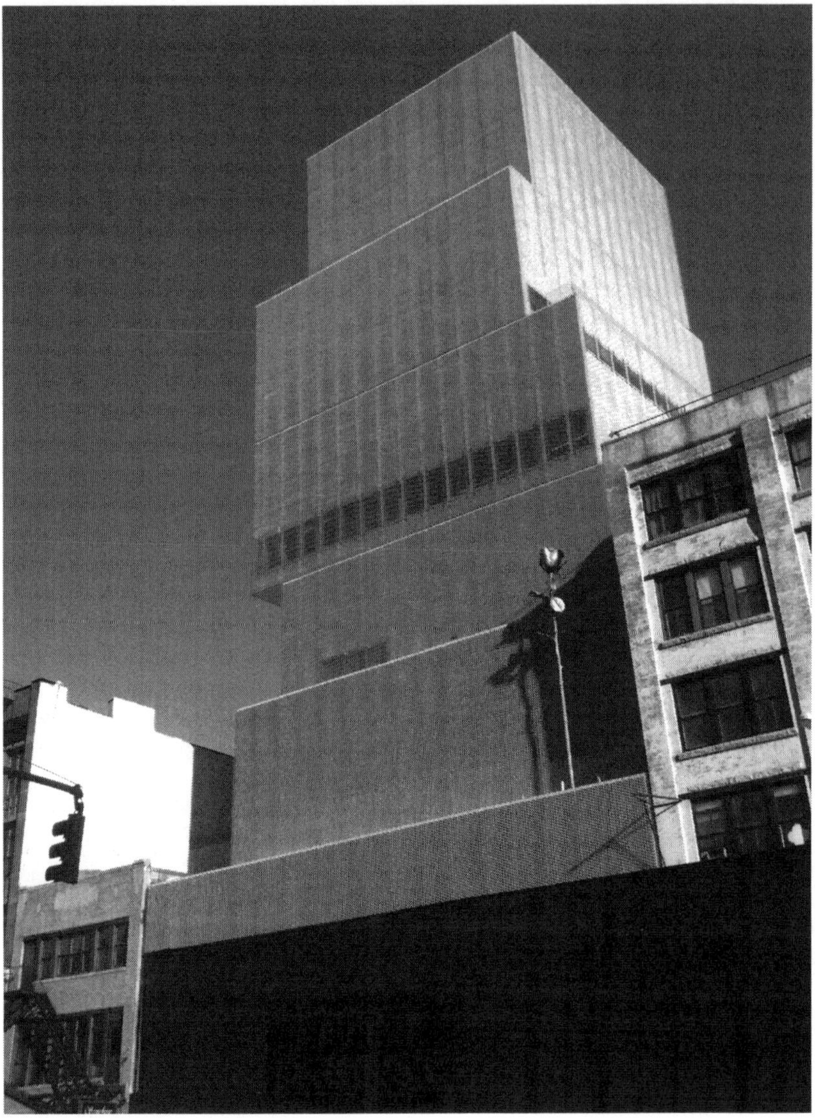

Figure 6. Kazuyo Sejima + Ryue Nishizawa, New Museum of Contemporary Art on the New York Bowery (2007). Photo by Herbert Lindenberger.

capital in Brazil, Brasília—where there was a will to style and also ultimately a rupture between the aesthetic and the function. Le Corbusier dreamed of building a city from scratch that aimed to unify shape and function. He wanted the buildings to harmonize with nature—city or otherwise. His planning of these small cities had to harmonize with the geography and geology (the material basis) on which it would be built. Then he would take into account this unity of shape and funciton, where the shape would allow the buildings to integrate themselves into the landscape *in an aesthetic* way, but with the aesthetic coming after considerations of geography and geology. (Those glass skyscrapers built in the deserts of Dubai clearly don't follow this principle at all.)

We also see the same wilfulness in the nineteenth century with Baron Haussmann's demolishing half of Paris to build huge boulevards for quick and easy movement of the punitive arm of the government so that its military and police could move quickly from one part of the city to another to squash worker revolts. This was urban planning determined by military and economic reasons. Then, in the twentieth century in Paris (after World War II) there was a law passed that determined not to separate the workers from others and to create mixed-income neighborhoods.

There are many kinds of urban planning, and they exist for many different kinds of reasons. With economic and other pressures, planning can and does deliberately separate form from function, leading to different kinds of discomfort for people.

HL: Whether it's for a commercial building, a museum, or a residential house, one needs the luxury of a good architect to prevent this monotony.

FLA: Even though we admire some architects, it's a very interdisciplinary art; the architect not only needs to have a full knowledge of material resistance (longevity and flexibility) as related to the geography and geology of the building site, but also many specialists who can furnish this information along with all those with the skills to execute the plan. Like the director of a film, the architect is a master of ceremonies. When architects don't use the knowledge of material specialists and engineers telling them what can and can't be done in practical terms, this can lead to disasterous results, as we see with Wright's leaky roofs.

HL: A typical city contains buildings representing a multitude of architectural styles from different periods. We are so accustomed to seeing, say, a Victorian structure next to an art deco, which will in turn be placed next to a tall glass tower, that we take in what should seem an incongruous sight without, literally, batting an eyelash. I think of this incongruity whenever I see one of those rare citiscapes, like Venice or small towns like Rothenburg, that are pretty much all of a piece. No art museum would juxtapose paintings in so incongruous a way.

FLA: Incongruity . . .

HL: Freud makes a point of this when he writes that Rome contains structures spanning well over two millennia—from ruins dating to the republican period down through medieval, Renaissance, and Baroque styles, not to speak of its many more recent buildings. He used the analogy, however, not to speak of architecture, the subject that concerns us here, but to illustrate his own main concern, the human psyche, which, as he explains, contains memory traces—all mixed together in seemingly random fashion like the buildings of Rome—from the various periods of a subject's life (*Freud Reader* 725–27).

FLA: Yes, and Gaston Bachelard likens our mental space to that of a house: the attic would be the frontal cortex and the basement that of the limbic system, to put it in today's parlance. Beyond the typical structure of a traditional house Bachelard doesn't venture into all those variations we see in modernist architecture and its stripped-down structures. I think of how Adolf Loos rejected ornament, famously creating a house for Dadaist Tristan Tzara that pushed exteriors with the aim of discomforting those passing by. Like other modernist architects of his day there was the seeming aim to create structures that overturned expectations of how we were to inhabit buildings.

HL: Upon first encounter, certainly. But then people gradually learned how to look at these buildings, like the house Loos designed for Tristan Tzara. I remember not knowing how to deal with Loos when I went to Vienna on a Fulbright in 1952. During my first few days there I saw the once-scandalous building, called the Looshaus, that Emperor Franz Josef ridiculed for its lack of eyebrows because there was no decoration above the windows. Since I'd had no experience with modernist architecture at that point, its deliberate simplicity made it look insipid to me—especially since it was facing the heavily ornamented, massive structure across the street and, for that matter, similarly ornamented buildings all over the area (figure 7). At the time the building went up Loos wrote a celebrated essay that associated ornament with crime—not, of course, crime on the streets but the crime of ornamenting a building!

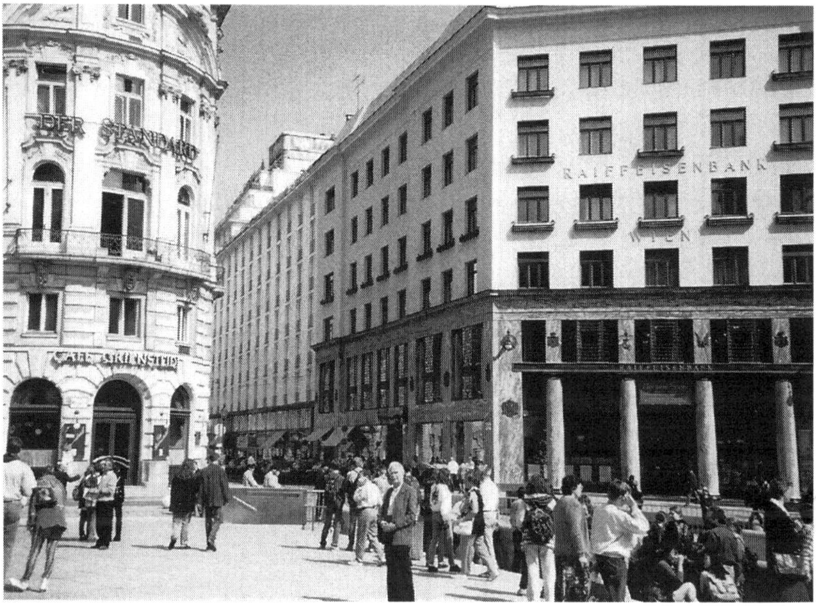

Figure 7. Adolf Loos, Looshaus on Michaeler Platz, Vienna (1910). Photo by Herbert Lindenberger.

My next, and only, subsequent visit to Vienna was some forty-five years later, by which time I'd become an aficionado of modernist architecture. Now the surrounding buildings bored me, and the Looshaus looked defiantly right. The irony of all this is that by 1952 I was thoroughly familiar with modernist poetry and was working in Vienna on my doctoral dissertation on the poet Georg Trakl, whose radical style I was explicating and defending and who, it turned out, was not only a friend of Loos but who actually dedicated the title poem of his second volume, *Sebastian im Traum*, to him. I had been trained to remain so specialized that it never occurred to me there might be a connection between what Trakl was doing so radically with poetic style and Loos, with architectural style.

FLA: Your experience, Herbie, has me wondering how much does our appreciation of that which discomforts rely on our cognitive appraisal system. Does the more we know about modernist architecture make us appreciate more how an architect willfully sets out to fracture function from shape?

I've been drawn to Loos as much for his disruptive designs as his life, particularly the way it wrapped in and around the life of Josephine Baker—the African American performance artist who also sought to *be modern*. Recall that she had "Sois modern" above the entrance to her Paris nightclub. Loos even designed and presented Baker with blueprints for a rather discomforting house—one that was never built.

HL: And biographical information can also be off-putting. Those stripes on the Baker plan have a deliberately scandalous look about them. Loos was also supposedly involved in a pedophile scandal. But I'm not going to call that relevant to his role as an architect. Frank Lloyd Wright and Louis Kahn, to speak of only two major modernist architects, had their own sexual scandals, and one of Wright's was with a client's wife, whom, to be sure, he subsequently married. And, unlike Loos, to be fair, Wright and Kahn sought out mature women who supposedly knew what they were doing.

FLA: The sordid lives of those who seek discomfort.

HL: Since we are concerned here with discomfort, let me bring up a point about architecture that's particularly relevant to Wright's work. I refer to his refusal to make many of his houses really comfortable places for their occupants to live in. I know that this statement flies in the face of Wright's influential notion that architectural form is related to the functions that buildings are intended for. But Wright had little respect for the needs of his clients—rather, he designed so that clients could accommodate themselves to his particular vision, comfort or not. (His clients usually were submissive and continued to speak fondly of him while putting up with whatever discomforts he had designed for them.) I suspect that Wright himself—at least to judge from his and his wife's bedrooms at Taliesin West, in which one wall was missing so that they could sleep in the desert air—didn't much care about his personal comfort. Worst of all were his kitchens, which were usually impractical and much too small. And the gorgeous chairs and benches he designed were hell to sit on.

FLA: Purposefully discomforting—or an ego getting in the way of practicality.

HL: He was notorious for his casualness about practical matters: there's the well-known story that when a client complained of rain dripping onto his desk, Wright replied, "Move your desk." His great house on the Stanford campus, the Hanna house, also known as the Honeycomb House because of its hexagonals everywhere, including the furniture, almost collapsed during the 1989 earthquake because it was

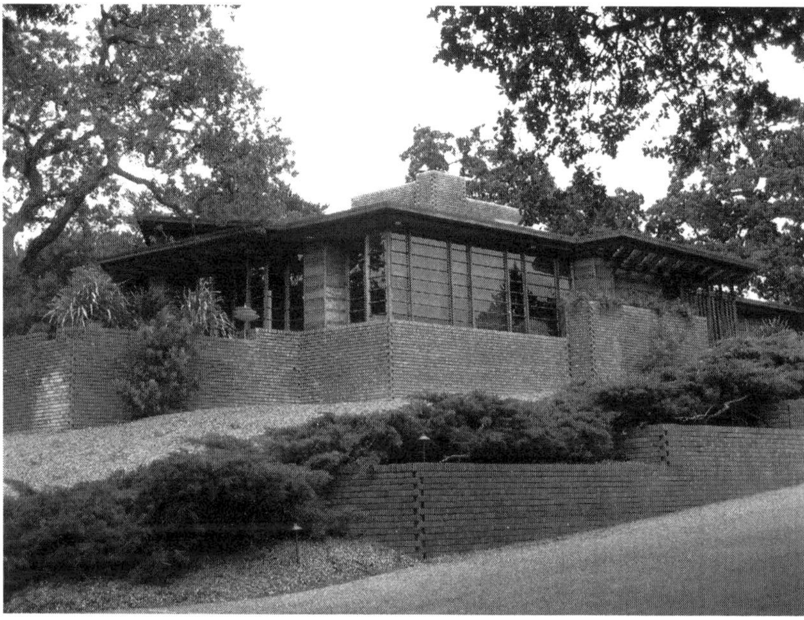

Figure 8. Frank Lloyd Wright, Hanna house, Stanford campus (1937). Photo by Herbert Lindenberger.

built of unreinforced brick, with its beautiful fireplace forced to offer support at once for the living and dining rooms and the kitchen (figure 8). Moreover, because of a slope on the hill upon which the house was erected, he had put part of the house on landfill, a dangerous thing to do in earthquake country.

I used to pass the house on my daily runs when I lived on Stanford campus, and while it was being repaired after the earthquake I sometimes talked to the workers, who complained of the shoddy construction around the foundation. I say all this in full awareness that seeing Wright's work over the years has provided me with some of the greatest aesthetic experiences of my life. I've sought out Wright buildings all over the country, seen all the Oak Park houses (most of these, to be sure, necessarily from the outside) and exulted over Fallingwater, the Guggenheim, and Taliesin West. He was very great, but I would not subject my family to the discomfort of living in one of his buildings. These buildings are a little like New York: you'd rather visit than live there. And the discomfort does not derive simply from the architect's frequent casualness about practical details: it also derived from

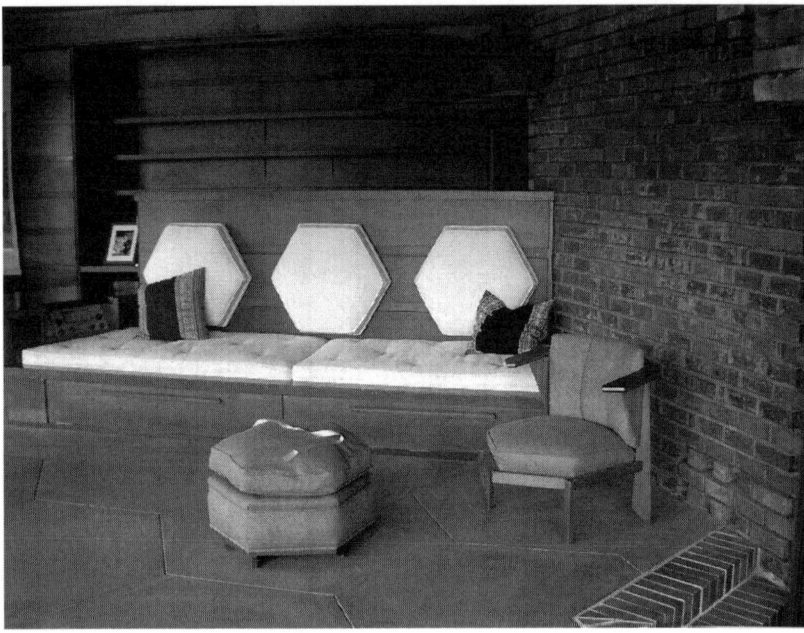

Figure 9. Frank Lloyd Wright, furniture designed for Hanna house, Stanford. Photo by Herbert Lindenberger.

Wright's desire to subordinate comfort to beauty. Look, for instance, at this furniture he designed for the Hanna house (figure 9).

Since I visited the house on various occasions when Stanford provosts were assigned there to live, I had ample occasion to try out the hexagonal furniture, whose discomfort should be evident even to those who haven't sat on these gorgeous pieces.

FLA: I think of another architect whose projects are theoretically engaging—even if discomforting—and that one certainly would not want to live in. Le Corbusier's first project for Rio de Janeiro (presented at a conference in Buenos Aires in 1929) was of a "building-viaduct" that would house residences underneath a raised highway stretching across the city. This was never built, but others have since taken up his vision, making in the 1960s and 1970s some of the most innovative yet discomforting buildings in Rio. And, as time has passed, they no longer instill a dizzying sense of discomfort. Rather, they've become monolithic concrete eyesores.

HL: I'm not familiar with these buildings but know how much of the innovative and utilitarian architecture of this period did not age well. There's a building like this on the UC Berkeley campus that, ironically, houses the architecture school. It has become one of the least aesthetically pleasing buildings on that campus.

FLA: While at Cal, several close friends spent their entire undergraduate lives confined within the discomforting cold concrete walls of Wurster Hall. I don't know how they survived. Like Joseph Esherick and others who designed Wurster, I think we should add Gaudí in the category of architects that seek to create buildings trying to eject us from inhabitation.

HL: Yes, and it bothers me to have to admit this, for each time I've visited Barcelona I've wanted to like his work but still found myself irritated by it. It was deemed eccentric in its time and somehow it never became absorbed within the history of modernism to the point that it ceased to seem eccentric.

FLA: I still can't wrap my brain around La Sagrada Familia in Barcelona.

HL: I've walked all over the roof of the Sagrada Familia church trying to accommodate his style to my normally welcoming sensibility. But those knobs with their eyelike slits never succeeded in establishing any new norm for me, which is what a revolutionary style ultimately succeeds in doing. Were these knobs attempting to scare their viewers? But asking a question like this is to assume a philistine stance, and that's not a stance I like to take. And then there are the towers, which rise before you like a garden gone wild (another philistine remark similar to the Austrian kaiser's making fun of the eyebrows missing over Loos's windows). Or to turn to another Gaudí building, the Casa Batiló (figure 10), are those balconies teasing you to guess what protrusions they represent (again, I've retreated into unthinking philistinism)?

As I look back at my reactions, what I find most disquieting is not the buildings themselves but the fact that I'm falling back on the clichéd thinking (or nonthinking!) that I associate with the detractors of modernism, or of art in general.

FLA: Ah, how Gaudí puts us into a tailspin—a battle between our emotion with our reason system that leads itself to a feeling of discomfort, Herbie. At least Gaudí triggers this struggle in us. I say this because most of the everyday architecture we experience—actually, that we are fully habituated toward—is dull because of its ordinariness or simply unappealing.

HL: Yes, most of the architecture we see every day, as I implied earlier (unless we happen to live in Venice, Florence, or some untouched village,

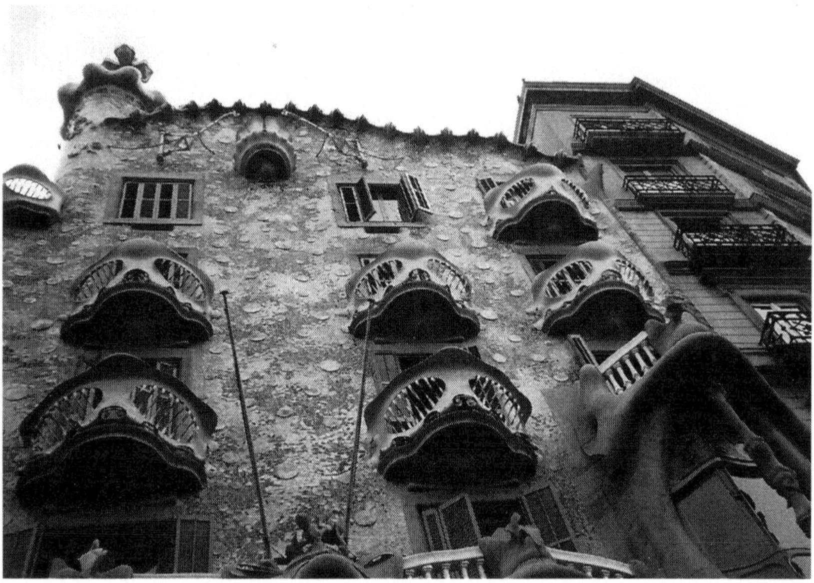

Figure 10. Antoni Gaudí, Casa Batlló, Barcelona (1904). Photo by Herbert Lindenberger.

say, in the south of France or Vermont), is either ugly or insipid. We get so used to this we don't realize that what we see is actually an insult to the eye. Bad architecture, moreover, affects us differently from other artistic media, for we're forced to live with it, see it along the street as we go out our door; as you mention, Frederick, it's likely that our neighbor's house or the one we live in is dull or distasteful; we pass awful buildings on our way to work, and once we arrive, we often do our work in a claustrophobic, ill-designed space. With other forms of art, you can take it or leave it. If you react badly to a film you're watching, you can walk out or stop the DVD player. With a confrontational picture such as Munch's *The Scream*—whose unpleasantness derives not only from the screaming woman but also from the prospective suicide at the left bending over the bridge railing—you can move to another picture if you choose to, though when I took the photo in figure 11 while this pastel version (1895) was on temporary display at the Museum of Modern Art, there were crowds of people who really didn't want to move away at all.

If a Bukowski poem upsets or bores you, you close the book—or throw it out! And you can usually avoid discomforting music unless

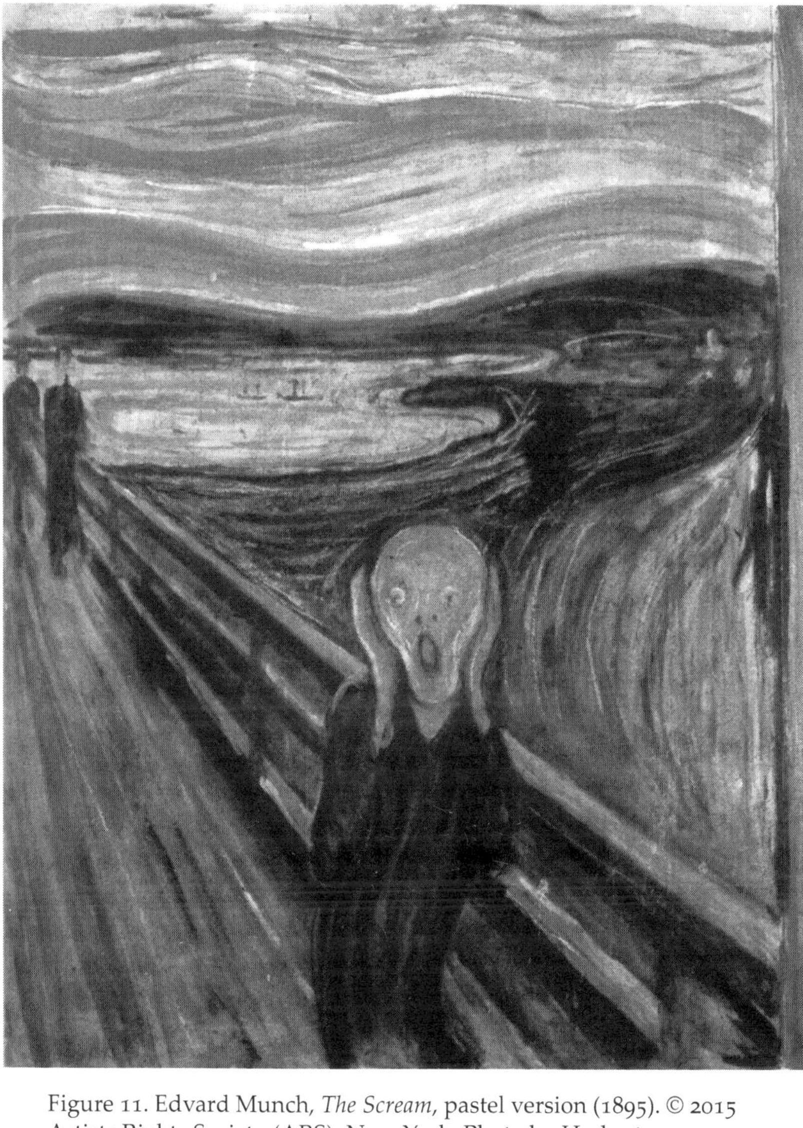

Figure 11. Edvard Munch, *The Scream*, pastel version (1895). Photo by Herbert Lindenberger.

the car next to you at a stoplight is blasting something maddening. But you're stuck with the architecture around you.

FLA: Yes, we're stuck with our buildings, Herbie. Unless of course one has the skill, time, and money (the class issue raises its ugly head once again) to deconstruct and reconstruct—or build from scratch spaces that *enstrange*. As a partial response to this need to modify architecture that we're stuck with, without moving walls or razing and then rebuilding habitable edifices, we move our furniture around to reexperience our otherwise fixed environs. Certainly money helps us to recreate—to *enstrange*, if you will—but we know all too well that money isn't a cure-all for the re-creating of ugly spaces and ugly architecture.

HL: Except for film, money plays a bigger role in architecture than in the other arts we're discussing. I leave out the astronomical figures that some people pay for paintings and sculptures these days—this money, after all, goes to the preceding owner and not to the artist, who got only what the original owner paid, which is usually only a small fraction of the later price. To build a good architect-designed house, one pays substantially more than one gets by going directly to a builder. When my family moved to the Stanford campus in the late 1960s, the best contemporary architect in St. Louis, whom we'd met socially while we were living there, suggested designing us a house. We told him our needs, which included having enough room, including play space, for a growing family. He made some sketches and then gave us a rough estimate of what we'd be paying. Although his ideas were genuinely appealing, it turned out that our budget allowed us only about two-thirds of the space we wanted. He then suggested we look around for the kind of builder who would be willing to make extensive modifications. Nearly all the models we saw by the Bay Area builders we sought out were so depressing that I wondered how we could ever live in one of their spaces (am I being unduly sensitive to aesthetic discomfort?). Finally we found a builder willing to let us modify one of his standard patterns, and we suggested a number of architectural details to his designer (he didn't have the credentials to call himself an architect), with the result that we got a large and aesthetically nondescript, noncontroversial, generally OK house, yet considerably below the standard of the work we'd seen by the St. Louis architect—or that of some Bay Area architects we might have had if we could have afforded them.

FLA: Budgets matter and so too does creativity, Herbie, and so too does scale. One can have a very pleasing house, but if it's a space that threatens to eject us and our everyday living needs because of size (too big or too small) we experience discomfort that can even turn into deep sadness or a sense of horror.

HL: When you consider large-scale architecture—whether commercial buildings or museums, to which some of the best architectural talent has been devoted in recent years—financial considerations put aesthetics to a grave test. Although we live in an age of celebrity architects—Gehry, Rem Koolhaas, Zaha Hadid, Renzo Piano, Daniel Libeskind, Norman Foster, Herzog & de Meuron, to name only a few, all of these from different countries—a large percentage of brilliant plans get scrapped for lack of financing. Architects, even the most famous, are forced into making concessions far more than other artists, but then the firms these artists create are actually business enterprises that have to make the usual compromises expected of a commercial venture. But it's not only money that gets in the way of aesthetic autonomy. Every architect has to contend with a multitude of pressures: the local building codes, the inspectors interpreting these codes, the preferences of planning commissions, the politics of the city council, the changing whims of clients. And then there's the problem when the money is about to run out, and this happens whether it's a family home or a towering high-rise: cheaper, aesthetically less pleasing materials need to be ordered; space needs to be constrained; the lovely facade that got the politicians and the financiers alike to come on board now gets scrapped. It's a wonder that anything really beautiful ever sees the light of day.

FLA: I know all too well in the countless houses I've designed and built that one can dream (and some dreams are better than others) all we want, but in the end it does come down to access to money, materials, and skilled labor. It might come down finally to whether or not there's a unity of form and function—and the lack thereof (even with lots of money spent as well as excellent materials and skilled labor used) can lead to extremely discomforting constructions. At a place like Stanford you and I had daily reminders of disquieting architecture.

HL: Yes, I've spent over half my life on the Stanford University campus, so I've had ample opportunity to admire the best buildings and suffer distress at the failures. The initial building project from 1887 to 1891, the so-called Inner Quad, is a masterly example of late nineteenth-century Romanesque (figure 12), and having my office in this complex for much of this period was sheer joy.

FLA: With the exception of the Quad, my experience of the campus has been increasingly of a mess of higgledy-piggeldy architecture.

HL: Yes, the buildings constructed since the Quad have turned out to be a

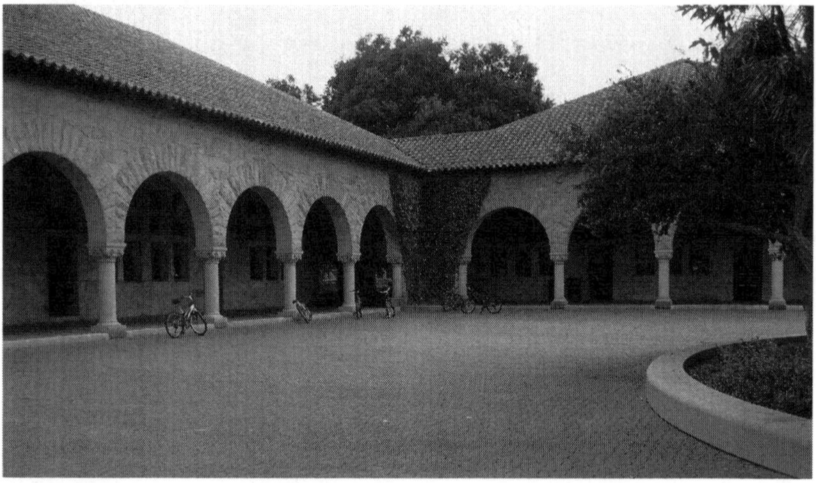

Figure 12. Corner of Stanford University Inner Quad, designed by Shepley, Rutan and Coolidge (1887–91). Photo by Herbert Lindenberger.

mixed bag. The custom has been that, whatever the architectural style, the sandstone walls and red-tiled roofs would be followed to achieve some sort of unity. But there has been no unity of quality. Most of the buildings constructed over the years have been dull, though a few have been downright hideous. One unfortunately overwrought construction of the 1960s, the former undergraduate library that the students, extracting the u, g, l, and y, nicknamed UGLY, was torn down in early 2015—less for the aesthetic reasons that would justify this than because the earthquake retrofitting it needed would not have been cost-effective.

FLA: The interior design is similarly disquieting, Herbie. Looking back now I think it might be less the anxiety about the PhD exams that made me nauseous and more the concrete, red carpets, and disorientating levels that caused this.

HL: We might consider this one of the many architectural sins that have been committed at Stanford. In the last decade or so we see this clearly as a consequence of the demands of donors along with the university officials who were too lily-livered to refuse a gift horse. Among the most egregious of these sins is a dormitory for law students that I have to pass, alas, when I drive to the campus. (Instead of going to a major architect, as it has, fortunately, with a number of fine recent buildings,

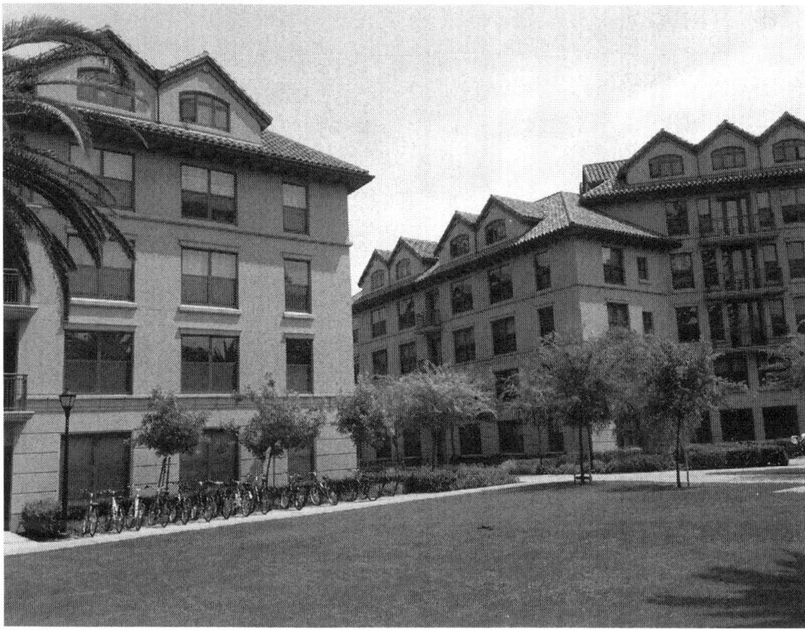

Figure 13. Stanford Law School dormitories, designed by Hoover Associates, architects (2007). Photo by Herbert Lindenberger.

the university hired a local firm, Hoover Associates, that had also designed the football stadium.) The cutesy little dormer windows over those massive piles are a joke—unintended, of course. A friend who also has to pass by regularly commented that every time she's forced that way she looks to see if the greenery has grown any. One might call this the ultimate test of bad architecture: the impatience that viewers experience waiting for trees and vines to hide the sheer ugliness of a building. The billionaire donor insisted on the site since he wanted the students to be within easy walking distance of the law school. There were protests from faculty members living nearby, for the site was too small to accommodate the amount of space needed for six hundred residents. The result was these big piles of buildings crowded against one another in the most ungainly way (figure 13).

With an ugly building a rich donor can flaunt his power more effectively than with a beautiful one, for he is saying, in effect, "I defy you to like this." And this monstrosity is only a few blocks from Wright's Honeycomb house, pictured earlier in this chapter: looking at the two is similar to Hamlet's comparing his father to his stepfather as "Hyperion to a satyr" (1.2.140). But money, as we know, speaks louder than beauty, and this donor's daughter, moreover, is on the university's board of trustees.

FLA: Money does not always lead to the building of an architecture that discomforts.

HL: That's true. Stanford has been getting some genuinely beautiful buildings to house the visual arts but only because, as you might expect, the sort of person offering many millions for art is likely to have taste, indeed, even to be an art collector. For instance, when the collector Iris Cantor gave a large donation for an addition to the Stanford Museum (now renamed after her and her late husband), she made the condition that the architect be the esteemed James Polshek. And right now, what, at least judging from the looks of it going up, will likely be an architectural gem, a new building financed by the collectors Deedee and Burt McMurtry and designed by Diller Scofidio + Renfro will house the art department; it is significant that this building, though sandstone in color, is ignoring the convention of a red-tile roof. And besides these there are also two excellent science buildings by the Norman Foster firm.

FLA: Yet we can't assume that having money necessarily equates with good taste. And while it is likely that a donor who is giving money to the arts possesses such taste, there's no reason that techies like Bill Hewlett, Dave Packard, Bill Gates, and Jerry Yang—to name only a few whose names grace buildings in Stanford's science and engineering complex—should feel any commitment to distinguished architecture. So the buildings named for them are a distinctly mixed bag.

HL: The Packard building, posthumously funded, turned out to be excellent, the Gates, an utter embarrassment. (If Steve Jobs had possessed a generosity to match his aesthetic sense—something he claimed was developed growing up in an Eichler tract house [Isaacson 7, 125]—a building bearing his name, quite unlike the Gates building, would likely have displayed the elegance of the computer products he brought into being.) And, of course, the taste that gets realized in public spaces has a good bit of back and forth transpiring behind closed doors. Even if a donor has good taste—or, to put it bluntly, a taste that matches my own—there are so many bureaucratic hurdles that you have to move through to create a new public space that the original concept can be lost altogether in the ugliness or, at best, the dullness of its realized form. This is to say, the big money that well-heeled donors offer can be a force for beauty, as with the museum addition and the art building, and it can also, as in all too many instances, be a source for ugliness or, at best, boredom.

FLA: Because of the enormous cost, public, habitable art brings too many cooks to the kitchen, including unfortunately those of the pencil-pushing type less interested in aesthetics. I've also seen on the Ohio State University campus a case where the donor, Dutch Knowlton, had explicitly written into the contract that a certain material and style be used and incorporated in the construction of the architecture building. The donor nearly pulled the millions required to finish the building when it was discovered that its facade was not marble and it didn't have any classical Greek stylistic elements. Today's architecture building (Knowlton Hall) has little to do with a classical Greek building. Knowlton Hall is a cast in place concrete building; as a result it is a free-flowing building with massive, open interior spaces and exposed post-tensioning structures that allow students to study the construction of the building while inside the building. However, a compromise was reached. After the fact, an aluminum system was used to suspend marble tiles to cover the curved building like fish scales; and, somewhat hidden at the street entrance, 5 giant columns were erected to ensure the presence of a classical element; they are Tuscan and Composite orders, so more Roman than classical Greek. To have these added, Dutch Knowlton took back $1 million of his original $10 million gift. Unfortunately, Knowlton died before he saw the completion of the building.

HL: We are touching directly on a central problem in the making of viable built spaces. Unlike the creation of paintings, poems, and music, executing a building, as we've mentioned, means constant compromising. Architects, even with the best of aesthetic intentions, are at the mercy of those financing their work, and the latter, if they run short of money, often ensure the failure of a potentially lovely structure even as it is being constructed.

FLA: Yet there are those like the lay builder Le Facteur Cheval, who built his disquieting edifice (*Le Palais idéal*) on his own steam—and stone by stone. It's actually one of the ugliest buildings I've ever seen (figure 14). He built it little by little out of objects he found here and there (during his daily mail round) and without any guiding aesthetic blueprint. It's this lack of aesthetic care that makes the house so discomforting.

HL: Keep in mind that it took Le Facteur thirty-three years to build this. It's more the exception that proves the rule. Modern-day, public building

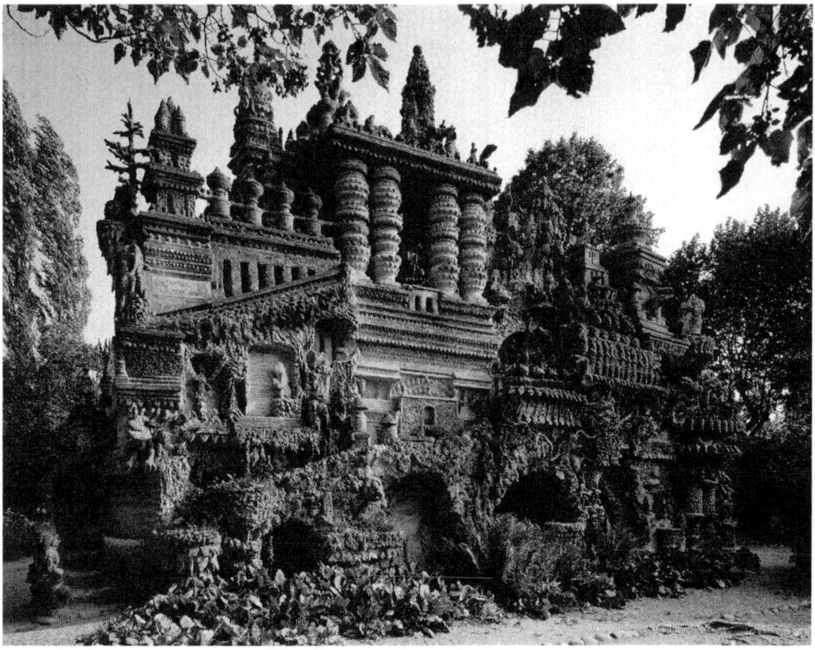

Figure 14. Segment of *Le Palais idéal* by Ferdinand "Le Facteur" Cheval, Hauterives, France (1879–1912). Erich Lessing / Art Resource, NY.

is a collective effort that includes many struggles between competing interests. This is what compromised Daniel Libeskind's prize-winning design for the World Trade Center's main building, for instance.

I went to an exhibit some years ago showing models by the various architects competing for the job. Libeskind's model was clearly the most exciting, and I felt gratified to see it win. But then the troubles began, many of them stemming from the developer who had rights to the land, and Libeskind was no longer listed as the main architect. From what I've seen watching the building go up, it will likely be aesthetically OK, as I like to say of buildings that neither excite nor depress me, but it won't embody the model I saw. Let me add that Libeskind can create discomforting spaces that are also aesthetically just right: I'm thinking of his Jewish Museum in Berlin, the building that made him a celebrity architect. This museum is full of narrow angles and cramped spaces that supposedly suggest the claustrophobic world of Nazi camps (figure 15).

FLA: I'm glad you brought up the Nazi death camps, Herbie. There's so

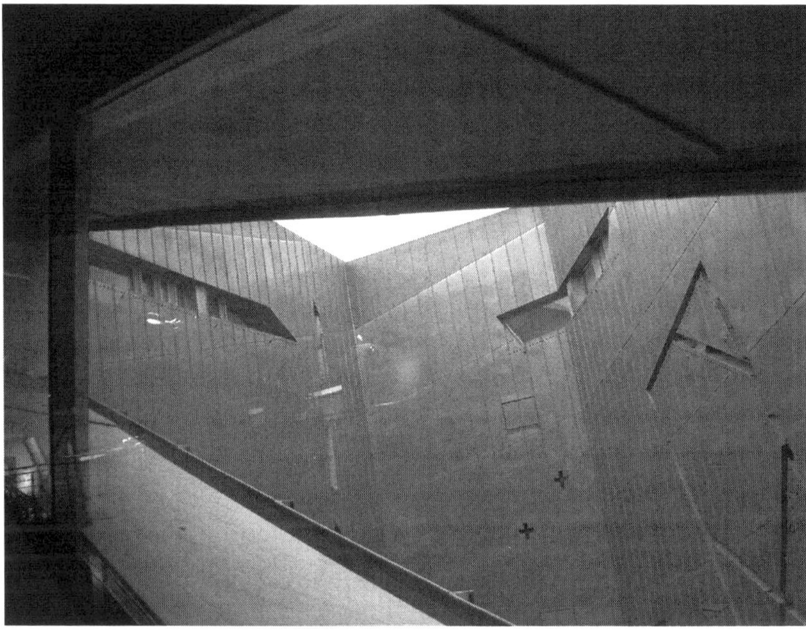

Figure 15. Daniel Libeskind, Jewish Museum, Berlin (2001), segment. Photo by Herbert Lindenberger.

much here to discuss in terms of how they were designed precisely to rupture this unity between form and aesthetics. Of course, there was ornament—the gate at Auschwitz's "Arbeit Macht Frei"—but as something pasted onto a built structure not aimed to house or provide a home, but to dis-house and murder.

HL: One notorious camp, Theresienstadt, actually was grafted onto a once handsome town built around 1780 to house Austrian troops. But the Nazis, who used this camp (which did not have its own gassing facilities) as a place to hold Jews before they were sent off to the actual death camps, kept some fifty thousand there at a time in quarters originally designed for only a few thousand soldiers. As you can imagine, it became a living hell.

FLA: No matter how much time has passed, this camp and the actual death camps continue to create discomfort and fear in us.

HL: The Berlin Jewish Museum, as I mentioned, and also the U.S. Holocaust Museum in Washington, DC, seek to evoke this discomfort and fear for visitors.

FLA: Pyramids like that of Chichín-Itzá in Mexico's Yucatan region were originally built to instill a certain fear in the observer and as a show of power. Today, we stand in their presence with awe.

HL: Yes, and I've managed to feel this awe as I climbed the pyramids at various Mexican archaeological sites. It surely added to the awe to know that in early times prisoners were often hurled to their death down those steep steps. We've been concentrating thus far on buildings from various cultures and periods that are fear-inspiring, heavy, made of concrete or stone. But what about the opposite sort of building: I mean the many buildings of the past half century that are essentially made of glass?

FLA: If used as the dominant material in a building, glass can itself be a source of discomfort. The early twentieth-century International Style found an affinity with the use of glass, blurring lines between public and private in disquieting ways.

HL: There are few movements of the twentieth century that have seemed as exciting to me as the International Style. Yet as with movements in any art form, the excitement wore off with time, especially since, during the later part of the century, those huge glass towers grew like giant weeds all over the world—in London, Shanghai, Singapore, Dubai, and in every U.S. city past a certain size. Although some of these buildings seemed just right, all too many were too high or too fat or too thin. And building walls of glass doubtless makes for a greater monotony than one finds in other architectural styles. People these days express their fatigue with the style. Yet one only need stroll past one of the most glorious examples, Mies van der Rohe's Seagram Building (1959) to note how delicately proportioned, how utterly beautiful it is (figure 16).

FLA: You find the Seagram appealing, and I find it rather disturbing. I think this is a question of size—at least for me. Let me elaborate. What looks beautiful in a Frank Lloyd Wright house—whether comfortable or not—does not necessarily look beautiful in an office building or an apartment building.

Size and dimension matter. The glass skyscraper is terribly monotonous and thus ugly—and very uncomfortable: can't open windows, and so on. Imagine this in Saudi Arabia: with the way glass reflects would be like living in a sauna; not to mention the Disney building in LA that seemed to heat sidewalks to the point of melting the soles of the shoes of passerbys. . This same glass structure in the size and dimension of a house can be quite attractive.

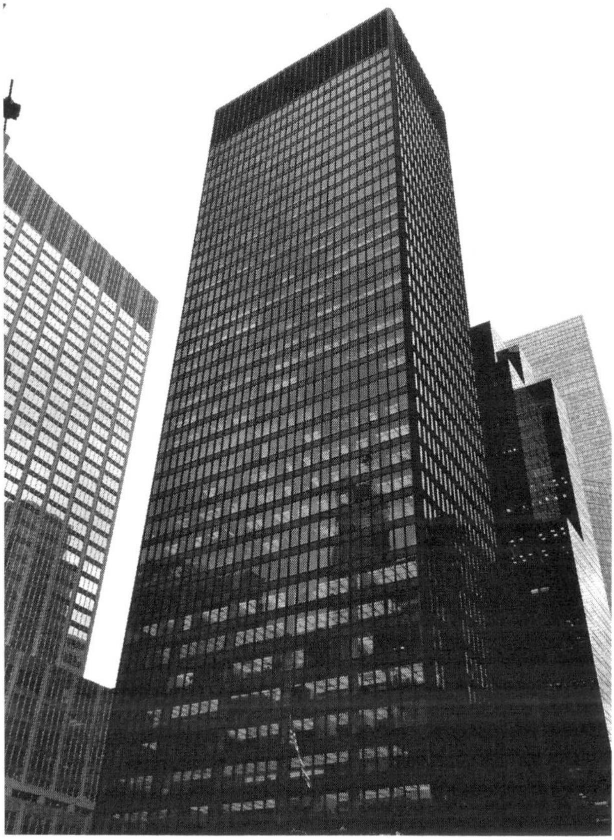

Figure 16. Ludwig Mies van der Rohe, Seagram Building, New York (1959). Photo by Herbert Lindenberger.

There's a difference in size between a house and an office or apartment building. There's also a difference in size between a house and a city. A glass building cam be terribly ugly, but imagine a glass banlieue (large Parisian suburb) where no privacy is allowed.

HL: Then let's look at a glass building that's really small: I'm thinking of the glass house that Philip Johnson built for himself (figure 17).

It's a wonderfully delicate building except, perhaps, for the heavy vertical corner supports, which Mies told his disciple Johnson were the weakest part of his design. In the International Style delicacy is of prime importance. Anything so awkward as these corner supports likely caused Mies van der Rohe grave discomfort.

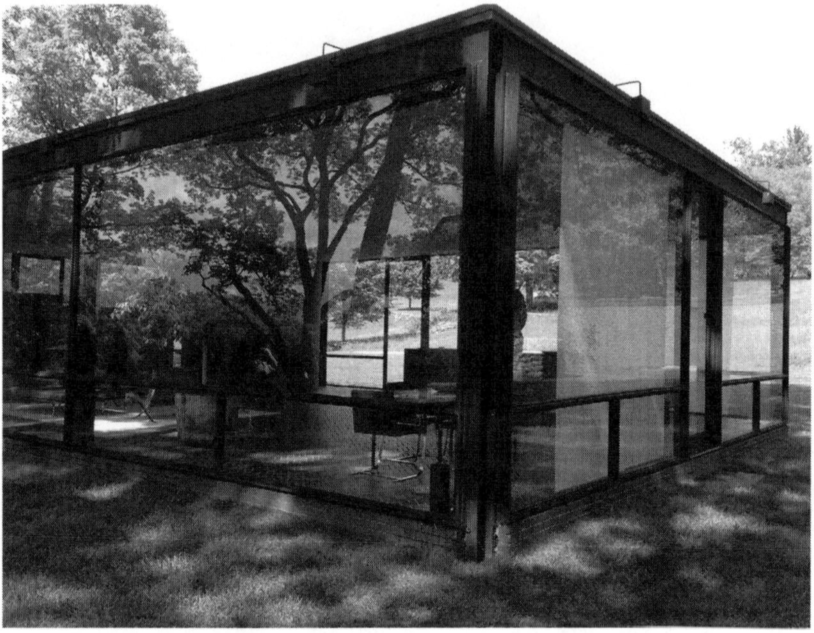

Figure 17. Philip Johnson, Glass House, New Canaan, Connecticut (1949). Photo by Herbert Lindenberger.

FLA: Just as size matters shape matters and also colors matter. It's not the same thing to have a whole house painted green and a whole building painted green and a whole banlieue painted green. Uniformity in color can also be a nightmare.

HL: That's why recent architects have been adding slabs of bright and varied colors to buildings.

FLA: Long before the glass high-rises, all manner of skyscrapers (as they were then called) sprouted up across American cities. Loos lost the 1922 competition for the Chicago Tribune Tower to a neogothic design by Raymond Hood and John Mead Howells. Had Loos's design been built it would have been a twenty-one-story Doric column clad in polished black granite. The soaring skyscraper would have been anchored deliberately to the earth as a monolithic obelisk.

HL: Since Chicago was the world's most pioneering city in modernist architecture, the choice of the neogothic design for the Tribune Tower represented a shameful regress—whether or not Loos's tower would have been an artistic success. That huge Doric column would likely have been derided as looking like a well-circumcised, erect penis.

FLA: On my last visit to Chicago I marveled at how ugly the Trump Tower was; a $750 million vanity project, the asymmetrically twisted and stepped polished steel and glass with its spire seeking to rival the height of the world's tallest buildings (upon then-mayor Daley's insistence).

HL: Possessing tallness is something that many cities, and especially their developers, desire. But then most people, especially men, wish to be taller than they are.

FLA: And perhaps they wish to be more beautiful or handsome than they are, too. Wright designed an inverted tripod to be a skyscraper that would be the social and cultural hub of his 1920s imagined and designed Broadacre City, Illinois. The materials used in the skyscraper and city would accentuate the exploratory possibilities of horizontal space: gold-tinted metal on facades would bring attention to the angular surfaces along balconies and parapets. Talk about defiance of the laws of gravity: horizontal space *in space*. How ultimately discomforting, however—even if only in our imagination.

HL: Somebody should put together an exhibition, with large-scale models, of the finest building designs by great architects past and present that never reached the stage of construction (and there are infinitely more designs to choose from than the number of buildings that actually saw the light of day!). In some cases, I suspect, we'd feel relieved that we don't have to live with a particular building, but in many, perhaps most, instances, the show would tell us what wonderful things we've missed out on.

FLA: Your mention of this feeling of "missing out on" leads me to think about those mausoleums built so others will not miss out on our presence in the world. In fact, Ferdinand "Le Facteur" Cheval wanted his ugly behemoth to be his mausoleum, but French courts wouldn't allow it. I think of others, however, like the narcos (drug lords) in Mexico who build their elaborate structures in cemeteries all over Mexico in anticipation of their death—and the impulse to not be forgotten.

HL: Anybody who sets up ugly memorials such as these deserves an eventual spot in some Dantesque aesthetic hell: indeed, being buried in a conspicuously ugly structure is hell enough. But remember, Frederick, as I mentioned before, there are also such wondrous buildings as the Taj Mahal and, on an infinitely smaller scale, Sullivan's Wainwright tomb—both of these, incidentally, commissioned by grieving husbands to commemorate wives who had died young.

FLA: From our homes and places of work to our built environments we experience the comforting and discomforting, the exciting and banal.

With few exceptions (those who choose the intellectual over the emotional, perhaps), we tend to choose (when we can) to inhabit built spaces that we don't experience as disharmonious. Like you, I'm intellectually interested in how Wright creates the illusion of defying natural laws. Theodore van Fossen (a builder and furniture maker who worked on two of Wright's projects in 1939 and 1940) designed an entire neighborhood in Worthington, Ohio, known as "Rush Creek." All the houses are built in the manner of Wright's Usonian style. I had the opportunity to buy a house there for a very good price. However, at day's end I would never want to be subjected to the physical discomforts experienced living in one of these houses. For all the will to style present in the realization of their construction, they eject humans like myself.

HL: That's the difference between architecture and painting. A beautiful building can, as with a number of Wright houses, give its occupants physical discomfort, but a beautiful painting hung on the wall does not affect the way we cook our meals, or sit on a built-in bench, or force us to wear sweaters because of an ill-designed heating system.

FOUR | Noise to the Ears

FREDERICK LUIS ALDAMA: Turning now to discomforting music, let's approach it on its own terms—as an aesthetic built out of the aural building blocks of reality and given shape by its own specific devices. Some shapes are decidedly disquieting. That is, to understand why some music triggers reactions of discomfort we should consider how its formal acoustic architecture operates as a cultural artifact from a compositional point of view. To this we can enrich our understanding if we consider music as a biological phenomenon in terms of production and reception. In addition, the tools offered by musicology might enable us to understand how discomforting music works within specific sociopolitical contexts. These threads, I suspect, will tell us much about the history of disquieting music.

HERBERT LINDENBERGER: Like art and literature, music has a history, but its expressive possibilities did not develop until relatively late in this history. In antiquity it played a subservient role to drama and dance, and it did not possess the technical resources to produce figures comparable to Phidias or Sophocles, whom, with our customary romantic vocabulary, we classify as "creative geniuses" on the order of, say, Michelangelo and Shakespeare. Although we revere such early composers as Josquin des Prés and Palestrina, it wasn't until Monteverdi, born three years after Shakespeare and long outliving him, that a composer could rival a major literary or a visual artist in range and power of expression.

In our first conversation I referred to Monteverdi's controversy with the pedantic critic Artusi, who objected to the fact that the composer's unresolved dissonances broke long-standing musical convention. But these dissonances, together with other techniques that Monteverdi employed—for example, his so-called *concitato* or agitated style—enabled him and later composers to vastly extend the expressive possibilities of music. And during the past two centuries composers have continued this expansion at a furious pace—Beethoven's insistently dramatic manner, Berlioz's loudness and orchestral color, Wagner's chromaticism and his leitmotivic mode of organizing a musical drama, Stravinsky's and Schoenberg's sonic attacks on their hearers' ears, not to speak of the jazz and later the rock musicians who found still newer ways to undercut the listening habits of their audiences. Each of these expansions created discomfort for many early listeners.

FLA: As your brief history points out, many disciplines can and should be brought to bear on the study of disquieting music. In each discipline within the arts there appear to be certain overlaps and cross overs.

Shouldn't we therefore consider similarities between the arts and how aesthetic artifacts are built to create new relationships between the subject (listener in this case) and the object (the music in this case)? That is, if we consider there to be a common ground in the making and experiencing of music as an aesthetic object, perhaps there is some fruit to bear if we compare it to some of the other arts. Perhaps, however, the differences are too *different*.

HL: Unlike the other arts, except perhaps for abstract painting and sculpture (quite recent developments, to be sure), music is not representational, though a representational element becomes manifest in song and in opera. This nonrepresentational element, moreover, may cause music to have a greater immediacy of effect on us than the other arts; certainly the stark power of music to move the emotions has been remarked upon throughout the history of Western civilization. And if music has this special power, then the unpleasant effects that it can exercise—effects central to our present inquiry among all the arts—can make it all the more dangerous (to put it in Plato's terms).

Let's remember that music during much of its history was not classified as an art within the educational system in the same way that the other arts were. The verbal arts—grammar, logic, and rhetoric—were part of the classical trivium, while music was classified within the quadrivium, which linked music with arithmetic, geometry, and astronomy, and this was because music, like these other areas, could be understood by means of its numerical relationships. Painting had no place in the educational curriculum, but by the Renaissance painting and literature were characteristically dubbed the "sister arts." It wasn't until quite late in history that music was viewed as comparable to, and commensurate with, verbal and visual art forms.

FLA: The history of art (that is, of all aesthetic phenomena) in all its guises is at the same time the history of the education of the senses. When I read a history of aesthetic phenomena I get the impression that some historians consider only a few of these senses, especially as shaped and experienced through time. But it's a history that involves all the senses.

I think you're right to state that music in the West was a very secondary artistic activity. The Greeks knew dance, but not ballet, which has its origins in seventeenth-century France; they knew music accompanying plays, but they didn't know of this music as an independent art—it was always linked to the chorus (whether a tragedy or comedy) or to dance. It's quite evident that people creating music, whether in ancient Greece, the Middle Ages or today, are always seeking to create something new and taking advantage of advances in technology and to educate the senses of their audiences with this newness. I earlier mentioned rock and roll. When it was first played, many considered it monstrous. This was not only because of hip gyrations that offended the more puritan of mind, but also the use of new musical technology. No matter how well one plays the acoustic guitar, it will not sound like an electric one; what you can do with one you can't with the other. In other words, it's a complex phenomenon where science and technology meet art. In music we have a concurrence, a meeting of very different elements: science and technology and art (in this case music); it is the meeting of the innovation (creative power of the artists) with the creative capacity of reception on the part of the audience. Because of the way the human brain works, if open to it, audiences can become receptive to something new; by being receptive to this newness, we are rewarded, and we continue to explore new possibilities. There is no linear progression per se from primitive to complex and artistically sophisticated and where things happened without our human trial and error in their attempt to find new shapes.

What we have is a complex combination of scientific and technical innovations made, therefore, by creative people in the scientific and cultural sphere. We have an education of the senses that affects the audience. However, it's also an education directed at the creator him- or herself: there's a feedback between the artist and the audience educating the artists. It is a very heterogeneous and complex situation; art history is the history of scientific and technical innovations *and* the education of an audience's senses—and, in turn, an education by this audience of the creator.

HL: Ernst Gombrich's great book *Art and Illusion* (1960) provided a powerful model for the history of styles by showing how each innovation seeks to "correct" what he calls the "schema" that characterized the preceding style (174) and also how the expectations (or "mental set") planted in us by an earlier style are subverted by a later one (58–62). A similar model had been created for the history of music a few years earlier by Leonard B. Meyer in *Emotion and Meaning in Music* (1956). In both these arts, as these books demonstrate, the new schema is often felt as disturbing to viewers and listeners.

FLA: The role of music in ancient Greece and that of modern-day cinema seem to share similarities: you can't create an atmosphere of visual horror, disquieting scenes, with "Singing in the Rain" as the background music. One has to create music and instruments and electronic means to create sounds that are as disquieting as those we watch. The basic principle here is the same as that of ancient Greek theater's chorus. Robert Rodriguez makes the music for most of his films, and he knows which sounds will fit in specific scenes. Modern-day composers inventing music are perfectly aware that certain sounds and their combination will produce a disquieting reaction in the audience, reinforcing the visual images of the film. Rodriguez deliberately creates disquieting sounds, but without giving them a status independent from the film. Yet, just like the Greek chorus, it is deliberately created to reinforce the dialogue, action, and so on.

HL: In a "mixed media" form such as film, the audience's main focus remains visual, and we don't think much about the soundtrack that a cunning auteur such as Rodriguez is barraging us with. Yet this soundtrack is constantly shaping our response to what we see.

FLA: While many since the Pythagoreans talked about the connection between music and mathematics, if we push a little harder, might we say that all the other arts are linked to mathematics and all the other sciences?

Earlier, when you compare music with arithmetic, geometry, and astronomy because of their numerical relationships, it's also important to point out that painting, for instance, in the Renaissance is to a large extent the result of a close and detailed observation of the human body and other bodies. Painting during this period demanded a careful use of geometry. You link music to numbers. With this you link composers with the exploration of mathematical properties of sounds and the combinations of sounds. This goes back to ancient Greece. However, painting during the Renaissance had an enormous surge in the West, linked to the deeper understanding of a work's geometric properties. The use of perspective is the use of geometry in painting like it had never been done before in terms of scale. Painting's immediate link is to geometry—as a field within mathematics. Furthermore, painting in the hands of artists like Leonardo was also directly and immediately related to the close study of anatomy. Not satisfied with just observing human bodies, some painters like Leonardo did dissections to see how muscles were constituted, and how the different parts of the body worked together to form the whole organism. We can't imagine Renaissance painting without this huge curiosity about the science that we find in anatomy, biology, and mathematics, but also the science you find in the chemistry of pigments as well as in materials that go into the making of builders: Leonardo was an expert builder, directing the building of ramparts so cannon balls would not perforate castles. This is why in Renaissance paintings, both in the foreground and background, we are given clues about just how much the painter knew about architecture.

This is to say, and we'll return to this in the following chapter, painting during the Renaissance and since then is directly linked to mathematics—and all the sciences like anatomy, biology, botany, and anatomy. All this comes together in the sculpting of Michelangelo's David or in the mold created by Cellini to make Perseus, as we already mentioned.

HL: Although perspective was abandoned by most modernist styles, a strong scientific motive remains within certain of these styles, for example, in the almost mathematical rigor with which Russian constructivist paintings and sculptures were shaped and in the ordering of pitches in serial music.

FLA: We mentioned in the first conversation in the book the creating of an aesthetic category for us to honor and study those artifacts built to trigger thoughts and feelings in us and that we could value regardless of their utility. This leveled the scholarly field between music and the visual and verbal arts—all were equally valid objects of study in their own right.

HL: Indeed, what we came to classify as art sometimes achieved its highest prestige if it had no use value at all. Once we had bundled these art forms together, we saw what they had in common: their ability to entertain us, excite our emotions, make us, we hoped, "better" people than we might have been without their mediation. But if, as in these conversations, we find that the arts can sometimes be downright unpleasant, the notion that art, and especially discomforting art, makes us better people would clearly need to be argued.

FLA: Indeed, today we see clearly (and with the corroboration of the work done in the neurosciences) the naïveté that feeds the argument that music or any art (discomforting or not) makes us better. I think we can let that rest. However, what's interesting for us to consider is how devices can be used to shape an aesthetic where the aural is the dominant building block being reconstructed.

HL: Whether or not we consider the aural to be dominant (to measure that we'd need to ask, "Dominant in what parts of the brain, and do these parts of the brain have precedence in any way over those that process other art forms?"), it is certainly true that the way we respond with our aural sense is different from the way we respond with our visual sense and whatever other senses are affected by the poetry or fiction we read. For one thing, our individual identities are more tied to—or threatened by—particular forms of music than they are to and by forms of art and literature.

FLA: During my father's young adult life in Mexico and for those like Tom Wolfe, Ken Kesey, and others in the middle to late 1960s there were these proto-raves where lights would project geometrical shapes on walls while the music played pieces like Iron Butterfly's 1968-released "In-A-Gadda-Da-Vida" that ran for about seventeen or so minutes (the entire side of a vinyl 33) when most songs during this epoch played for about two minutes. Such songs were made to be listened to when viewing geometric ("psychedelic") paintings while you were high on marijuana or even after dropping acid to induce states of synesthesia. All this was created for a synesthetic experience where sight and sound would seem to overlap in our brains. It's not that one was hallucinating; it was that the music was becoming images. This all would seem to indicate that we might take with a grain of salt the sharp distinctions made between aural and visual senses—and precisely because of the phenomenon of synesthesia. The music reinforces the disquieting effect of the images in this synesthetic experience.

Moreover, William Sargant's book *Battle for the Mind* (1957), which explores such mind-bending techniques as religious conversion and brainwashing, can still teach us much about many other phenomena—artistic, especially. Just as repetition can be one of the techniques used to induce hypnotism, so too do we see its use in poetry. I think of the repetition (and syntactic inversion) that T. S. Eliot employs in his *Four Quartets* (1945). Indeed, Eliot's dronelike, inexpressive reading creates a semihypnotic state for us listeners.

HL: Hypnotizing listeners, if they are willing to be hypnotized, can be a powerful tool for a composer. I mentioned earlier the hypnotic effect of operas such *Pelléas et Mélisande* and *Saint François d'Assise*, which many listeners reject just as subjects of hypnotism sometimes refuse, consciously or unconsciously, to respond to a hypnotist. The hypnotic spell is central to the effect that minimalist composers such as Steve Reich, Philip Glass, and the early John Adams sought. People who refuse to be hypnotized by this music usually complain that "it doesn't go anywhere." Hypnosis is fine if you respond and a big bore if you don't.

FLA: Add this to the deep thumping beat you hear in techno music. I've just heard this same thumping beat overlaid on Bach, Beethoven, and Mozart. We know from Sargant's work that the repetition of a beat sends listeners (and he did his research in churches) into a hypnotic trance.

HL: As soon as musical works got longer, composers learned that they could control their listeners for an hour and more by means of musical hypnosis. I think it begins with Wagner, who keeps you going for more than five hours in his final work *Parsifal*, which operagoers either like or hate depending on their willingness to be musically hypnotized. It's no wonder that Debussy looked back to Wagner's example when he composed *Pelléas* or that Bruckner used an essentially Wagnerian method to write his repetitive symphonies that are more than an hour long.

FLA: In the nineteenth century, for every individual who went to hear a Wagner opera there were likely hundreds and thousands who read novels and short stories. Just as Wagner for a long time was difficult to assimilate and created what listeners considered disquieting music, during this period there were also the invention and growth of the horror short story in Edgar Allan Poe, for instance, and the development of all kinds of disquieting short stories and novels (many concerning the disturbing possibility of our encountering a double) such as Bram Stoker's *Dracula*, Stevenson's *Dr. Jekyll and Mr. Hyde*, and Wilde's *Dorian Gray* that were just as disquieting as Wagner. Such authors reflected social situations whereby their own identities were in question; where they could no longer feel confident in saying I am who I am—*ego sum qui sum*.

HL: Wagner had toyed with Gothic horror early in his career in *The Flying Dutchman* (1843), but his later work can be related to a large number of nonmusical developments: after all, Wagner had considerably more intellectual curiosity than his fellow composers. The *Ring*, for instance, as I worked out in detail some years ago, is suffused with the new discipline of Germanic philology together with its accompanying medievalist and nationalist baggage (see *Opera in History*, 134–59). And the chromatic style he developed in *Tristan* can be related to matters such as the German Romantics' obsession with the relation between love and death and the insatiable fruitless yearning afflicting Schopenhauer's philosophy—both of these helping shape the excruciating Tristan chord that so discomforted its early listeners.

FLA: There is much cross-pollination in artistic creation that seeks to discomfort. That is, the maker of art doesn't exist in a void. All artistic creation is linked to social life in general, including science and technology: from the first arrowhead that our ancestors contemplated with awe to Poe to Wagner. This, together with the fact that the brain doesn't operate as if it were made of separate, airtight chambers. All parts of the brain are linked, even if we have certain areas of dense concentrations (modules or networks). It is because of this networked brain that we have phenomena such as synesthesia and hypnotism. And this is reflected and materialized in the arts generally.

HL: Synesthesia, by means of which all the arts commingle promiscuously, was first suggested in a literary work, *Kreileriana*, which is centered around an imaginary composer, Johannes Kreisler, and was written by a great writer, E. T. A. Hoffmann, who also happened to be a good, though minor, composer. Then the term was taken up by Baudelaire and Rimbaud (see Lindenberger, "Literature and the Other Arts," 382–83) and later applied to the way Wagner works on his listeners. During the nineteenth-century synesthesia craze nobody of course knew what we've been discovering about the brain, but obviously these writers must have intuited the networks that we now know exist.

FLA: While the brain works as a networked whole, there are concentrated areas of networks that focus on vision and language. It might be that these areas do not react as dramatically as the areas through which we process music.

HL: Just look at how we often shape our identities by the music we identify with; I don't believe that our literary and visual experiences have quite this power to shape us. Not that we're programmed in any genetic way to identify with a particular type of music. Rather, the influence of friends and of particular moments in our lives is crucial to how our ears learn to hear. And this often means excluding music antithetical to a taste to which you have attached yourself.

FLA: Herbie, you point to something very important here. That while our senses are at the bioneurological level by and large the same in all human beings, their education varies between individuals and from one historic moment to another. For example, if one's hearing has been "educated" by listening to Chopin in late twentieth-century Los Angeles, it will differ from that of a person who has never listened to Chopin and has been "educated" only by Mexican *corridos* or Mexican boleros or Mexican pop music. However, as it is obvious from the biological point of view, nothing would impede the latter individual from becoming "educated" by Chopin. The same applies to all the other senses. In matters of taste, the particular (local) and even the idiosyncratic may become universal even when biologically based.

HL: Indeed, we are not genetically programmed to like Baroque music or Italian opera or jazz, but certain experiences early in life set you up for some possibilities and exclude other possibilities. I have friends who don't want to hear any music after Bach and Handel, others who are willing to listen to anything up to 1800, but nothing Romantic or modern, please. And then there is the bulk of the contemporary classical audience that wants anything from Haydn and Mozart up to the end of the nineteenth century; these folks will only accept music later than this if it eschews excessive dissonance, so the later, more populist Copland and much of Benjamin Britten are OK with them.

And then there are those who don't want to hear any vocal music, which they claim hurts their ears or embarrasses them. I have a friend who belongs to this antivocal contingent, and she also likes nothing before, say, 1760 or after 1900. She was in Boston a few years ago visiting her niece and nephew, who both play with the Boston Symphony. That week their great conductor at the time, James Levine, was doing a concert performance of Schoenberg's *Moses und Aron*, and my friend felt forced to attend. She told me afterward that she suffered immeasurably throughout the performance.

One can also turn chronology in the opposite direction and cite the aficionados of contemporary music who wouldn't be caught dead listening to anything from earlier centuries. Recently I attended a four-day festival staged by the San Francisco Contemporary Music Players featuring what they call electronic-acoustic music—which means you hear live players whose music is filtered electronically not simply to augment the sound but, even more important, to play with the sounds emanating from the players. Thus, as a I watched the harpist (an old friend, so that's why I had my eyes on her) in a telling piece by the Finnish composer Kaija Saariaho, I could hear the sounds she was creating bounce back and forth among different parts of the large pavilion in which the concerts were held. Yes, the music would be considered "difficult" and also "discomforting" by the vast majority of concertgoers, not only because of its high volume but also because it offered none of the traditional satisfactions of harmony, predictable dynamics, or infectious rhythms. The festival called itself "Sweet Thunder," a delightful oxymoron that suggests these discomforting effects were somehow mitigated by a certain sweetness, though I confess that my ears, though quite receptive to a number of pieces, failed to perceive anything in the least bit "sweet." Still, the devoted (though small, to be sure) audiences, most of whom kept coming back day after day (with twice two concerts in a single day) would likely have found anything before Anton von Webern simplistic and boring. Actually the earliest composer they played was Edgar Varèse, who, though wildly experimental with the orchestra during the 1920s, did not possess the means to have his sounds filtered electronically until the 1950s—after which he succeeded, as in his *Déserts*, with which one of these concerts ended, to rouse his audiences with a resounding bang.

FLA: In a massive way that goes beyond the concert hall audience, the Beatles did something rather amazing when they invited Ravi Shankar to play his sitar. For the generation of youth in the 1960s this was the discovery of a whole new musical world, leading to their being receptive to music that at first sounded foreign to the ears.

HL: During the past half century music has indeed become globalized. The undermining of the Western tonal system that Schoenberg initiated at the start of the twentieth century was continued later in the century by the introduction of musical sounds and structures from many non-Western cultures.

FLA: One sound that opened ears to new ways of aural experience was the Algerian music known as *rai*. It grew in cities among the urban poor, decrying colonialism and postcolonial aftermath. In the 1990s it became very popular among the *pied noir* and youngsters generally in France. The musician Aldo was one of those in the limelight during this period. In fact, many of the important rai musicians were murdered in Algeria. The traditionalist Algerians hated the music. It was identified with challenging traditionalism and with rebellious youth. What's interesting is that rai itself is already a mixture and conflation of East with West in terms of music: it brings Spanish, Jewish, Arabic music traditions together. As it moved from Algerian cities, as a cultural form it moved from the urban working and impoverished classes into the middle and even upper classes. It embodies this formulation of transculturation in the convergence of cultures—a process conceptualized and analyzed in the work of Fernando Ortiz in the early twentieth century—for instance, in his *Cuban Counterpoint: Tobacco and Sugar* (1940).

This phenomenon of transculturation (the basic phenomenon in the development of culture within and across countries) is found especially in music; in literature it of course happens, but not to the same degree of penetration that we see in music. Once a style of music, shape, or style of music becomes popular, it no longer depends on any kind of linguistic tradition. Rai songs appeared in Arabic, but also in German, French, and Spanish.

HL: When literature tries to assimilate a foreign model, it has to rely on translation, which doesn't work when the sound patterns in the model are crucial to the effect. Music does not demand translation, and even if the words of a song remain in a foreign language, the listener usually gets enough from the music alone even without understanding the words.

FLA: We may be beating around the bush here, but I think we're also talking about how identity attaches itself to music. You've given some examples of how cliquish folks are about the music they listen to. I think of what happened in the UK in the 1960s and 1970s when there were rockabillies, the mods, and punks, for instance, and never would the music cliques mix. In fact, like gangs based on territories we know today, they would even go to battle with one another. Of course, the ska that the mods listened to was already a mixture—Jamaican reggae beats are quite dominant here, for instance. So while music itself is transcultural, listening cliques or communities do form, and some quite rigidly.

HL: Of course, there certainly are sociological reasons that influence, indeed, often determine what our ears cannot tolerate. When I lived in Italy I discovered that many intellectuals refused to attend the opera, or often to listen to anything vocal at all; they claimed to prefer German chamber music to everything else; and it quickly became clear to me they were reacting to the fact that opera in Italy had always been a popular form associated with people of a different class from theirs. Our musical identities are intrinsic to our personal identities. And this is especially evident in popular music, where, in contrast with the classical world, in which we identify with particular periods of music, or with particular instruments, we identify instead with particular musical groups. And feelings run very high in the world of rock, in which the groups you listen to often determine friendships. A heavy-metal rock fan, for example, is not going to want to share a bed with somebody expressing disdain toward this group. But unlike most people I know, I lack a firm musical identity: I subscribe to such diverse groups as the Philharmonia Baroque Orchestra and the San Francisco Contemporary Music Players, just described above. The devotees I meet in the lobby during intermissions want to talk only about the particular style of the group we are hearing, and I generally have to go along with this, since if I told people in the Baroque crowd how much I'd enjoyed the Contemporary Music Players' performance of, say, Boulez's *Le Marteau sans maître*, they would consider me hopelessly promiscuous. For these contemporary folks the Baroque stuff must sound tame, trivial, ultimately beside the point.

FLA: Rockabillies would never get into bed with mods, even though if they considered more attentively how their music is given shape, they would realize that they share more in common than not in terms of music's transculturation. I'm sure there are many hormonally charged youngsters who have shared a bed in spite of fundamental differences in musical taste, Herbie. Of course, sharing a toothbrush might be a different matter.

HL: The toothbrush, I agree, is a better analogy. Sharing a toothbrush can awaken disgust—that strong emotional response we discussed earlier—more easily than sharing sexual intimacy.

FLA: Your mention of heavy-metal rock, however, is particularly resonant. It's a music that was very much part of my generation but that I never liked. I tried, but I always felt beat up by it. I experienced it as an aggressing noise. Is noise *noise* across all time and place? Or do we make sense of noise in different times and places?

HL: Noise is very much culture-bound despite the fact that our brains have similar means of processing what we hear. Think of the Indian music you occasionally hear: it does not give you a beginning, middle, and end the way that Western compositions throughout all periods do. If we complain that a Philip Glass piece lacks the structure we demand in music—that a minimalist piece of his goes on and on with only the most gradual changes—that's doubtless because he spent time in India learning its music while he sought to break away from the serial style dominating American and European music in his youth. The musical conventions of a particular culture become embedded in people's brains at an early age, just as the languages we grow up in do. The Western tonal system, with its alternation between dissonant and consonant chords and its drive toward closure, seems "natural" to us just as the systems guiding, say, Chinese and Arabic music seem natural to people in those countries. (To be sure, Western music has, in recent years, become so popular throughout the world that an Indian or a Japanese listener's ear may well be better attuned nowadays to the Western rather than to his native system.)

FLA: How might our perception of distasteful, disharmonious music interrupt our sense of temporality?

HL: Much of the so-called advanced music of the past century eschewed the temporal dimension central to tonal music since the Renaissance. It's interesting that Schoenberg, even in his twelve-tone period, still retained the structure of traditional forms. His last two quartets, both of them serial compositions, simulate the temporal development of sonata form—but only simulate, for sonata form is dependent on the chordal progressions that the twelve-tone method had abandoned. Schoenberg's serial successors, Webern and Boulez, no longer attempted any traditional temporal development, and listeners, I suspect, have had an even harder time with these later composers than with their leader.

FLA: It has been suggested that Adorno's philosophy could be described as *atonal* and indebted to the compositional techniques of Schoenberg.

HL: No accident: Adorno studied music composition for several years with Alban Berg. And both Schoenberg and Adorno—each in his own medium—are difficult to process.

FLA: And so too is the Austrian artist and composer Peter Ablinger difficult to get our ears around. His career has focused nearly exclusively on noise, yet he claims not to be interested at all in *making new*. He remarks, "I do not believe in the new. At best, I believe in a renewal in the sense of a permanent process, in the sense of an equilibrium. Renewal is needed for things to stay the same." He even proposed a method for listening to noise.

HL: Ablinger is clearly working in the avant-garde tradition (if one dare link these two seemingly antithetical words) established by Cage and in which random noise is treated as intrinsic to a composition, as in the latter's *4′33″*. In *Instruments and Noise*, for example, seven instrumentalists playing music from Ablinger's notated score alternate with, or are interrupted by, crowd noises emanating from loudspeakers. Whether or not Ablinger has "made it new" or has suggested a mode of "renewal . . . for things to stay the same," is not a vital question for me. Since this and other pieces are designed for a formal concert milieu (even one specializing in new music), he has simply shown that random aspects of life outside the world of art can be absorbed by this world. The street noise, in short, has become a formal part of a musical composition.

FLA: And there's Luigi Russolo, who wrote his *Art of Noises* manifesto (1913), insisting on the autonomy of the artist in his choice to integrate noise into musical composition.

HL: Russolo was merely anticipating by a few decades what Cage and his successors were to do. But then 1913 was also the year in which Marcel Duchamp, who was to exercise an empowering influence on Cage, exhibited his upside-down bicycle wheel atop a stool, which, by dint of his calling it art, achieved aesthetic status—and the few later copies that were made (the original having been lost) are now safely ensconced in art museums.

FLA: In between the generation of Russolo and Duchamp and the era of Cage we had the introduction of musique concrète—or concrete music. Indeed, French composer Pierre Schaeffer theorized the collecting of concrete sounds in lieu of notating musical scores. And, advances in recording technology (microphones and tape recorders) facilitated the capturing of these sounds from any and all places. There was a time (more at the tail end of my father's generation when he was a teenager) in Mexico City when it was fashionable for artists to have this so-called concrete music play in their studios. I've heard stories of painters working with great concentration in their studios while the sounds of rain, wind, doors slamming, motors revving, you name it, would be heard playing in the background. Some concrete music was edited to create a montage effect—a motor revving juxtaposed with the sound of a water drop; others were simply recorded and played back in the raw.

HL: In both cases, what was produced is music that is simply the organization of sounds, wherever they may have come from. And it's not all that different from a visual artist like Gabriel Orozco (whom we'll take up in the next chapter) organizing found objects.

FLA: Yes, at this most general and abstract level, we have the organization of sound-events that are natural (not made by a musical instrument per se) to create music. While the fad of concrete music passed, we see traces of it in the music of Tom Waits, for instance. He would incorporate the sounds made from scraping washing boards or bending saws and the manipulation of any other object he might find around his house and barn to accompany his guitar playing and singing. He often recorded in his barn, incorporating, say, a rooster's crow into his compositions.

HL: There are no limits to what can be metabolized in the creating of acoustical art.

FLA: Yes, earlier we talked about the way the Beatles metabolized the sitar from India and the way rai metabolized acoustical art from Israel, Spain, Algeria to create a new form of music—a form of music that was persecuted for years, then transformed into a music enjoyed by myriads of youth in Europe. And rai in turn has been metabolized by other musical traditions since.

HL: I suspect that the metabolizing of earlier or distantly foreign styles is part of the "natural" history of the arts.

FLA: In this metabolizing process, however, homogeneity can also appear. That is, there are no limits to what can be metabolized in music—just as there are no limits to what can become boring and commonplace in music. Even something like too much randomness becomes boring. Whether in the background while painting in a studio or listening more attentively, when we are surrounded by a composition of random sounds we might be distracted for a moment by its novelty, but, after a while, we want to get away from it.

HL: It has the same effect as repetitious sounds. We tire of it (unless of course the repetitions are part of an intended hypnotic effect).

FLA: Earlier I mentioned our shared acoustical neurobiology that springs from our common evolution as a species. We evolved sense-meaning mechanisms that attached to different sounds: abrupt, short, loud sounds as warnings and slower more regular sounds as soothing. When a composer willfully puts together sounds he or she can direct our emotions and thoughts in specific ways.

HL: We see a neuroscientist like Dan Levitin build entire arguments around the way our brain arranges basic elements of sound into higher concepts such as meter, harmony, and melody.

FLA: Our listening to music involves multiple sound dimensions such as tone (a discrete sound), rhythm (the duration of notes and how they group together), tempo (overall speed or pace), contour (notes going up or down), timbre (the difference in sound between instruments), loudness (physical amplitude), spatial location, reverberation, and pitch. Just as random sound can be carefully orchestrated to become a composition where the elements combine and form relationships that give rise to those higher-order concepts in the brain such as meter, key, melody, and harmony (what we call music), so too can sounds be carefully orchestrated to form relationships of disorder.

HL: Absolutely! This is when the untrained ear might hear Webern and Boulez as noise—and the trained ear might hear carefully organized musical compositions.

FLA: Those composers who seek to trigger comforting emotions in us know well (even if at the intuitive and not neurobiological level) that repetition in music creates emotions of satisfaction, but that in order to help us recognize the repeating units, composers insert differences or variations; that is, they build in units of difference to give our brains something to measure the repetition against. It makes sense, then, that to give shape to sounds that defy meaning and that trigger emotions of discomfort requires a willful lack of repetition in a composition and instead the stringing together of seemingly incoherent acoustical phrases.

HL: And certainly one of the several things that make Schoenberg's *Erwartung* so discomforting is his refusal to repeat musical themes. (A distinguished recent performer of this piece admitted that, in the absence of any repeatable melodies, she had to struggle to learn each of the pitch intervals by heart.) But this lack of repetition is only part of Schoenberg's discomforting game in this seminal work. Remember that *Erwartung* is also an exercise in female hysteria. In fact, recent research (see Carpenter) has shown that Schoenberg's librettist, Marie Pappenheim, a young medical student at the time, was a cousin of Bertha Pappenheim, who was the Anna O in the Freud-Breuer *Studies in Hysteria* (she was actually Breuer's, not Freud's, patient). The libretto contains all sorts of echoes of the Anna O case history as well as of other case histories. Schoenberg, who at the time was still suffering from the effects of his wife's affair with the painter Richard Gerstl, is inducing in us effects analogous to those that Breuer was describing in his patient. *Erwartung* is certainly disquieting, but then so was Anna O's illness, not to speak of Schoenberg's family crisis. To give a positive note to this, I might add that Bertha Pappenheim recovered, moved from Vienna to Frankfurt, and became a prominent fighter for women's rights! And Schoenberg's wife came back to him after a few months, while poor Gerstl, as a result, committed suicide at twenty-five, and Schoenberg recovered sufficiently to become, with his rival Stravinsky, the greatest composer of the first half of the century. But the listener, on the other hand, never quite recovers from *Erwartung*, composed soon after this family crisis.

FLA: One certainly might not like it, but one might also be fascinated by it, just as we are with his theory of a twelve-tone system (consonant and dissonant made equal in his chromatic scale) introduced in 1923 and that promised to give us a new system comparable to the old tonal system.

HL: Perhaps we get too caught up in the term *like*, which implies that a piece has to satisfy the pleasure centers of the brain. My reactions to *Erwartung* amount to something considerably more than what you call "fascination," a term that implies one is keeping a certain distance from the object. But I get wholly caught up in this piece—as well as in many other difficult, though perhaps less astringent, works—in a way that goes far beyond fascination. Hearing a challenging piece makes me want live my way into it, inhabit it, whether or not the music accepts my presence.

When I developed a taste for this type of music—and this was in early adulthood, well after I had become familiar with the earlier classical tradition—it's likely that some area of my brain came to respond favorably to this particular form of noise. I even remember my first powerful experience with "difficult" modern music—a performance of the Bartok Fourth by the Julliard String Quartet at Antioch College when I was eighteen. All my fellow students who were present seemed to go through a similar experience, and we talked about our experience a lot. (When I heard the Bartok Fourth played just a few months ago, it struck me as easy as pie.) I think the same thing happened to some (though not most) pop-music fans of my generation who'd been nurtured on swing and bebop and then, during the 1960s, became converted to rock bands. It was something new—loud and shocking—to their ears, but they came to relish the experience (you may note that I'm avoiding the word *like*).

FLA: There are trends in music and the arts generally shaped by economic interests. In fact, we see often how this can even lead to the championing of a cultural object that in actuality discomforts. I think readily of the Frida Kahlo industry that appeared in the 1980s with many (especially feminists) championing her more out of fascination than like; her paintings of medical instruments and the inversion of bodies would likely not appear on living-room walls. In this senses, liking and disliking require less functioning of the neocortex. We can simply disregard it. Fascination and intrigue require much work on the part of the executive brain; this is why we pay close and careful attention to the music. The mental attitude of *like* doesn't imply *enstrangement*, whereas *fascination* does—a state of mind that requires us to focus on the discomforting object.

HL: Those few works like *Erwartung* or *Finnegans Wake* that we never fully assimilate suggest that there can be a permanent *enstrangement* between us and these texts. But for me it's still something more than what I consider "fascination," which, as I said, means that you keep a certain distance. I think of myself as thoroughly caught up in these difficult works: as I said earlier, I'm inside them, struggling to cope with them, not caring in the least whether I can ever feel "comfortable" with them.

FLA: Just as happened to that generation who grew a taste for rock, so too have some of us (myself included) developed a taste for what at first felt like an assault on my senses: Tom Waits's compositions made out of his raspy, sandpaper grinding voice and barnyard (chickens etc.) and wrenching household and toolshed noises. I also grew accustomed to the discomforting sounds of Waits in Robert Wilson's musical fable *The Black Rider* (1990–2012)—what I suggestively call elsewhere a pop opera and that played for years in Germany.

HL: And which played briefly in San Francisco, where I went twice to hear Marianne Faithfull sing Tom Waits's songs in her own aging, raspy voice—and together with the gloriously slow stage movements typical of Wilson, you had a strange sort of ritual, deliberately ugly—or at least anything but "lovely"—sounds and sights that define an experience like no other. And behind this one recognizes the scenario coming from Weber's opera *Der Freischütz*, whose uncompromisingly Romantic music contrasts sharply with this often grating score.

FLA: Interesting that you mention Marianne Faithfull. The youthful Faithfull (when she was hanging out doing drugs with Mick Jagger and others) had a quite "lovely" voice; I liked her songs and singing because it was easy to the ears. It was when she returned later to the singing circuit in the late 1990s as a much older woman and chose to sing songs by Kurt Weill and Bertolt Brecht—well, she's no longer a singer I "like." Rather, I'm *fascinated* by the way she phrases the songs. While she was easy to the ears as a young singer, she's a much more interesting singer in her mature years.

Another musician that spans these decades and with whom one is likely more fascinated with than inspired by is Frank Zappa. When I was a young teenager, my cousin Ilena was obsessed with the Sicilian American Frank Zappa (he grew up in El Cajon, California, so maybe we can include him as an honorary Latino too). She was a bit older than I and going through a rebellious phase. She loved the fact that his music was deliberately unharmonious. One of his songs was unlistenable unless you somehow managed to figure out how to play it backward on the record player.

HL: Much rock can be disquieting, but Zappa occupies a special place, I suspect, because of the insistence with which he sought to needle his listeners.

FLA: Intermixed with Zappa's rebellious, gritty urban soundscapes ("Trouble Every Day" comes to mind) were soundbites (quotes) from Varèse, Stravinsky, and Webern. He collapsed highbrow with lowbrow to create music that was self-consciously critical of consumer culture.

HL: Let's call Zappa a crossover artist who was trying to give us new sound experiences while influenced by and quoting from difficult modernist composers who were themselves creating new sounds. And new sounds are what classical music has been foregrounding above all during the last couple of decades. It hardly matters whether these sounds come out tonal or not—often, in fact, there's a mixture. But they don't cultivate a particular "method," as Schoenberg did.

Indeed, there's no reigning "style" that one can discern today as one could in most past periods. Even if you can't define a style as such, the one thing that characterizes recent composers—for example, the British Thomas Adès, the Finnish Kaija Saariaho, and the Argentine Jewish Osvaldo Golijov—is a search for sounds that will hit their audiences in a striking and unexpected way. They're not afraid to use electronic means to help create these sounds, and they'll "cross over" when convenient, as Golijov does with Yiddish, Spanish, and Latin American popular forms. (There's a group called the Spectralists—with which Saariaho has been associated—for whom the exploration of sounds you think you never heard before is central.) For listeners wedded to Brahms and earlier, these current composers are not likely to make much of a dent, but they are considerably more digestible at first hearing than, say, the serial composers of the 1950s and 1960s were.

FLA: While certain compositions seek to be indigestible, the method and means for creating this are infinite. Because they are infinite, they are also impossible to transcribe and thus not learnable in a formal sense.

That is, music that discomforts defies the making of (the need for, even) a reproducible methodology.

HL: Schoenberg and his disciples actually did create a method they considered reproducible—to the point that textbooks were written to teach composers how to do twelve-tone music. Once Schoenberg had died and was no longer his rival, the aged Stravinsky (in 1951) studied one of these textbooks so that he could adapt Schoenberg's method to his own needs—though the result was compositions that sounded much more like Stravinsky than like any of the German or American serial composers.

FLA: The unlistenable does not mean *unreproducible*.

HL: Indeed! Let's return to what we said earlier about Schoenberg and Cage. We used their names as shorthand for the Unlistenable, or at least the tough-to-listen-to. But using their names in this way is also falsifying their actual careers. The early, pre-atonal Schoenberg wrote lots of listenable—if not necessarily simple to listen to—pieces like the first quartet and the first chamber symphony plus at least one really easy piece that still gets played all the time, namely, *Transfigured Night*. But even during his long nontonal period he composed occasional tonal pieces. Moreover, the nontonal pieces differ greatly in the difficulties they cause in their listeners. *Erwartung* may stand at one extreme, but then there are the five nontonal sets of solo piano pieces, which, after no more than a few hearings, are quite enjoyable (to use a word rarely associated with this composer). I might add that Schoenberg himself believed that with repeated hearings his nontonal pieces would become more pleasing (if not precisely like mother's milk) to his listeners, but that has obviously not proved to be true.

Perhaps if he had known about the experiments that Levitin and his fellow neuroscientists performed, Schoenberg would have realized that Western listeners' brains want to have their pleasure centers rubbed. They crave the sort of experience that *Twelfth Night*'s Orsino calls the "food of love" that

came o'er my ear like the sweet sound
That breathes upon a bank of violets
Stealing and giving odour. (1.1.1 and 5–7)

In short, we customarily demand that these pleasure centers be awakened, and that's our right—just as it's our right (at least if you have a doctor's prescription) to pop Prozac into our mouths.

FLA: And how much sweeter that sound of Schoenberg's tonal pieces might be after we've popped a nontonal pill of Cage.

HL: With Cage, who was Schoenberg's student for a brief time but was wholly different from him, there's also an early listenable period. The difficulties arrived around 1950 when Cage turned to chance operations (partly a response to the self- and will-lessness he sought after studying Zen Buddhism). Before that, when his conscious self determined all the notes, he was relatively accessible, though admittedly eccentric to the ordinary listening ear. The percussion pieces from the late 1930s and early 1940s are exciting and, for me at least, thoroughly enjoyable works, as are the great *Nocturne* and the *Sonatas and Interludes for Prepared Piano*. For the latter Cage "prepared" the piano with rubber erasers, metal pieces, and the like stuffed under the strings to give the instrument a less resonant and more percussive effect. The effect is quite wonderful once the listener gets used to the weird sound generated by those erasers.

FLA: And Cage's *Nocturne*?

HL: Yes, this composition, written for violin and piano accompaniment, and which, in my recording, times in at four minutes, twenty-eight seconds, just five seconds short of *4′33″*, has all the sweetness that Orsino asks for in music. And, at the other extreme, let's not forget a chance-operations work such as *Europeras* (1987), for which Cage, as with *4′33″*, composed nary a note (see Lindenberger, *Opera in History* 240–64). Here, instead of composing silence, as it were, he used sounds from famous operas—namely, familiar arias that his singers, and not Cage himself, were asked to choose. But the orchestral accompaniments to these arias got totally scrambled by means of chance, and although the listener can discern, say, Rossini's big Figaro aria behind all that noise, the result is sheer cacophony. Yet Cage gave the audience something to hold on to by means of the stage actions and scenic constructions, which, to be sure, were also determined by chance operations, with the result that everything, according to reports, seemed amusingly zany.

FLA: There is that element of chance that can and does change our experience of such musical performances, turning the intended discomfort into one not only of comfort but also of bellyaching laughter. Social context and its unintended surprises can change the experience of a piece, but so too can historical circumstances. I'm thinking of Beethoven's Ninth Symphony that we now know was performed annually on Hitler's birthday. How might history change our experience of the original?

HL: The Beethoven Ninth is a cultural icon that suits the most diverse purposes. Tolstoy, in his foolish book on aesthetics, chose this piece as his prime example of why classical music was so bad: it was incomprehensible to the masses of ordinary people, he said correctly, and if something didn't please the lowest common denominator, it was by definition bad. The Nazis embraced the Ninth since this icon represented the greatness of German culture. But then it also got played triumphantly as the Berlin Wall came falling down.

FLA: I think also of the character Alex DeLarge in *A Clockwork Orange* and the shock treatments he received while the Ninth plays—his favorite symphony.

HL: Icons obviously serve many purposes, and film, with its ability to tie the visual to the aural and generate new meanings for both media, can take full advantage of these icons—the Blue Danube, for instance, in *2001: A Space Odyssey*, and the Beethoven Ninth, in a thoroughly unpleasant scene, as you remind me, in *Clockwork Orange*.

FLA: The Ninth in *The Clockwork Orange* contradicts all those old and renewed formulations that art is by definition uplifting; that it somehow makes you a better, smarter, more empathic person. (Recall all those industry ploys to get parents to play Mozart and classical music generally to babies developing in the womb.)

HL: I too once believed that exposing a baby to Mozart would work wonders for the child's musical and mathematical powers, so I played Mozart to my son constantly while giving him the bottle late at night when my wife was already asleep. As it turned out, math turned out to be his weakest subject, and although I took him to operas and concerts when he was a child (not to speak of playing classical recordings while we were at the dinner table), by the time he turned twelve he deserted Mozart for Pink Floyd and the like.

FLA: Some research shows a marked increase in brain activity that indicated greater emotional processing when music excerpts were played together with pictures as opposed to situations when pictures were shown without music (T. Baumgartner et al.).

HL: That may explain why opera often feels more intense than music you hear in the symphony hall: apparently the visual dimension creates a mixture that hits the brain with greater voltage. Same with film and ballet: imagine films without music to help direct the drama to the intended places in the brain—even silent films had their live organ-playing to help do the trick. Jerome Robbins's ballet without music, *Moves: A Ballet in Silence*, forces you to concentrate only on the dance movement, and the effect at first is a bit unnerving. And then there's Merce Cunningham, who with Cage, his musical director during the earlier part of his career, instituted the policy that there be no relation between the dance and the music, which, indeed, often were conspicuously at odds with one another. The result was an altogether cooler, less intense experience—just the opposite of the emotionally charged experience, both visual and aural, that you had with Martha Graham's group, with whom Cunningham had performed before he went off on his own.

FLA: Herbie, I must confess that I find myself more and more turning off the radio while driving because pop and rock increasingly sound like atonal *noise* to me.

HL: The interesting thing here is that pop and rock are usually tonal, though the effect they have on us—the noisiness, the screechy sounds—is much like that of atonal music. If someone had heard a fully tonal rock song at the time Schoenberg broke with tonality, it would have bothered the ear just as much as Schoenberg's music did. I might add that, just as millions of people all over the world have come to find the loud and seemingly uncomfortable sounds of rock pleasurable, so it's become possible to introduce supposedly "unmusical" sounds—the kind that musique concrète cultivated—into classical compositions that find considerable favor with traditional-minded symphony audiences. I'm thinking particularly of the young composer Mason Bates, who, "playing" his computer with the orchestra, introduces conspicuously "nonmusical" sounds such as a glacier calving, an early-model automobile cranking up, and particles colliding at Fermilab. For his piece *Alternative Energy* he searched through junkyards to find metal objects that his orchestra percussionists could use. I've heard him cheered wildly by audiences, and you know why? He's composing beautifully crafted tone poems, full of good tunes, and nobody ends up feeling in the least bit uncomfortable. As a musically conservative friend put it after hearing a Bates composition, "This is the first time I've ever really enjoyed this kind of a piece." Yet to the extent that his pieces are full of those sounds from the everyday world that John Cage cultivated, Bates belongs to the progeny of Cage (who of course was never cheered by this type of audience and would likely have disdained Bates's work!).

FLA: The cheering audience *knew* what it was hearing. I likely would not. It has to do with experience, certainly, but also one's mood at the time of reception. I might hear the sound coming from the radio as noise because I'm not in the mood to *listen*. All that's going on in and around me, including everyday traffic, might shade with negative emotion whatever it is that I'm listening to on the radio.

HL: Let me add that the discomfort we feel in musical works is not limited to composers like Schoenberg and Cage whose sounds are difficult to process. A musically communicative composer such as John Adams became a source of controversy in late 2014 when his opera *The Death of Klinghoffer* was given its first production at the Metropolitan Opera. Protesting crowds gathered outside at the first performance, which was interrupted inside as well by hecklers—and all because the opera was supposedly "anti-Semitic" in the way it depicted the terrorist killing of an elderly Jew. In addition, scheduled radio and television broadcasts were canceled. I had attended the opera's first production in 1991 and, despite the fact that the Nazis' killing of all my aunts, uncles, and cousins in Germany should have made me sensitive to the issue, it never occurred to me that this work was in the least anti-Semitic. Uncomfortable, to be sure, as a considerable amount of the world's great art is. But the complexity with which *The Death of Klinghoffer* explores the plight of both the Palestinians and Israelis at the same time that it condemns the terrorist act indicated by the title was especially lost on the protesters, many of whom admitted they had never read the libretto nor heard the music. Whereas these folks should have found their discomfort in the way that the work, both verbally and musically, opens up and analyzes some of the touchiest issues of our time, they allowed themselves the luxury of simply crying foul about what they imagined to be an ethnic insult. At least those, like most of my friends, who complain about twelve-tone music have listened to it enough to feel some physical assault on their ears. I'd also like to make a pitch for what you call "negative" emotion. I'm not saying it's necessarily good for the soul, but somehow, as I've indicated above, I often get what others must take as a perverse satisfaction out of it. Perhaps I'd need to subject myself to an fMRI to help explain this, and then they might find an area of my brain that responds positively to what's negative for others. But if there's a good pitch to be made, I'd speculate that cultivating uncomfortable music is a way to stretch one's thinking muscles, to explore feelings you never believed you had in you, to confront your own capacity to induce—as I've tried to do in this conversation—discomfort in others.

FIVE | Retchful Art

FREDERICK LUIS ALDAMA: Herbie, let's turn our attention to painting and then photography. Some research (V. S. Ramachandran, for instance) shows that people prefer art that is prototypical and that preferences are influenced by prototypicality—the mind/brain's construction of typical versus atypical concepts and cases (faces, shapes, objects, and animals, for instance). So what are we to make of the nonprototypical, or art that makes us want to retch?

HERBERT LINDENBERGER: Feeling comfortable with the prototypical is merely to say that people viewing visual representations want to confirm their expectations of what the external world looks like. The same is true of their attitude toward literary fiction, but only to a degree. Readers are willing to let authors stretch their imaginations beyond realistic representation—which has made fantasy possible throughout the history of literature in what we call "romance"—and it persists in a big way today in, say, the Harry Potter books and in science fiction. There's no real equivalent in painting: the monstrous faces that romance is loaded with are relatively rare in visual art, which, as you say, demands a measure of prototypicality.

FLA: Much has been made about the nonprotoypicality of the eighteenth-century German sculptor Franz Xaver Messerschmidt's busts. We recognize them as human faces, but we do a double take to try to figure out where the line blurs between the ordinary and the strange—monstrous, even (figure 18).

HL: These are the sorts of heads one can imagine—at least among the villains—of literary romance. Still, none of the bad guys in, say, Tolkien or Rowling is as shocking as a Messerschmidt sculpted head. And when captured in stone, mad heads like these are a good bit harder to take than if they were painted two-dimensionally in oil. These heads are much like what I remembered when my college psych class was taken on a field trip to what in those days was called an insane asylum; that was before they had psychiatric drugs to mitigate the effects of

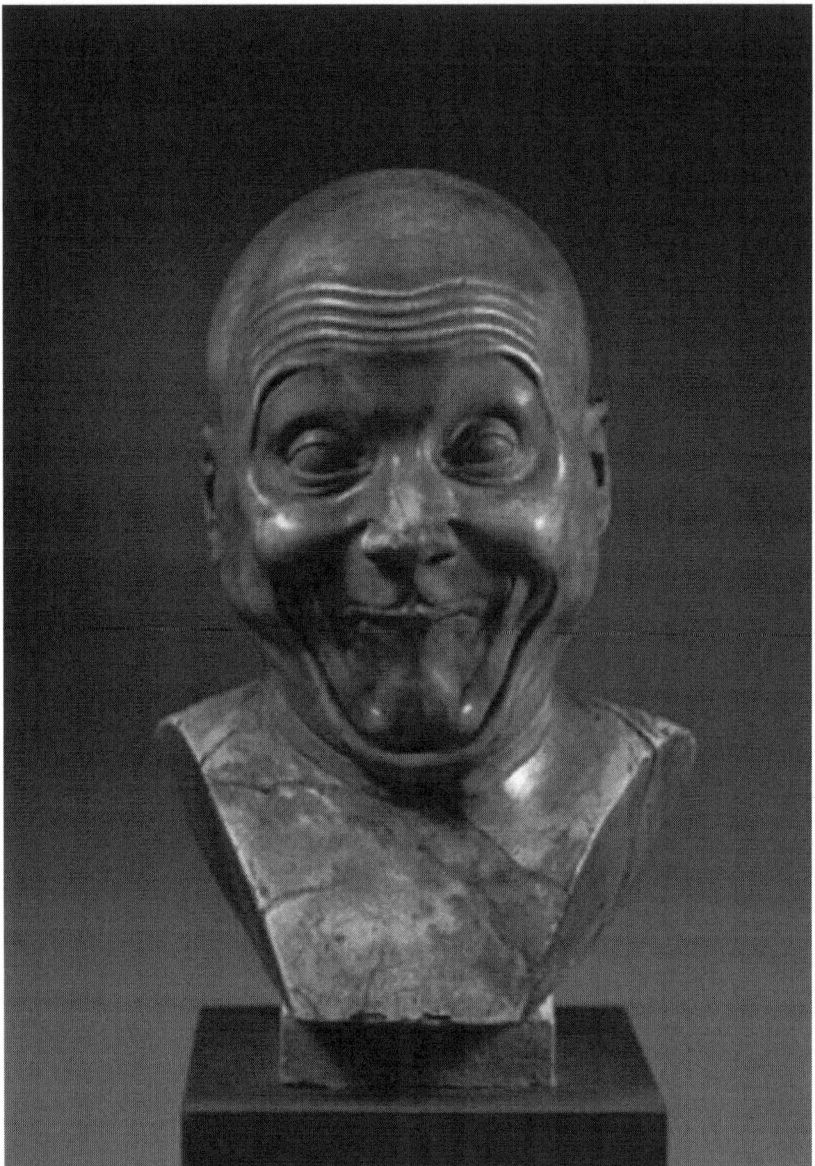

Figure 18. F. X. Messerschmidt, *An Intentional Jester* (1770). Oesterreichische Gallerie im Belvedere, Vienna. Erich Lessing / Art Resource, NY.

mental illness, and the people we viewed looked every bit as scary as this Messerschmidt bust.

I experienced the same discomfort with the Messerschmidt bust when I recently visited the Stanford Museum and ran into two of Robert Arneson's sculptures. One of them (see book cover) is an obvious self-portrait (the artist's reaction, according to the label, to a fight with his first wife), and the other is named *Global Death and Destruction*, supposedly what happens to a head in a nuclear war. Arneson specialized in the uncomfortable—to the point that his commissioned portrait of George Moscone, the San Francisco mayor who'd been shot to death in 1979 by a disaffected former county supervisor, was rejected by the Moscone family. Not only did Arneson inscribe "Bang Bang Bang Bang" on this artifact, but the face was distinctly unflattering (but then what do you expect from a sculptor who was so nasty to his own face?). Instead of being housed in the convention center named after the martyred mayor, the Moscone bust now sits in the San Francisco Museum of Modern Art, where it cohabits with other discomforting modernist sculptures.

FLA: I wonder, however, if our experience of discomfort with the sculptures of Arneson or Messerschmidt arises from our distinguishing between a prototypical (ordinary) and nontypical face. Perhaps the monstrous is less in the DNA of the object (the blurring of lines between ordinary and nonordinary) than in the way that Arneson or Messerschmidt establishes a new relationality between the sculpture and the viewer. The disquieting effect takes place *in* the relationship, and not necessarily in the object or in the mind of the viewer. That is, the prototypicality that is countered with Arneson or Messerschmidt leads to a nonprototypical encounter (and expectation of this encounter) that dashes to the ground our usual encounter with art, whereby we seek to gain a soothing and contemplative state of mind along with a pleasant feeling. Another way to think about this might be to say that while I'm fascinated by the sculptures I would never place them in my living room.

HL: There's all sorts of provocative art I'd place in my living room if my wife were willing to put up with it. But she feels much the way you do, Frederick.

FLA: Yes, cohabitation presents its own set of inhospitable problems, Herbie. Let me further clarify. It's not so much a discomfort that arises out of a proximity to a real-world representation, but rather how the artists create a specific aesthetic relationship. While I don't want Arneson's and Messerschmidt's works in my house, I am willing to observe and establish a relationship of nonrejection of these art objects. That is, I can put front and center an appreciation of how this aesthetic relationality of discomfort is constructed.

In this sense, our discomfort with art is at once similar to (and different from) our encounter with the disquieting faces of *real* people. We are accustomed to seeing certain kinds of faces in our everyday encounters in the world. When we come across a face that seems out of place, say, we might be taken out of this customary relationship. We might notice the face. The last time I took Corina to the ballet one of the ushers was a black man who suffered from vitiligo (loss of skin pigmentation that's beyond his control and not, say, the deliberate, will-to-style tattooing of the face we see with others) and he had all sorts of huge warts growing in and around his face. I noticed on Corina's face and gesture a simultaneous fascination with looking at the fellow—and a deep discomfort. I can say that I shared the exact reaction with Corina. Children feel discomfort when encountering something new and difficult to comprehend. While she showed a deep interest (in the sense of a scientific interest) in the usher's face, she didn't attach with this an aesthetic judgment.

HL: You bring up an apt point. Indeed, unnerving as those Messerschmidt heads may be, they are just an extreme example of what we feel when we look at real-life faces; whether it be the faces I encountered in the insane asylum, or the face of the fellow you and Corina saw at the ballet, or artistic representations like those of Messerschmidt or Arneson, we react the same way.

FLA: Neuroscientific research more than supports this.

HL: Yes, and remember that facial recognition belongs to a specialized area of the brain, the fusiform gyrus, which, some have speculated, may have been developed in the course of evolution so that an animal could easily protect itself from potentially hostile members of another species ("I don't recognize his ugly mug and therefore it scares me").

FLA: Yet there is an important difference. In art the artist carefully distills from the building blocks of reality to re-create an aesthetic object that aims to direct our emotional reactions of desire, disgust, and repulsion, and all the others. Arneson's and Messerschmidt's sculptures (and art generally) are a distillation, then re-creation of our (Corina's) reaction to the disquieting, but in a carefully directed way that breaks with the prototypical aesthetic relationality—with the result that the newly established aesthetic relationality leads to our enstrangement.

In the making of these sculptures, the artists also seek to add something new to the universe. Of course, because of this goal to bring something new into the world they are not willing to obey any laws or rules that would govern their activity; they don't feel obligated to apply the common doxa that, in creating these sculptures, they don't have to take into account the prejudices and worldviews of the viewers. Thus, they can and do fight against the moralization of art and the aestheticization of reality. Recall Leni Riefenstahl's 1934 film of the Nuremberg rally, *Triumph of the Will*. The intrusion of the aesthetic into the political domain is always nefarious.

HL: Most of the portraits by famous painters since the Renaissance—by, say, Raphael, Leonardo, Gainsborough, Sargent—were strongly idealized (Frederick, you use "distillation" to describe this process), which is not surprising in view of the fact that their sitters expected to be seen at their best, or even better than they actually were. But then note when Goya, as was often his wont, gives us an ugly queen (figure 19) within a supposedly flattering official portrait (the current British royal family would scarcely tolerate a painter so realistic about their none-too-handsome looks).

And note how disconcerting (at least to us if not to their first viewers) the dwarf's large face seems next to that of the lovely Infanta in Velazquez's *Las Meninas* (if this dwarf [figure 20] appeared in a photograph looking straight ahead, we might ascribe it to Diane Arbus).

FLA: What you describe, Herbie, is precisely how Velázquez distills, then re-creates, in order to trigger a particular emotion of discomfort in us. Of course, much has been written on *Las Meninas*, including by Foucault (3–16), who identified carefully how its composition exemplified the bringing of something absolutely new into the world. Indeed, this painting is not only an important stylistic innovation within this branch of art (painting) but also in its new way of looking at things: while it seems mimetic (a complex composition in the way the geometry is constructed), there are many layers, including Velázquez in the background center, and in the foreground what we see is not aristocracy but rather the dwarf and dog. (Compare this to Rembrandt, for instance, who painted high-placed officials and the bourgeoisie, and we see how radically new this painting is.) Velázquez gives expression to a sociological reality that is at once present and absent in the painting: the fact that royalty was being pushed into the background—and even out of the society entirely.

For me, the discomfort doesn't come from the dwarf and dog in the

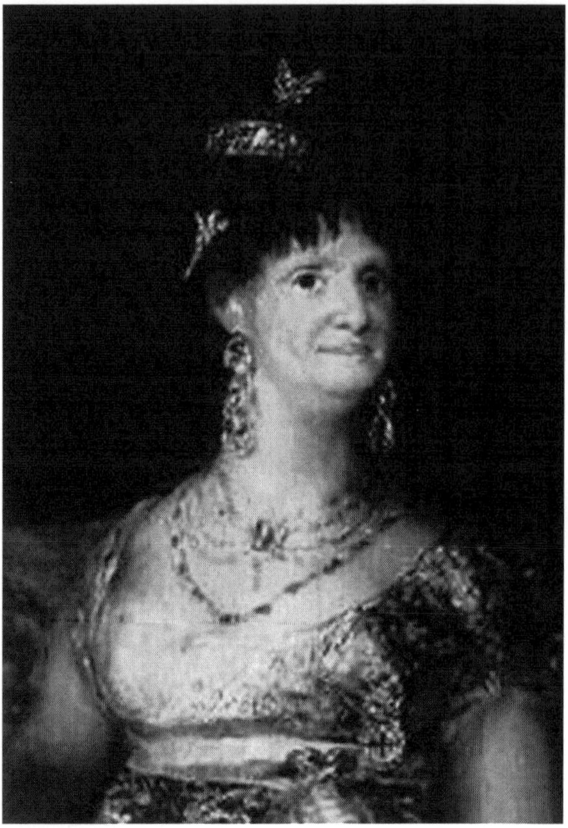

Figure 19. Francisco Goya, *Charles IV and His Family* (detail showing Queen Maria Luisa), Prado (circa 1800). Album / Art Resource, NY.

foreground. What's actually disturbing is the newness in the composition as a whole and the placing of the dwarf in the foreground as well as the placing at the center of the creator himself, who is also at the origin of the light. It was during a trip to the museums in Madrid that included the Prado over a decade ago that I realized in my face-to-face encounter with this painting that Velázquez was using shaping devices to innovate and make new a composition that displaced a long tradition of royalty portrait painting. I realized at that moment that the painting was disturbing beyond the big head of the dwarf.

HL: The first time I got back to Madrid after reading Foucault on this painting I spent an hour in the *Meninas* room, oblivious to all the other people going in and out. I suspect it was Foucault's captivating take on the painting, more than the work itself, that set off a disturbance. But the "large" dwarf still seems to me the most disturbing element here.

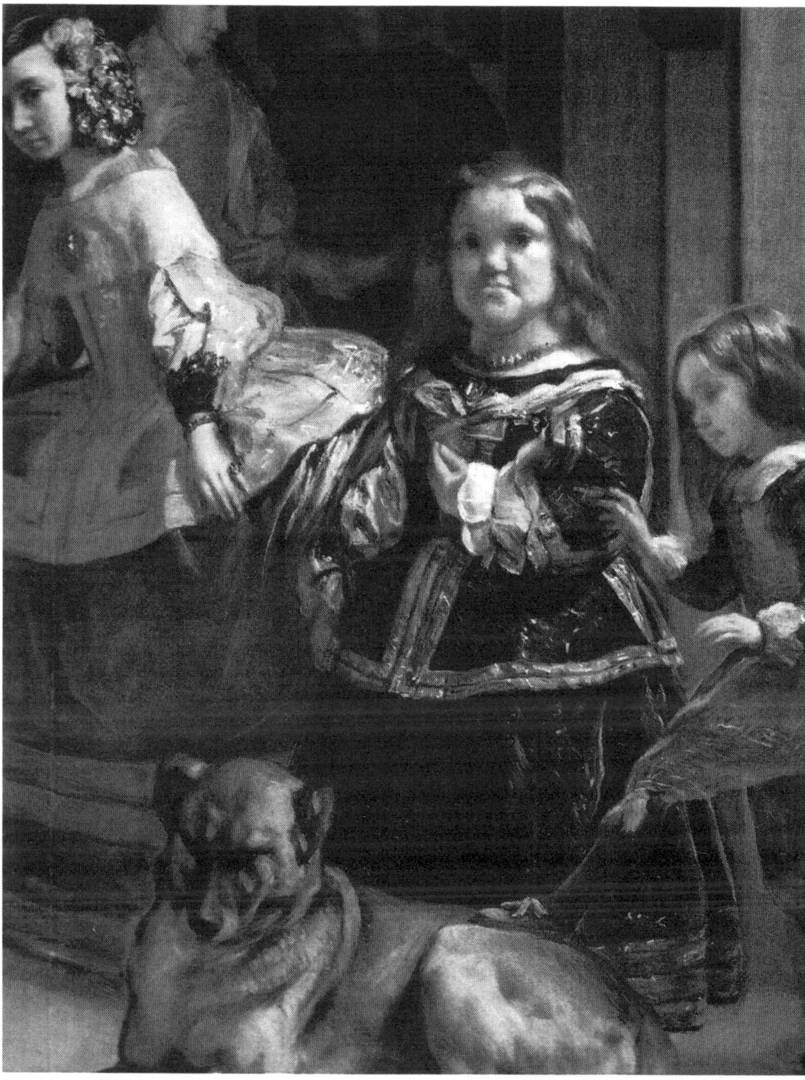

Figure 20. Diego Velázquez. *Las Meninas* (detail showing dwarfs), Prado. Album / Art Resource, NY.

Let me add that the great Spanish painters from Velázquez down through Picasso were very knowing about how to disturb us by means of faces. If Goya's formal portraits disturb in a peculiarly subtle way, the faces in his so-called late Black Paintings have nothing in the least subtle about them. And every time I see them in the Prado their power to upset seems as strong as ever. My first time there predated your visit by several decades. In 1953, during the depths of the Franco regime, I was taken on a tour by a guide who seemed reluctant to have to lead us into the room housing these horrifying pictures. She made all sorts of excuses in advance: Goya was infirm and depressed at the time, she told us, and, after all, he was painting myths that were familiar to everybody. It's as though Spanish national honor was at stake for her. Shocked though I was by these paintings, which I had never seen reproduced before—not even in the art-history survey I took in college—I thoroughly enjoyed them (and in my usual perverse way). Many years later, when we took our six-year-old son Michael to see the Black Paintings, he totally flipped when he saw Saturn devouring his child (figure 21).

How much scarier can a painted face get? And doubtless the idea of a father eating his kid had special resonance for a little boy.

FLA: There is this horrible expression on the face of Saturn when about to devour the child. It's terrifying to me—and would most certainly be terrifying to my daughter (she has not seen it). But what compounds the terrifying effect is the blackness of the background, underlying the bleakness of what's happening in this scene of scene of pedophagy. (I think of your earlier mention of Munch's *The Scream*; he chose to create a background filled with tumultuous waves of red, yellow, blue, and green to intensify our experience of the figure's discomfort.) At a further remove from Goya's realism, we have Picasso's discomforting art.

HL: Picasso, we now recognize, was one of the greatest portraitists in the history of art—despite all the distortions one can usually recognize which of his women he was painting—and surely one of the most unnerving things about early cubism must have been the paintings and sculptures of his then-mistress Fernande Olivier (figure 22).

If the lady had really looked like that, she would not likely have attracted the painter sexually. Compare this with a precubist portrait (1905–6) in which she appears as she "really" was (figure 23).

FLA: The objective of the artist is to keep us on that tightrope of *enstrangement*; to maintain a degree of interest and energy involved in the work. However, when it's disquieting art I think repeated exposure is less

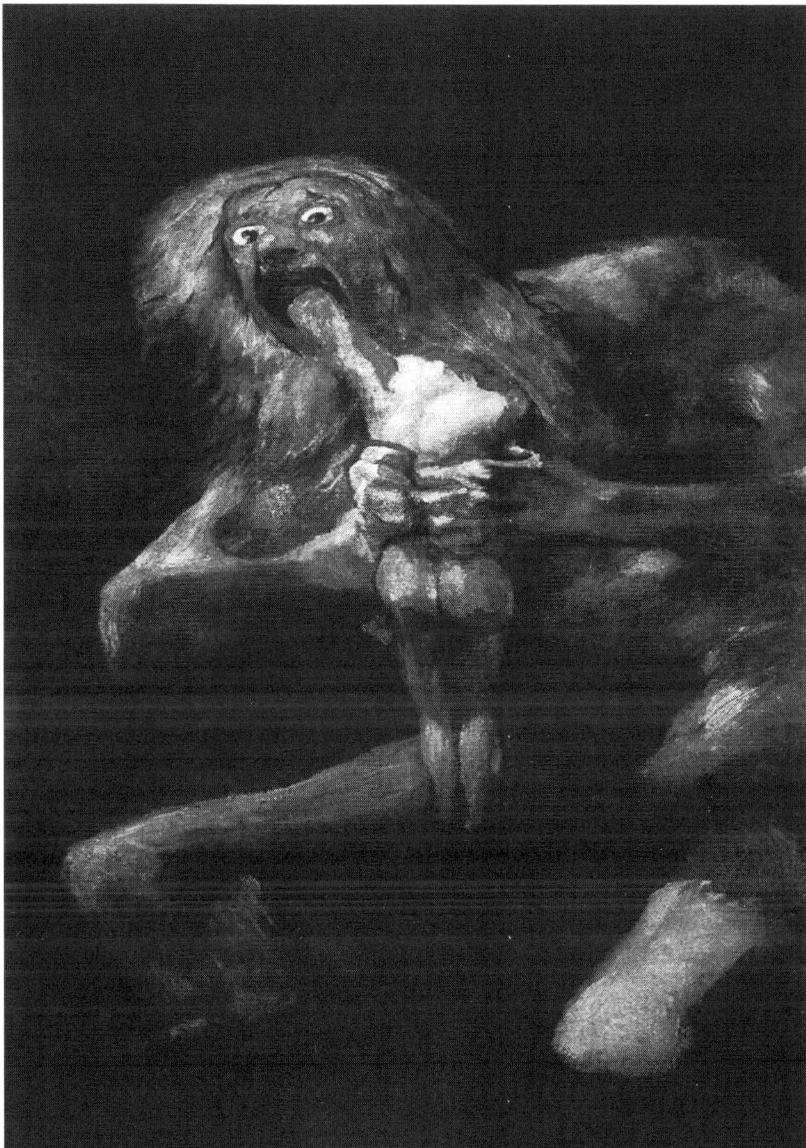

Figure 21. Francisco Goya, *Saturn Devouring His Children*, Prado (1819–23). © Museo Nacional del Prado / Art Resource, NY.

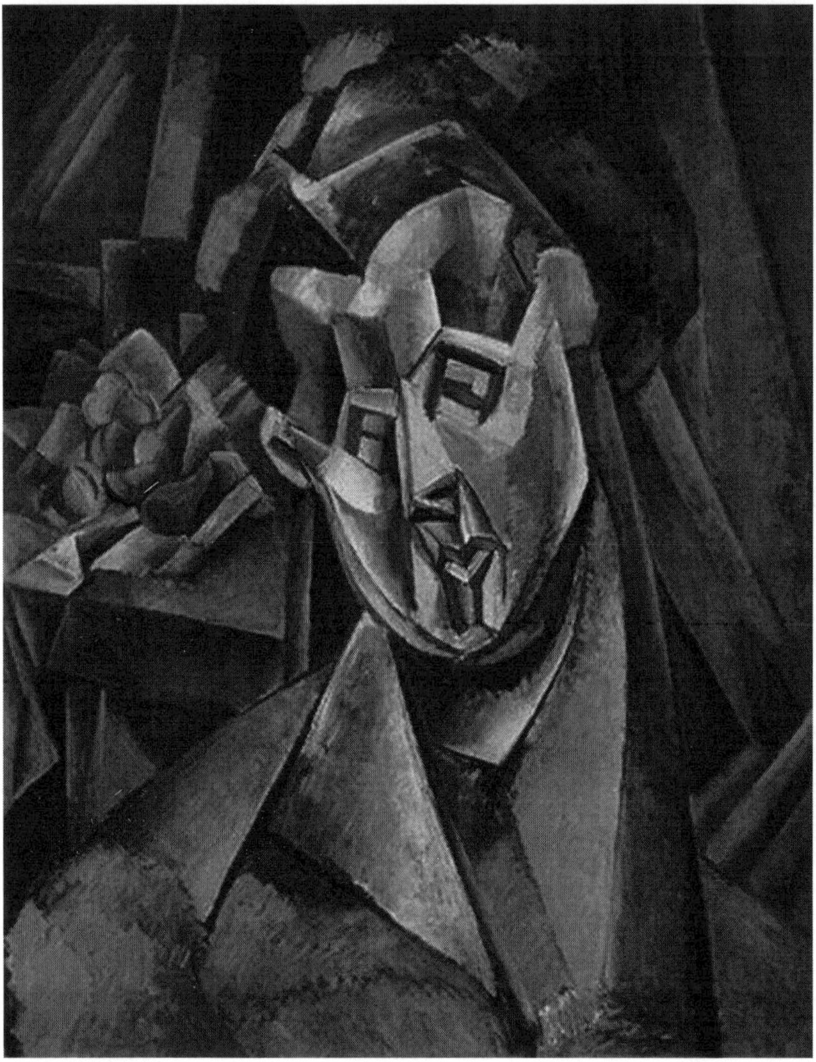

Figure 22. Pablo Picasso, *Woman with Pears (Fernande)*. © 2015 Estate of Pablo Pocasso / Artists Rights Society (ARS), New York. Digital Image © The Museum of Modern Art / Licensed by SCALA / Art Resource, NY.

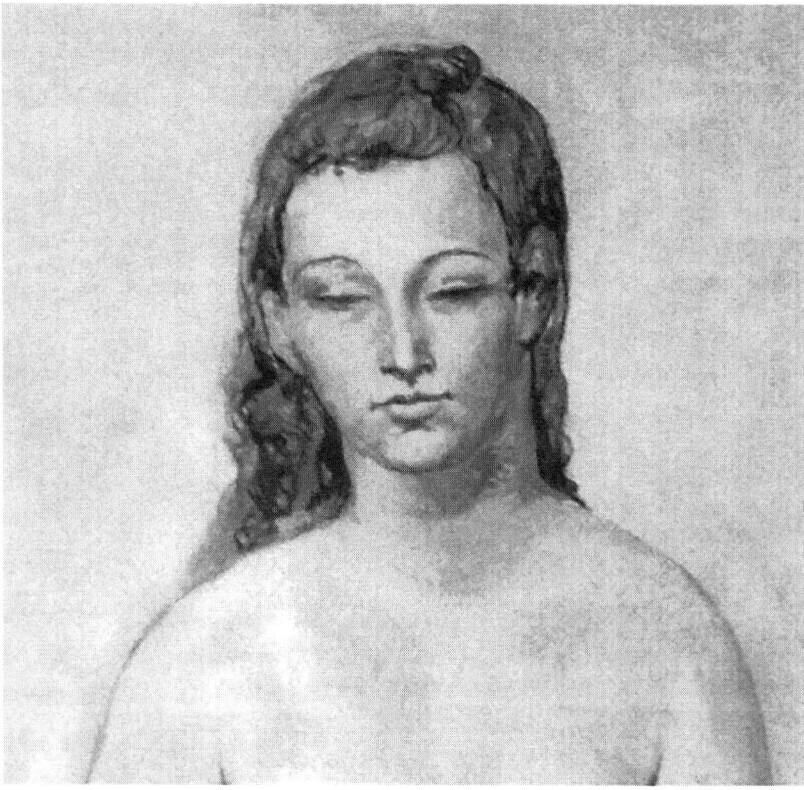

Figure 23. Pablo Picasso, *Nude with Joined Palms (Fernande)* (1906), detail. Art Gallery of Ontario, Toronto. Photo by John Ashkenas, with his permission.

likely to transform into an experience of monotony. No matter how many times we look at such forcefully disturbing works of Picasso (the cubist painting of Fernande "with pears," above) and Goya (his Saturn) they remain disquieting. Yet I became habituated to the framed poster of Munch's *The Scream* that I had hanging in my office. Unless a student pointed it out, I stopped noticing it altogether. I wonder how artists create such a strong aesthetic relationality between the object and the viewer that certain discomforting art manages to withstand the monotony that sets in with our repeated experience.

Milanese painter Giuseppe Arcimboldo's vegetable portraits seem to still trigger a deeply disturbing experience—and this especially when we contextualize his work within the less disquieting (bland,

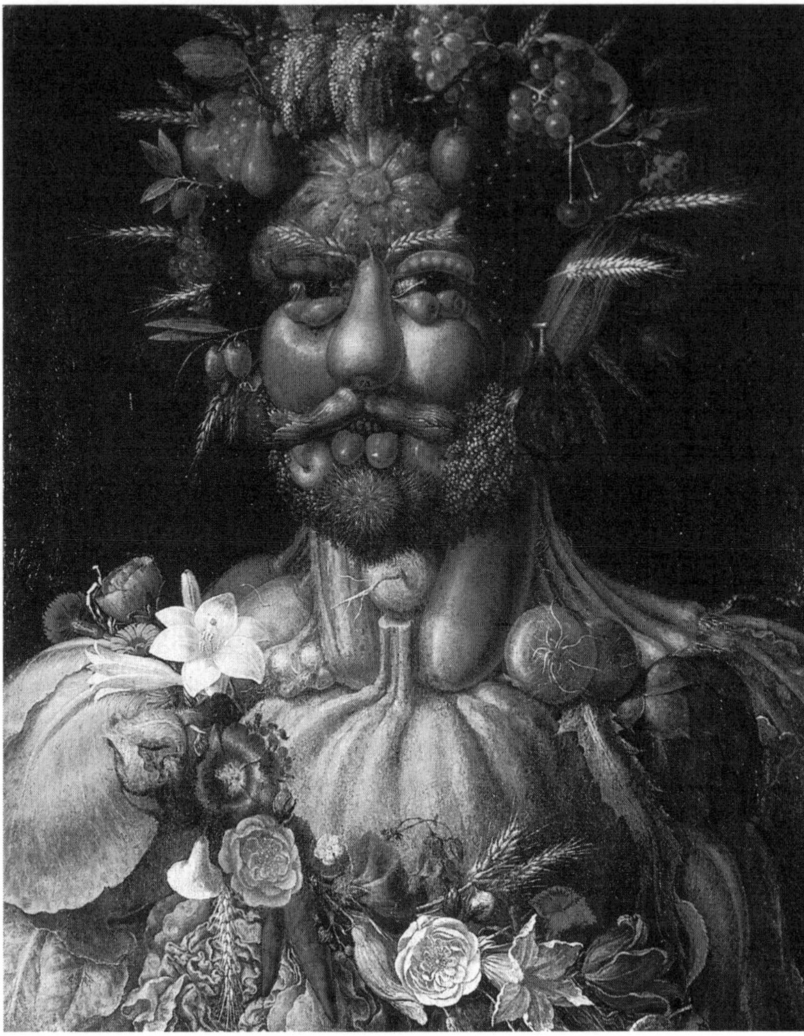

Figure 24. Giuseppe Arcimboldo, Rudolf II posing as Vertumnus, Skokloster Castle, Sweden (1590–91). The Art Archive at Art Resource, NY.

even) art of his day. He transformed fruits, vegetables, flowers, and animals into extremely discomforting portraits. In his portrait of Emperor Rudolf II posing as Vertumnus (1590–91) we recognize the individual plants and fruits (beautiful?), but as a gestalt that forms into a human face that is positively nightmarish (figure 24). I'm repulsed to the point of near vomiting, Herbie.

HL: The individual bunches of fruit, if isolated, might seem "beautiful," but heaping them together and centering them around a grotesque face creates a significantly more unpleasant whole than if the fruit or the face were presented individually.

FLA: Perhaps certain works are more transitory in their effect. We appreciate how in some of Picasso's works he made it *new*, but we experience this in a more intellectual, less emotional way than when we first encountered them.

HL: As with all the arts, most discomforting works become absorbed, as it were, over time and lose something of their bite. That's true of a lot of Picasso, but the late pornographic stuff still hits home as much as ever. And each time I go to MoMA and look at *Les Demoiselles d'Avignon* the ladies seem just as unpleasant as they did for me at first viewing when I was still a teenager (figure 25). If the real women with whom the young Picasso copulated at the Avignon Street (Calle Avinyó) brothel in Barcelona had looked like that, the establishment would not have done a very good business.

The only difference between then and now is that the demoiselles no longer hit me with a feeling of shock; but they still make me cringe when I examine them close-up. Of course the cubist distortion of objects upset people as much as facial distortion, but the latter, I suspect, has maintained a greater power to disturb over time. Think of the power of caricature, which seeks to undermine its object by treating real people's faces in the cruelest possible way. King Louis-Philippe, by dint of his unfortunate jowls, will forever remain in collective memory as the pear he became by means of the drawing by Charles Philipon—later redone by Honoré Daumier. And since Obama stepped into his shoes as president, there's been no end to how cartoonists exaggerate his negroid features.

FLA: Daumier belonged to a nineteenth-century artistic environment where artists were seeking to give art more abundant possibilities of expression. At the same time he was astutely critical of the nineteenth-century social and political environment. The great achievement of Daumier was his ability to focus on physical traits (and not just the face) and exaggerate features. His caricatures that render scenes from Rabelais's *Gargantua and Pantagruel* are hugely innovative. His making it new was a close observation of the model that would normally lead to a mimetic form of painting and drawing, but instead of seeking the mimetic he exaggerated and deformed physical traits. For his contemporary audiences, this exaggeration made the caricature look like a more realistic (more mimetic) portrait than the individual.

Finally, in Daumier we see not only a distillation of the body and

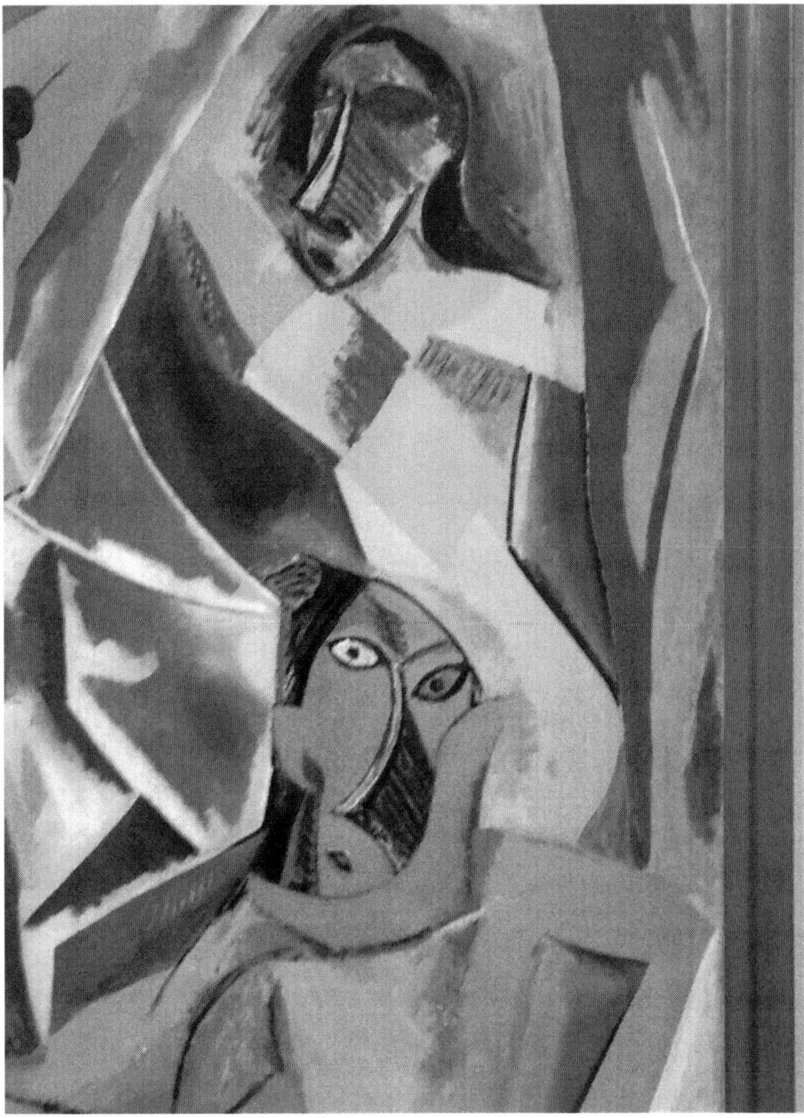

Figure 25. Pablo Picasso, *Les Demoiselles d'Avignon* (1907), detail. Museum of Modern Art, New York. Photo by Herbert Lindenberger.

the face, but more importantly the accompaniment of a specific way of seeing things whereby the mimetic gesture turns into a huge exaggeration of selected physical traits of the portrayed person; through this distillation and exaggeration Daumier was seeking to uncover a truth that is greater than the truth obtained by any strictly mimetic procedure (portraiture in painting and photography). It's this will to give the viewer a truer representation of a character than that which would be obtained by strictly mimetic methods that makes caricature a new disquieting art that has lasted so long. Those caricatures of Obama that you mention certainly extend this tradition so fine-tuned by Daumier.

HL: Discomforting things in all the arts become absorbed for us in varying ways. Remember that Wagner's notorious Tristan chord, which appears at the start of *Tristan und Isolde* and is not resolved until the end—four and a half hours later—was excruciating for many early listeners, but by the beginning of the twentieth century it had become associated with eroticism—as in Thomas Mann's novella *Tristan*—and before long it became just a moment, a crucial one, to be sure, in a work that listeners find "exciting," but not necessarily disturbing. In several earlier conversations I suggested Schoenberg's *Erwartung* as an example that has not lost its bite. I don't think the process by means of which visual art works on us over time is that different from music or literature.

FLA: I think of art that discomforts in the work of Hieronymus Bosch, Peter Brueghel, and then Arcimboldo, Dalí, and Remedios Varo. In each we see the building of a system of art that discomforts in ways that transcend time (history) and space (geography). As I just mentioned earlier, there is newness that glows bright, then quickly fades like a fad, and there's newness that traverses the centuries.

HL: Bosch and Brueghel—at least those works like the *Triumph of Death* and *Dulle Griet* in which Breughel was working in Bosch's mode—retain an extra level of disturbance for us through the fact that their imagery was adopted by the surrealist painters. As a result, the sharp disturbances that emanate from Miró, Dalí and Yves Tanguy are then read back, as it were, to the odd shapes and doings of their originators, who then seem even more potent than ever. Both Bosch and his successors cultivated, among other things, bulbous shapes that pretend to be natural but that also trigger in the viewer a certain dis-ease (figure 26).

What is there about a bulbous shape that gets to us? Is it that its shape triggers something deep as in our encounter with a fungus or

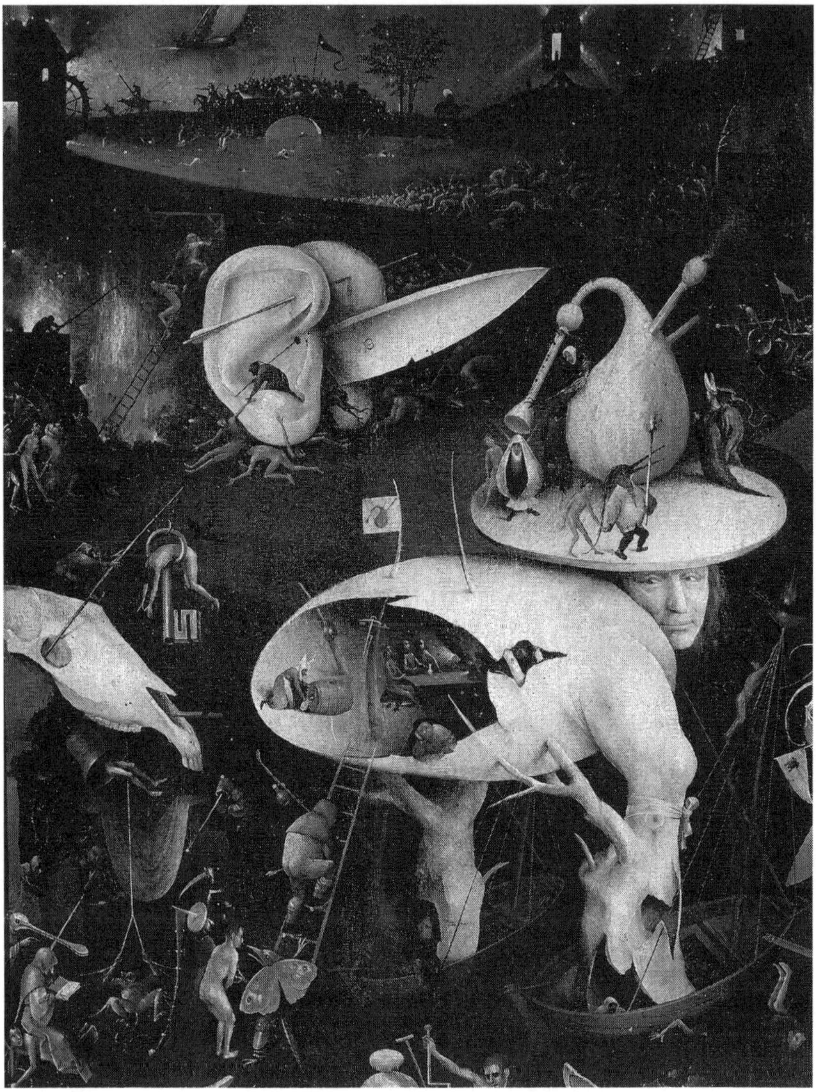

Figure 26. Hieronymus Bosch, *Garden of Earthly Delights* (circa 1505–10), detail from right-hand panel, "Hell"), Prado. Gianni Dagli Orti / The Art Archive at Art Resource, NY.

spilt blood or a festering wound? Is it that something supposedly "natural" will keep growing like a cancer? And when, as in the center of this Bosch painting, the bulbous shape is attached to a human form, do we fear for ourselves? And note how there is a bulbous quality to other objects within the painting—the ears, the vessel atop the woman's head. When we see such bulbous shapes we can imagine them opening, as here, to issue all manner of rank, festering objects.

FLA: Or consider another section of Bosch's triptych *Garden of Earthly Delights*, which features naked figures often kissing and fondling, but not in an erotic or sexual way. Rather, as disturbing oddities: flowers emerging from somebody's bottom (figure 27); a giant cherry and blackberry appearing for no particular reason. Yet the colors and drawing (a sense of animation?) delight. And nothing is haphazard or by chance here. Bosch carefully selects colors, symbols, organic entities (oft-grotesque and gargantuan animals and mutant humans) to direct our meaning-making mechanism and emotional response.

HL: What's interesting especially is that unpleasant things don't happen just in the right panel, which depicts hell, but in the central one as well, and this is supposed to be a garden of "delights." Not only do we find those bulbous shapes here, but also when we see flowers sprouting from anuses we know we've entered a domain in which we don't care to dwell for very long. But hell as such gave license to painters throughout the Western tradition to let themselves go with whatever they could to frighten their viewers into maintaining the moral conduct that the church expected of them. Every painter commissioned to do a Last Judgment, even an ordinarily gentle one such as Giotto, could concoct the usual horrifying images—like the people hanging from a branch by their tongue, hair, and genitals—on the painting's right side (figure 28).

FLA: The Renaissance is an obviously quite unusual period. After centuries of the Catholic (and other) church's religious dogma (dictatorship) and the courts that imposed on artists what were respectable and usable shapes in both content and form, there emerges an epoch of freedom from the dogmatic worldview. As you know, during this new period, as capitalism developed and there appeared more mercantile and financial capitalists, there arose the new benefactor system. The result: the appearance of a myriad of new forms of expression by artists who craved a total freedom in art and the expression of secular themes—even in religious art. With new technical means (pigment and perspective, for instance) Giotto's religiously themed art was

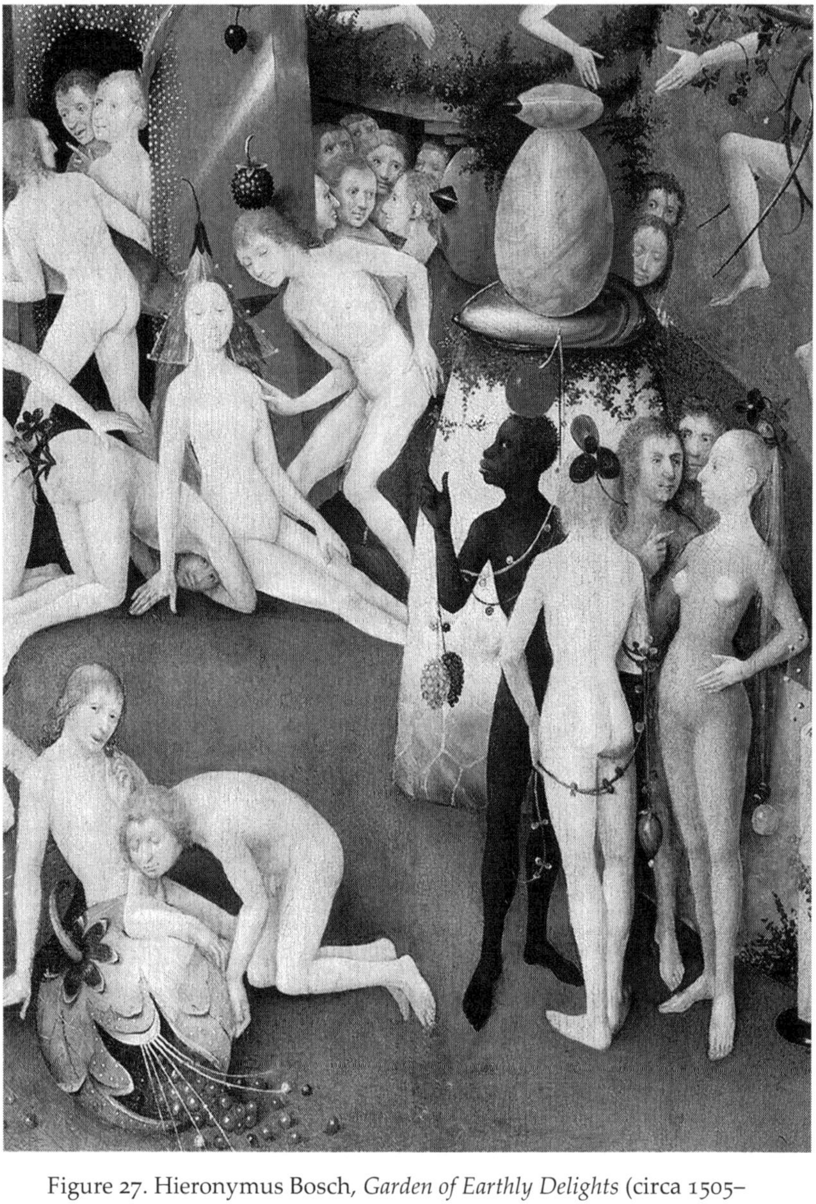

Figure 27. Hieronymus Bosch, *Garden of Earthly Delights* (circa 1505–10), detail of central panel, "Allegory of Luxury," Prado. Gianni Dagli Orti / The Art Archive at Art Resource, NY.

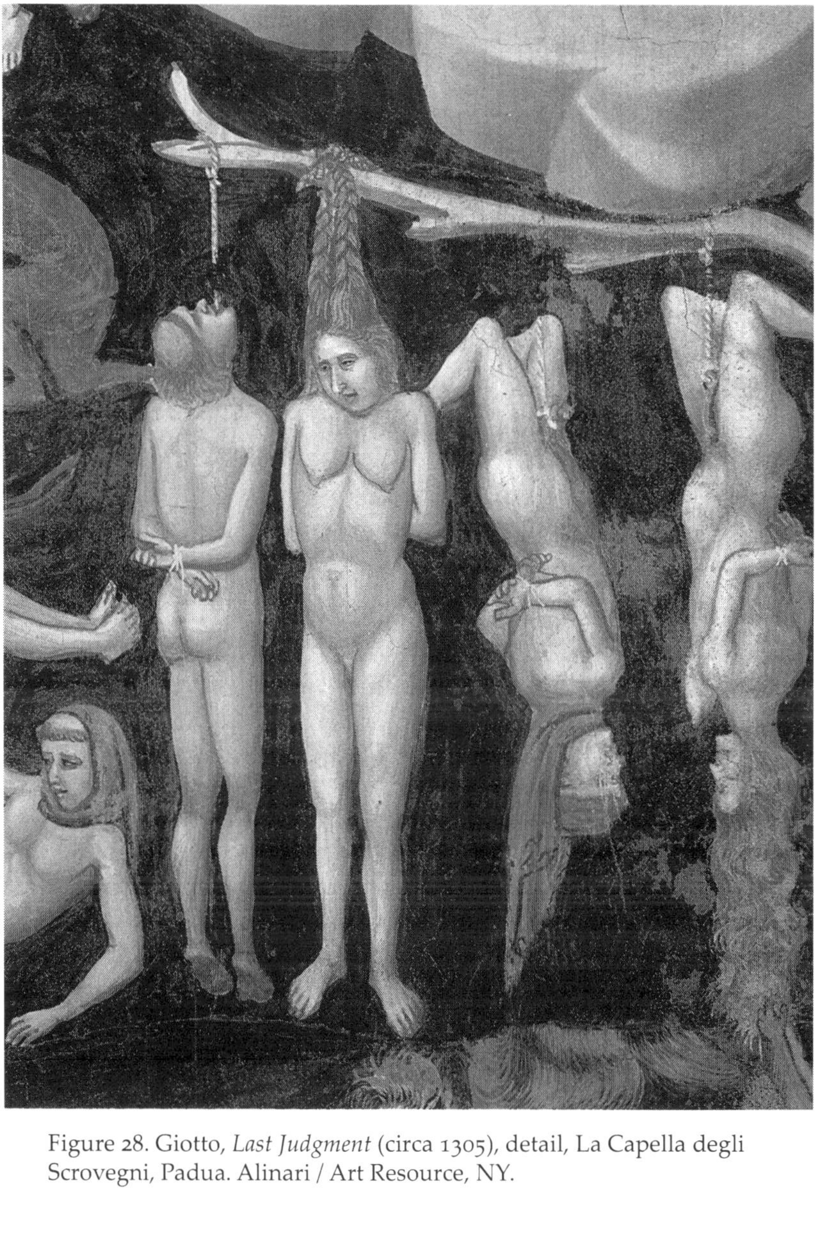

Figure 28. Giotto, *Last Judgment* (circa 1305), detail, La Capella degli Scrovegni, Padua. Alinari / Art Resource, NY.

quite new and disquieting—even presenting a secular worldview. In other words, there's a huge sea change in the way Giotto paints hell with those of the medieval artists (the latter, with their lack of perspective, use less rich colors and less layered forms). The ingredients of Giotto's hell are anything but a stereotype or monotonous experience, as had become the case with the medieval artists.

HL: It goes without saying that from Giotto onward hell in art creates much more interest in the viewer than that far duller place known as heaven.

FLA: To repeat some of what I've said before. There's this aspiration to make new and to enlarge the number of artistic options open to the artist. Sometimes this constant search for the new leads to dead ends; this could be the result of being too idiosyncratic à la *Finnegans Wake* or through repetition. Once Pollock achieved his drip paintings or Picasso hit the high mark of cubism, why do it again? They opened possibilities for art and at the same time closed them. There are other options (perspective, for instance) that open possibilities and continue to do so without becoming monotonous or dead-end idiosyncratic.

Since the Renaissance, art governed by a worldview of a total anarchy in art has constantly searched for means to make new and to enlarge an artist's options. This ambition is even more patent in the twentieth century with its myriad approaches and creations. Some approaches to making art have led to dead ends, in the sense that use of randomness in the making of art (Pollock's drippings, for instance, or John Cage's chance-determined graphic art) becomes redundant rather swiftly. In the search for new aesthetic relations artists reach dead ends *and* at the same time reach methods and shapes with much more lasting value. Within this framework, artists seek to make art that is deliberately disquieting. The question becomes, then, does this disquieting art open new modes of expression or does it lead to a dead end? Does it maintain its disquietude? Clearly, there's a shape-giving method and outlook that preserves its *newness* from one artist to another and from one century and socioeconomic situation to another. But there are other disquieting artistic shapes that don't have this kind of future. Picasso's cubism is done once, and that's it. If I were to bring a cubist approach to my art today, I would be doing a retro art. The same with Malevich's *White on White*: if I do it again the result is that I painted the wall or canvas white—there's no art in it.

HL: But the young Rauschenberg did it again, and even more radically, in *White Painting* (1951), which, as mentioned earlier, was made up of three canvases (this is only one of five versions) that used latex paint to avoid brush marks and thus eliminate any sign of a will to art. But of course this attempt to be antiart is just a new twist to the will to art.

FLA: The will to discomfort in art seems to have more traction (reproducibility) when we move more toward the representational end of the painterly spectrum. We have a Goya who created certain artistic shapes that traveled through the centuries and that have found many fruitful materializations. We can say the same of Munch where we see his influence on Richard Gerstl, then Schoenberg, who picked up a brush to create some rather disturbing art like *Gaze* (figure 29):

HL: It's as outrageous as his earlier work *Erwartung*, though perhaps not as immediately disturbing since you look at a painting for just a moment, but if you had to gaze at *Gaze* for the twenty-five minutes or so that *Erwartung* lasts you might well get freaked out. Both Gerstl and Schoenberg—the latter, though a decade older, had sought advice from Gerstl on how to paint—represent the beginnings of expressionism, a movement that, as it developed in Germany during the next two decades, contributed some of the most discomforting paintings and prints in the history of art. You mentioned having Edvard Munch's famous *Scream* on your office wall in Boulder. Munch (not to speak of Van Gogh) showed the early expressionists the way.

Gerstl's own self-portraits are actually his scariest works. He painted Frau Schoenberg somewhat more flatteringly than her husband did, but then he had fallen in love with her at a time when she had become alienated from the composer. And this was also the year—1908—that Schoenberg abandoned tonality. Disturbing art and disturbing music! And disturbing personal stuff as well!

FLA: Artists such as Munch, Gerstl, and Schoenberg (when not busy composing his music) took up the brush, but others chose different shaping tools to create disquieting art depending on the medium they're working within. Gabriel Orozco has used everyday garbage to create art—an art that might not disturb at first sight, but that does so once you discover that it is made up of trash, some quite toxic, at least in its earlier life.

HL: Many modernist artists, especially since the late twentieth century, have proudly made things out of detritus. Although they want the viewer to know their material's commonplace, sometimes even unsavory, origins, they usually—though not always these days—do things with this material that lift it, so to speak, into the traditional realm of art—if only, perhaps, because they exhibit it in an institution known

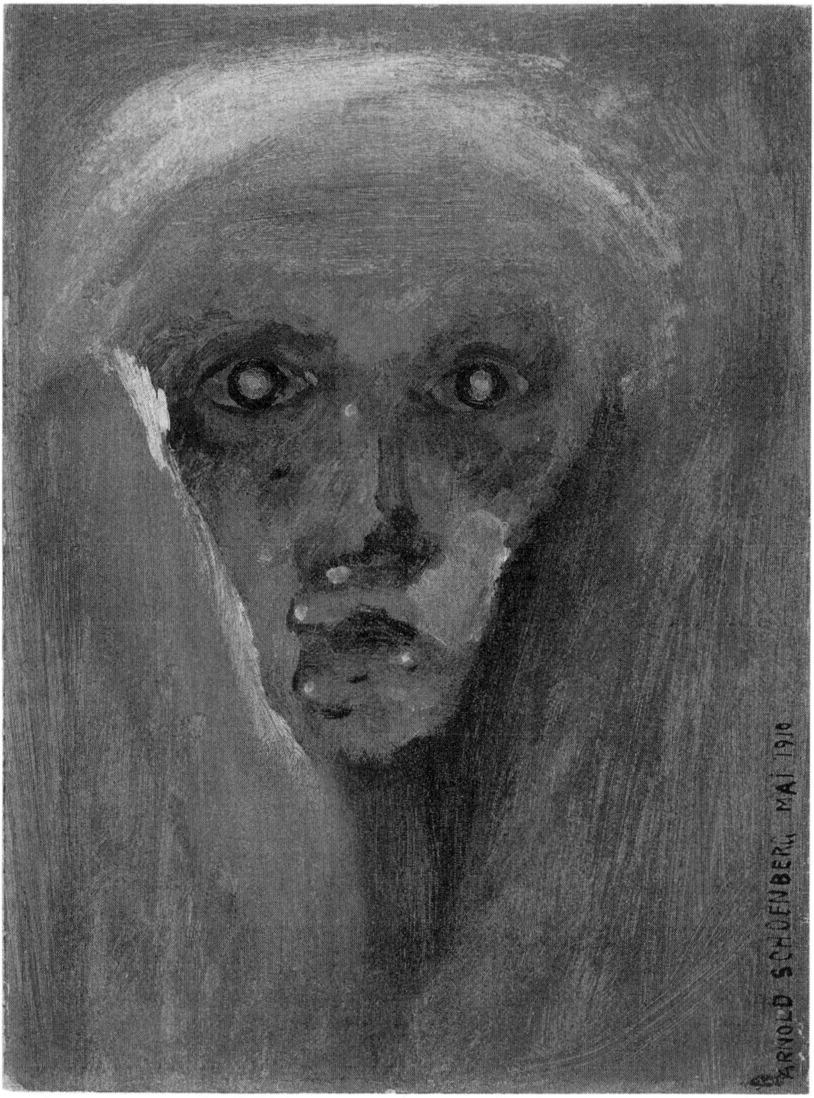

Figure 29. Arnold Schoenberg, *Gaze*, Arnold Schönberg Center, Vienna. © 2015 Belmont Music Publisher, Los Angeles / ARS, New York. Photo courtesy of the center.

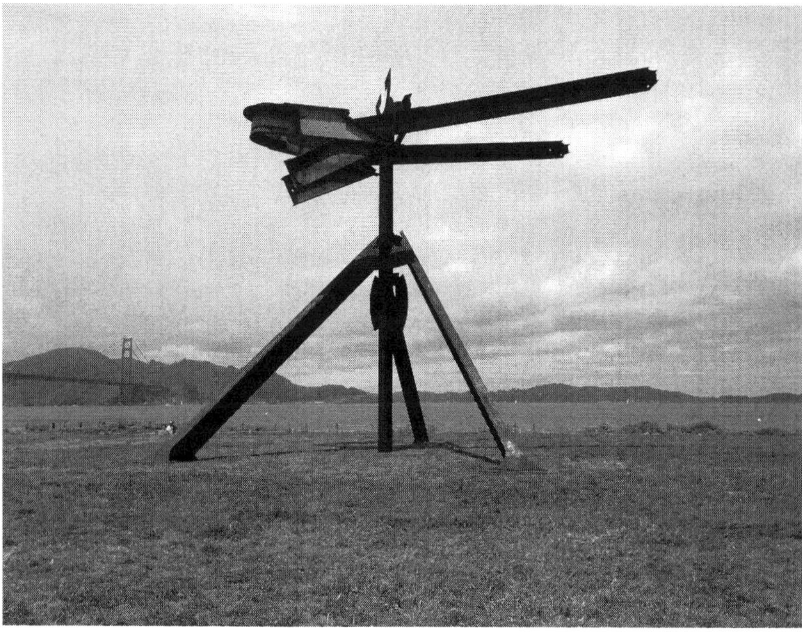

Figure 30. Mark di Suvero, *Huru*, exhibited at Crissy Field, San Francisco, 2013–14. Photo by Herbert Lindenberger.

as the art museum. Orozco's *Asterisms*, gathered in Baja California from industrial waste that had floated east across the Pacific, are neatly ordered according to color and shape. As a result of this careful ordering they don't really disturb. In fact, they are more likely to do the opposite: to elicit a response such as "lovely." Just as Mason Bates, as we saw, can make the sound of an auto cranking up aesthetically pleasing by means of the musical context in which it is embedded, so Orozco can make garbage lovely. But this word would not fit Mark Di Suvero's huge and powerful sculpture *Huru*, made from pieces of discarded industrial metal whose status as waste remains evident here (though not in other, similar pieces that he has painted in his standard orange color) through the rust gathering along it (figure 30). When spectators say, "But that's just junk," they are of course technically correct.

Even people who have seen a lot of late twentieth-century art often find Di Suvero's constructions challenging, for he is showing his viewers that the most unexpected materials can be turned into something that, if not "beautiful," breathes the aura of the "sublime." (It's like some contemporary poet listing the treasures within his garbage can in regular meters.)

FLA: We might ask, what gives Di Suvero's and Orozco's discomforting works their status as a work of art, Herbie? Orozco seeks to obtain an aesthetic result—a relation between the viewer and the object(s) and in this relation for the viewer to find the object fascinating in its discomforting properties. However, what allows Orozco to establish this relation between the object and the subject who applies aesthetic judgment is the institution of the museum. It's the museum that encourages the aesthetic relationship with the object. Otherwise, this relation is not established or not necessarily established. Likewise, when an artist puts a turd in a box and then sets it at the entrance of a room in a museum, you can attach the tag of aesthetics to it and thus call it a work of art. That it resides in a museum is an invitation to establish an aesthetic relation with the turd and the box and to see them as aesthetic products, namely as what we honor as art. This invitation could not exist before the institution of the museum in 1753—when the first national, public museum was established in London. These new ways of creating art can only appear as artistic objects because of the existence of this institution.

There was a leap in the twentieth century (and perhaps only since Duchamp's readymades) whereby artists realized that the artistic qualities of the art were neither in the object nor in the subject—but in us as viewers who have both accepted and rejected the work. It's in the specific construction of the relation between object and subject that there is an aesthetic—to the point of even educating audiences of how to determine this aesthetic relation. In art, the museum has become a mediator (even educator) of this process. It invites the public to see the object (garbage or turd) from a different perspective—from an aesthetic perspective.

HL: This institution also exists outside the museum in your private home whenever you hang something like your child's latest kindergarten painting or a nasty, unwarranted email from your boss on the wall over the fireplace. (Hanging things on the refrigerator door doesn't count, since that space by convention wouldn't be used for aesthetic purposes.) But then private quarters have long been museums of sorts, whether a royal palace in the sixteenth century or a Dutch middle-class home in the next century.

FLA: I wonder then, how much the museum might become a crutch to the art, Herbie. Does that which impresses us in a museum not have the same effect outside the museum? How many of these discomforting aesthetic products cease to have an aesthetic relation once outside of the museums? And we might consider the museum's function to be spread into other extratextual contexts such as information gleaned from the Internet or pamphlets, brochures or plaques that identify for us how we are to perceive the aesthetic relationality.

You mentioned Di Suvero's *Huru*—industrial art that you and I both encountered during one of our many walks in the area near the Golden Gate Bridge known as Crissy Field. It stands outside the institution of the museum, but its discomfort arises only once I've read the extratextual information (brochures, plaques, etc.) that describes how it seeks to dynamite social conventions concerning propriety. It seeks to create discomfort only after we know its intent—and not so much in the art in and of itself. We are supposed to *think* more than feel in our experience of the art once we learn that it is made of the wasteful by-products of capitalism.

HL: For the most part the art we call discomforting tries to challenge what we think of as "official" morality, to shock us into rethinking the moral notions we take for granted. When Mapplethorpe was shown during the 1980s, many art consumers were hostile toward homosexuality to a degree that they are no longer so today. But the classical beauty that his photographic style cultivated, as you implied earlier, worked to undercut some of the moral shock that many culturally "advanced" people felt (though not perhaps the congressmen who made such a fuss about the federal funds that were used to support his show). Analogously, the celebrated trial of *Madame Bovary* at the time of its publication (1857) put to a test the automated responses that most middle-class people felt not only toward adultery but above all toward how one talked and wrote about this subject. There have of course been all sorts of ways that art has confronted standard morality.

FLA: Artists who choose to depict the savagery of war, for instance.

HL: Indeed, Goya was the first major visual artist to exploit this—before that, war was usually depicted in its more noble aspects, as in Velazquez's *Surrender at Breda* or West's *Death of General Wolfe.* But Goya let himself go in his print series *Disasters of War* (1810–20), which shocks the viewer in much the same way as earlier depictions of hell. War is hell, the saying goes, and both sides of this equation elicit the cruelest images that the artist can muster up. Moreover, both war and hell images work to shake up the viewer's moral frame—the first, to warn what lies in store for humanity if it keeps up this madness, the second, to warn what lies in store for you if you do not lead a properly moral life.

FLA: The morals you mention are but one small ingredient of art. Nothing is foreign to art. Nothing is beyond the bounds of art. All that is human, including all scientific, technological products of human activity plus social, political, economic human activities are all fodder to art; art nourishes itself from everything out there, metabolizing everything out there in its search for the establishment of an aesthetic relation. As we discussed already, Goya's and Daumier's art is packed with religious and political content. Art can be used for didactic purposes to the degree we see with Goya where he felt compelled to write subtitles to his art to provide his viewers with a compass direction for registering its political worldview. Art can be about the consequences of not leading the moral life, but it is in its bountiful appetite to metabolize and make new all aspects of our existence that makes it essential for the making of *the good life*. This can and does of course include artists who choose to give shape to and make new our perception of war.

HL: Whereas the Napoleonic Wars that Goya depicted were cruel enough, the far bloodier World War I elicited powerful images from German Expressionists such as George Grosz, Käthe Kollwitz, Max Beckmann, and, above all, Otto Dix. They all had something big to say about the war. Dix's series of fifty prints entitled *The War* could easily have appeared in an earlier hell panel, as in the depiction of a wounded soldier in figure 31.

FLA: Just as artists can choose to re-create the experience of war, so too they can re-create all other subjects and experiences—even those considered sacred (religion) and foundationally pleasurable (sex). I think of Tania Kovats's *Virgin in a Condom* (1994) where the artist pulls a condom over a statue of the Virgin Mary that's immersed in yellowish (pee?) liquid.

HL: It's another example of contemporary artists' need to shock. This has been especially true since the 1980s. These artists have steadily raised the ante about how to get to us when we've already become inured to the shock effects of an earlier artist. One of the interesting things about Kovats's *Virgin* is that she was stolen from the Sydney Museum of Contemporary Art soon after being exhibited there. Theft makes the story all the more piquant.

FLA: Oddly, I find myself feeling moved by British artist Damien Hirst's

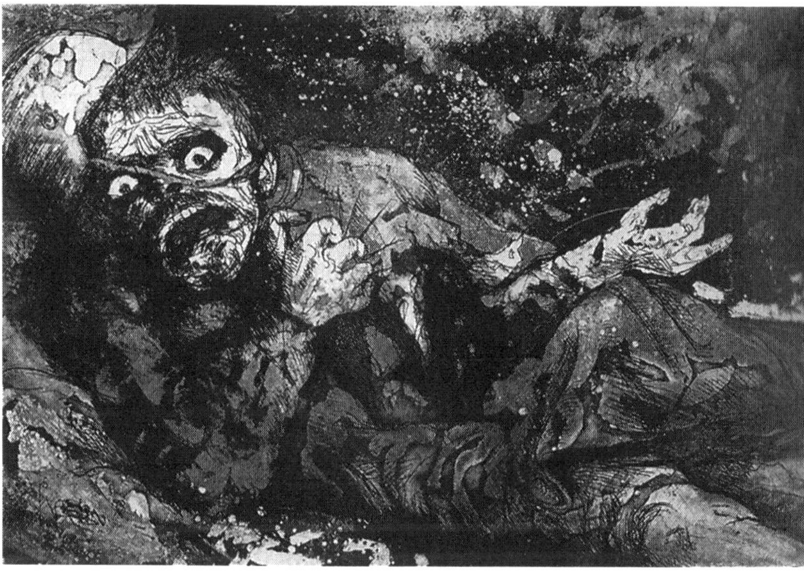

Figure 31. Otto Dix, *Wounded Man*, from *The War* (1924). © 2015 Artists Rights Spociety (ARS), New York / VG Bild-Kunst. Bonn. Digital Image The Museum of Modern Art / Licensed by SCALA / Art Resource, NY.

installation called *A Thousand Years* (1990)—even though it's of a putrescent cow's head. In my mind, Hirst manages to put beauty in the same ring (boxing) with the ugly. Although with much diminished use of lighting and lensing devices used by someone like Hirst, it repulses the viewer, especially with those insects hovering about the head (figure 32).

HL: I prefer not to get caught up in that old aesthetic term *beauty*. After all, its supplementary term, *sublimity*, in the early years of aesthetic inquiry referred to artistic artifacts that were not considered beautiful as such. We tend to classify things like the cow's head or, for that matter, the animals he actually pickled, as "conceptual art." Since these artifacts are bought by collectors—at enormous prices, to the point that Hirst has shown how artists can become successful capitalists—and housed in museums, they can be called art, at least from an institutional point of view. This so-called conceptual art, which is sometimes, though not necessarily, disturbing, doesn't easily invite traditional terms such as *beauty* or even *sublimity*. One can't find what people

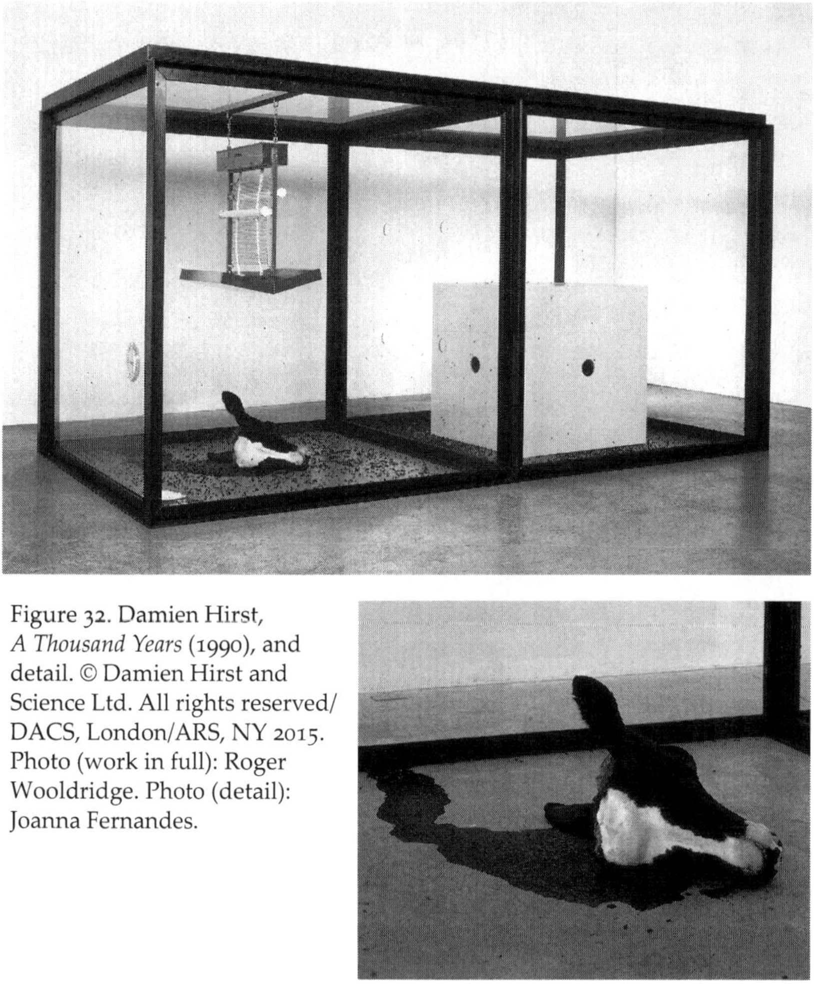

Figure 32. Damien Hirst, *A Thousand Years* (1990), and detail. © Damien Hirst and Science Ltd. All rights reserved/ DACS, London/ARS, NY 2015. Photo (work in full): Roger Wooldridge. Photo (detail): Joanna Fernandes.

characteristically call "redeeming" features here. But it manages to draw you in, make you react (even if negatively), force you to ask what the term *art* means, how this meaning has changed over time, why you are getting so angry at this art (whether or not you are willing to call it art). At one point in an interview Hirst declared, "Great art is when you just walk round a corner and go, 'Fucking hell! What's *that*!'" (Hirst and Burn 93 [italics Hirst's]). The discomforting shocks that Hirst seeks in his work are evidently necessary for art to be "great." I might add that at one point the real cow's head, which had become too putrid for gallery visitors, was replaced by a prosthetic head (180–81).

FLA: Fair enough, Herbie. We've already mentioned the importance of the rise of institutional space we call the museum. Here again we see how the institutional space around the work becomes an aide—maybe even a crutch—to establishing an aesthetic relationality. The space determines how we are to apprehend the object of the putrescent cow's head. As we asked earlier, what happens when this object is taken out of the museum? Actually I just read in the paper that a New York financial mogul has shocked his neighbors (not to speak of passersby) in Old Westbury by displaying on his front lawn a huge Hirst painted bronze sculpture of a pregnant woman with an exposed fetus. It's a good bit more discomforting to see potentially nauseating art in an upscale residential neighborhood than in a museum, whose institutional conventions allow you to display whatever is new, no matter how shocking. Do the putrescent cow's head and the pregnant lady on the lawn really open possibilities for artists in the future? Does Hirst's creating of the new in art really establish a lasting, contextually transcendent aesthetic relationality? We might ask the same of Andres Serrano's *Piss Christ* (1997), where we see a crucified Jesus in a tank of pee. If either of these is taken out of the museum setting—or even positioned on a wall that's too large and that dwarfs the photograph—there is no longer this mediation and thus no longer the bridge that connects object with subject and thus there's a rupture of the aesthetic relation.

HL: Museum curators nowadays (unlike those in earlier days when paintings were simply hung without any notion that how and where they're hung influences the viewer's reactions) have the power to control the way we look at and judge them by moving walls, repainting walls, and choosing the works that surround a particular painting.

FLA: The Catholic church tried to prevent the exhibition in Australia's National Gallery of Serrano's *Piss Christ*.

HL: But attempts at censorship usually backfire on the censors, since nowadays the notoriety that a censorship scandal creates only serves to draw crowds—as at the Mapplethorpe show in 1989 mentioned earlier—and also to raise the censored artist's prices. Yet there's also a recent example of a potentially discomforting show that was canceled before crowds even had a chance to turn up. I'm thinking of what happened in Mexico City early in 2015 when the Museo Jumex (financed by the fruit juice fortune) refused to open an exhibition of the veteran Austrian conceptual artist Hermann Nitsch, whose blood-spattered paintings, as well as his depiction of the Last Supper characters shown as anatomical figures revealing their musculature, were deemed too upsetting in view of some bloody recent drug-related events like the abduction of forty-three college students. As far as I could tell from the *New York Times* story on the show's cancellation (see Burnett), there was nothing particularly pornographic or blasphemous—as there may have been with Serrano's picture—about Nitsch's work, but the museum was simply trying to mitigate the discomforts occasioned by real-life violence by protecting the locals from any aesthetic discomfort they might experience at the show.

FLA: Herbie, with this last-minute cancellation of Nitsch's show I suspect it's more about the Museo realizing it wouldn't make any money, more than it was anything else. You see, shows like Nitsch's are not crowd-gatherers as such, and in Mexico the people visiting the Museo Jumex are in any case rather scarce. The museum is in the newly gentrified but out-of-the-way Polanco—a very posh barrio that is not visited by the kind of people who go to the other, more appealing museums in more appealing parts of Mexico City. If they had to pay Nitsch for a show that would not attract a big audience nor create any kind of stir in the mass media, it would simply be a big flop, a big nonevent—a big failure costing a pretty penny. If the exhibit fails to spark a scandal and thus give Nitsch the kind of advertising that might open a patron's wallet, then why bother having a Nitsch show?

This said, there's some truth to the reasons given by the museum for the canceled event: Mexico has seen too much violence. The violence the Mexican people endure daily, however, goes way beyond anything a performance or installation could show. In this sense, it would be redundant for Museo Jumex to show anything from Nitsch or from the many others doing the Nitsch sort of thing.

Herbie, shall we move our discussion back across the Atlantic to the topic of *art brut*—a term coined by Jean Philippe Arthur Dubuffet (1901–1985), friend of Artaud and supporter of Céline. While Dubuffet himself created deliberately unappealing portraits using thick oil paints mixed with sand and gravel, he used this term to identify art he collected drawn by psychiatric patients, prisoners, and children. Is art made by disquieted minds *disquieting art*?

HL: Not necessarily . . . In fact, the poems that Hölderlin composed after he had become insane are simple, benign, and dull, more inane, shall we say, than insane—while the poems of his still-sane preceding four or five years are among the most difficult, disturbing, and sublime poems in the German language. Dubuffet's own paintings were long considered unpleasant, but they now seem much milder than they did when new—a lot of the controversy had to do with the materials, like the sand and gravel, that he used, as well as the in-your-faceness of his faces. I remember seeing a whole roomful of Dubuffets at the National Gallery in Washington a few years ago and marveling at how comfortable I now felt with them. He was a really wonderful painter. By contrast, Dubuffet's British contemporary, Francis Bacon, whom I also love, has not lost his sting. His portraits seem just as mean as they ever did. Bacon himself was near the lower end of the scale for looks, but in his self-portraits—not to speak of his portraits of others—he went out of his way make himself look as unpleasant as possible (figure 33).

Similarly with Willem de Kooning's Woman portraits that have continued to rankle feminists for their alleged misogyny (figure 34).

Right now Bacon is going for record prices in the auction houses, and De Kooning's have long been in the stratosphere.

FLA: During the year off that I took before going to graduate school, I spent a lot of time in and out of museums in California. I remember being fascinated by an exhibit at the LA County Museum of Art that juxtaposed asylum artists such as Wölfli, Martin Ramírez, and Johann Hauser with artists like Paul Klee, Alfred Kubin, and some surrealist artists. This was the early 1990s, during a time when it seemed the fashion to collect and exhibit asylum art as the embodiment of art that discomforts.

HL: As I look at the three asylum artists you mention, the one thing they have in common is the use of lots of meticulous detail—which is also true of the supposedly "sane" Klee and Kubin. One would need a good bit of experimental evidence to know whether a particular mental condition has any real relationship to the sort of art that the patient produces. From a consumer's point of view there might be a certain prestige in owning good art created by the mentally ill. (The relatively simple, nonrepresentational paintings that De Kooning did during his many years with Alzheimer's are much prized, though considerably less so than his earlier, more complex—and controversial—Woman paintings.) Even if the art itself is not discomforting, our knowledge of its creator at the time can make the viewer uncomfortable. But the most discomforting modernist art has come from people like Bacon who were not mentally ill by the usual definition. Given the prices that Bacon can command, I'm sure these pictures are not purchased simply to go into some collector's storage facility. Perhaps people put their least pleasant paintings in private rooms that their guests never see unless they're on their way to the bathroom.

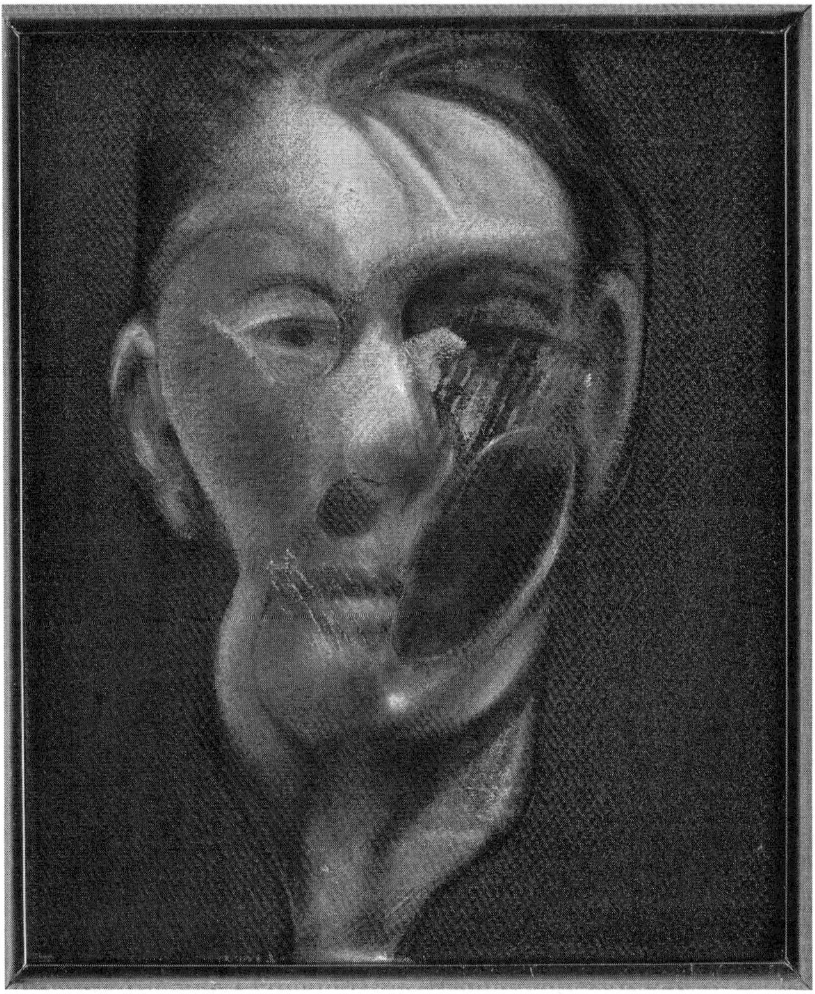

Figure 33. Francis Bacon (1909–1992): *Self-Portrait*, 1976. Oil and Pastel on canvas, 34 × 29.5 cm. Inv. C.76.2.3. © The Estate of Francis Bacon. All rights reserved. / DACS, London / ARS, NY 2014. Location: Musee Cantini, Marseille, France. Photo Credit: Bridgeman-Giraudon / Art Resource, NY (ART92471).

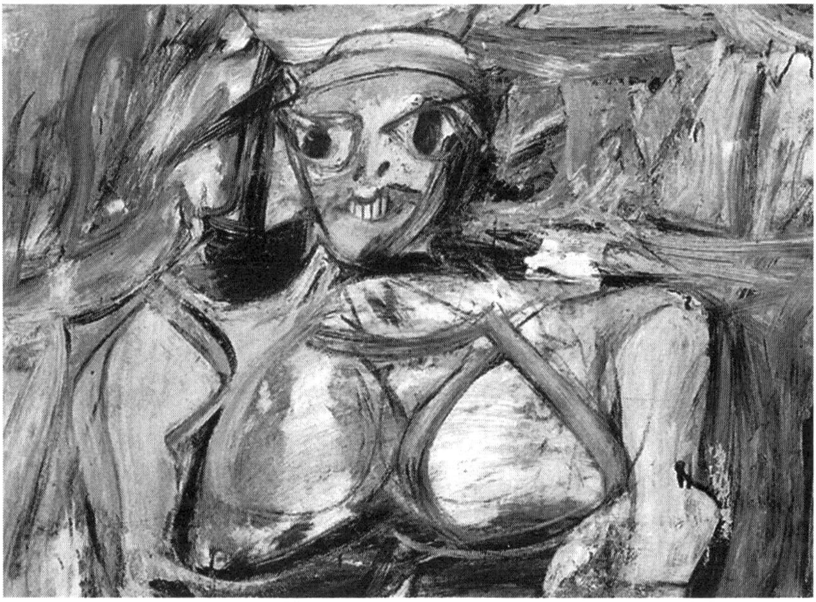

Figure 34. Willem de Kooning, *Woman I* (1950–52), detail, Museum of Modern Art, New York. Photo by Herbert Lindenberger.

FLA: Yes, such as Courbet's *Origin of the World* that we discussed in an earlier part of our conversation. Before André Masson, Lacan's brother-in-law, had it removed and replaced by another painting, Lacan had it hanging in his country house—and likely, with its 1.5 million franc price tag, one of the reasons he had had to make his therapy sessions more efficient. Its realism is nearly photographic, and a reminder that any and all objects—the female form in this case—can be created in such a way as to trigger feelings of discomfort.

HL: Discomfort for some people, mainly women, as I mentioned earlier, but erotic comfort for straight males.

FLA: In the same vein as *L'Origine du monde* some find Egon Schiele's paintings also disturbing. I find his paintings of men and women at once fascinating and off-putting. His colors are extraordinary. His use of red, for instance, over the genitals is beautifully disquieting. When I actually saw them in Geneva I was surprised at how small they were; the impact of the image on my mind when I first encountered them in a book made them seem to be much bigger.

HL: I attended a show of Schiele's portraits at the Neue Gallerie just as we were getting this book ready for publication. And I too was struck by the colors. In the watercolor called *Die Traum Beschaute* (*The Woman Seen in a Dream*) the most erotic elements—lips, breasts, and the conspicuously flaunted vagina—are highlighted in outrageous orange and pink (figure 35).

The two pieces—Courbet's *Origine* and Schiele's watercolor—use altogether divergent styles—one hyperrealistic, the other sketchy and contorted—to elicit similar effects, whether erotic or repugnant. I should like to say "extra-artistic effects," but that isn't accurate since you can't sustain a distinction between seeing art "as art" and seeing it as, say, sexual stimulant. The art we view affects us in many ways, bodily and intellectually at once.

FLA: I want to say that there seems to be a form of voyeurism with art that tends more toward the realistic end of the representational spectrum, but what if we were to turn *L'Origine du monde* upside down or sideways and imagine that it was painted from a different angle? Isn't the effect on us different? That is, while hyperrealistic (as compared to the Schiele, say) and its focus entirely on the pubic area, the painting above all displays the care that was lavished on it. Courbet's choice of perspective suggests a mystery hidden under the pubic hair—and, as a result, we feel ourselves invited to look at the pubic area with an intrigued and redoubled interest, one that draws us all the more into the painting. There is no way we can remain aloof or indifferent to this work. We are literally moved by the realism of the painting—and, I would add, especially by the angle Courbet chose to depict its content.

HL: The hyperreal in the format of photography—by means of its pretense to be "real"—can often exercise a more powerful effect than painting or printmaking. It's not just with freaks and the deformed and aged, but also with the horrors of war. The Goya and Dix prints mentioned above are horrifying enough, but think of the effect of Margaret Bourke-White's photos of Nazi victims taken as the American army was still fighting in Germany. Bourke-White's photos exercised a profound effect, for they were the first visual news—this was before television, after all—that Americans received about what the Nazis had actually done. For me, at least—and this may be because members of my own family were among the Nazis' victims—no picture of freaks is as potent as these photos.

FLA: In photography we find both testimony and false testimony—from those photographs taken in the concentration camps to those, like Joe Rosenthal's *Raising the Flag on Iwo Jima,* which, we now know, was

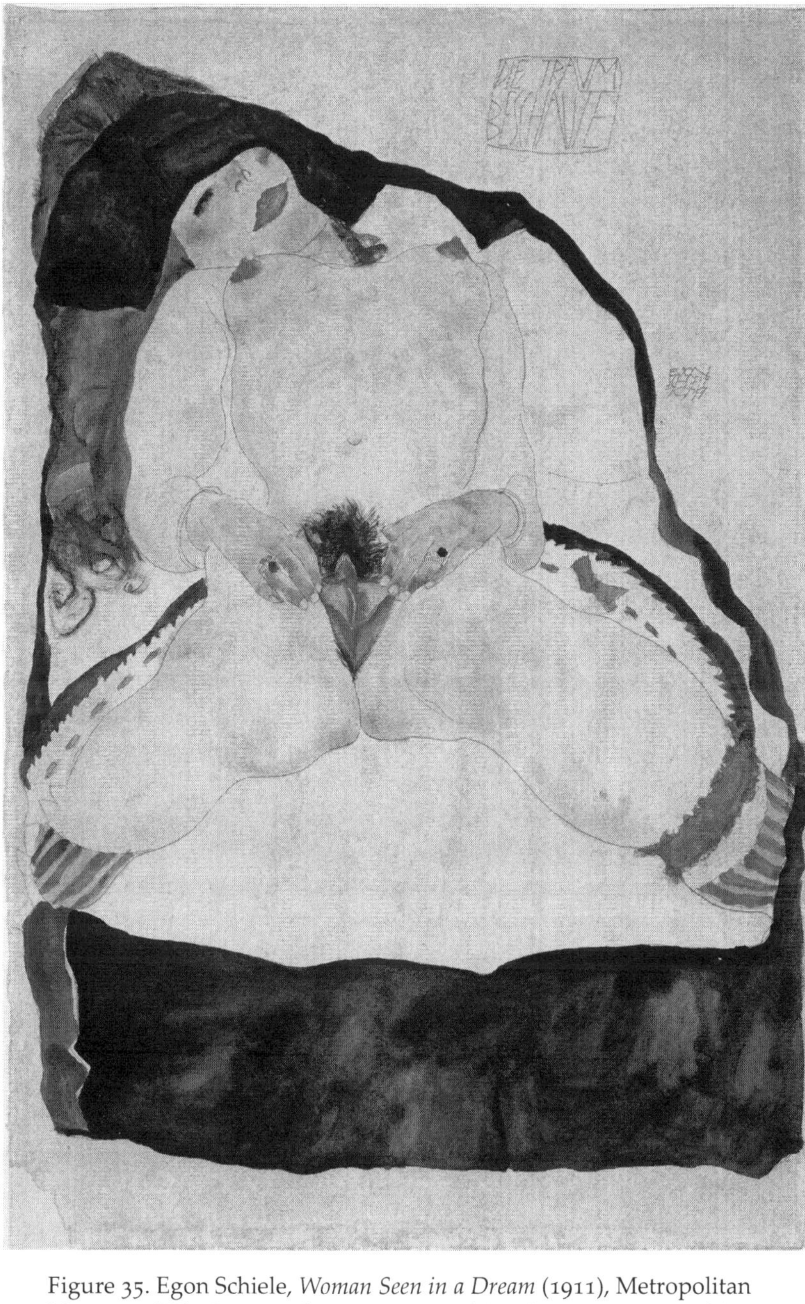

Figure 35. Egon Schiele, *Woman Seen in a Dream* (1911), Metropolitan Museum. ©The Metropolitan Museum of Art. Image courtesy of Art Resource, NY.

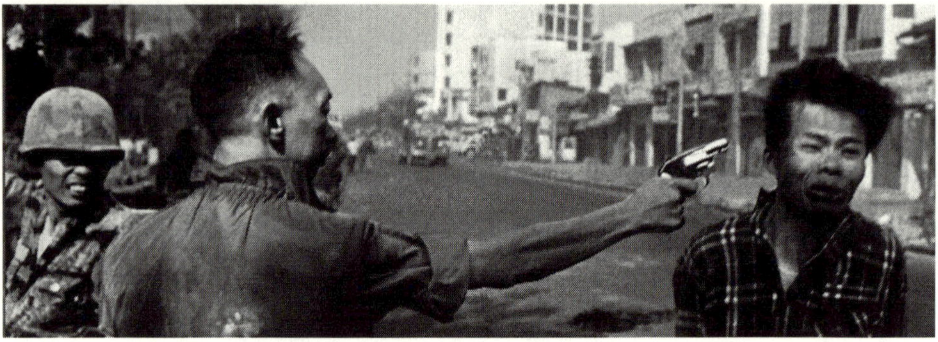

Figure 36. Eddie Adams, execution of a Vietnamese (1968), detail

actually staged. What they share in common is that they are necessarily small fragments of reality; the photographers (improvised or staged) use a lens that captures a fragment of reality and thus necessarily leaves out everything that is outside the frame. The photographs capture forms (geometry, if you will) and light in specific combination as delimited in space (a fraction of reality) and time (no movement actually seen, only suggested, as with Rosenthal). The specific combination can lead the viewer to establish an aesthetic relation with the photograph—and this even with extremely discomforting images such as that of the chief of police killing a Vietnamese civilian—a photograph that helped turn the American public against the brutality of the war (figure 36). It's testimonial photography where we suffer the shock of horror.

Yet the composition (the photographer's choice of angle, light, etc.) leads us to establish a certain aesthetic relationship with the photograph. The photographer in the face of something horrific not only knows he/she is giving testimony to this event, but knows that he/she is making an aesthetic object out of this testimony. It becomes more than a randomly taken photograph but rather an aesthetic object—even though the content is so absolutely disquieting. In fact, sometimes the fact that there is an aesthetic intention in the taking of the photograph may make it seem outrageous and immoral—even inhuman.

HL: Ever since aesthetics claimed a place in philosophy during the eighteenth century, there's been a lurking question about whether and how it is related to that other field within philosophy known as ethics. That photograph of a Vietnamese being shot gives the question a new twist.

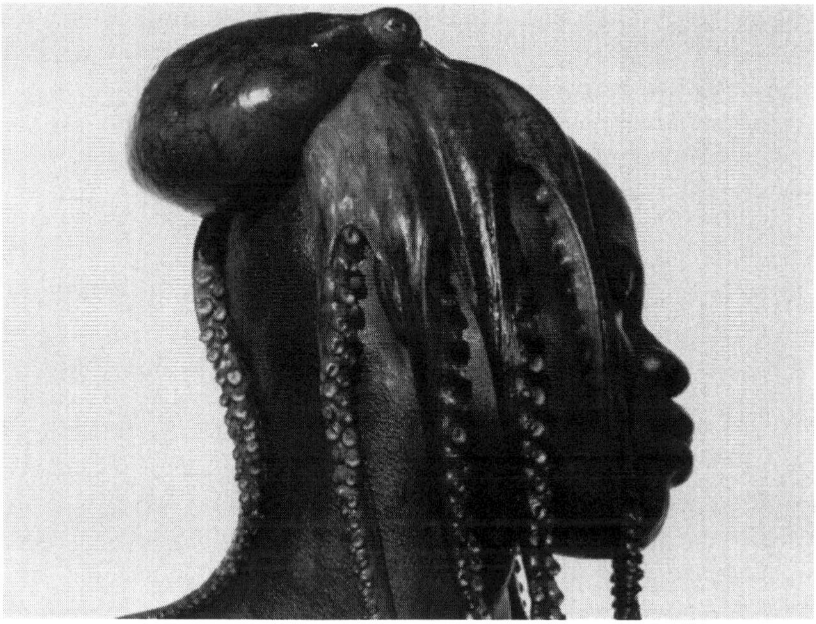

Figure 37. Herb Ritts, Djimon Hounsou (1989), detail

FLA: We discussed Mapplethorpe earlier, but I also think of the reception of some of Herb Ritts's works that were considered outrageous—immoral even. I think of his choice to create a composition that combined the disquieting, bulbous shape of an octopus with that of a black, sculpted body (Djimon Hounsou). Some asked if it was ethically correct to photograph a black man in such a discomforting (animalistic) fashion (figure 37).

HL: Frankly, I don't find this particularly discomforting, though the octopus has the bulbous shape we noticed as something distinctly unpleasant in Bosch. Ritts's photo is in the best surrealist tradition, and surrealism proved most inspiring to photographers such as Man Ray, whether or not they used it to disturb.

FLA: Or there are the less exoticized but nonetheless disturbing photographs of the quotidian by Diane Arbus. She takes as her subjects little people, circus performers, transgenders, Siamese twins. Her usually grainy, very rectangular photographs seem to at once push us away and pull us in. That is, they disturb in their testimonial role (like those of the concentration camp mentioned above). At the same time, because of its testimonial role (their content) the shape-giving impulse and the will to style that moves and to a large extent determines the way the photographs are taken has a specific role: to establish a special, aesthetic relationality with the present and future viewers of the photograph. Arbus wants the photo to connect with the viewer, but not just in any way—in a specifically aesthetic way. This is where the presence of a will to style intervenes, and why Arbus (and Ritts, and Mapplethorpe, and others) receive criticism for aestheticizing the content.

HL: It's in what you call the quotidian that photography has long pursued a special mission—that is, the ordinary life of anything but ordinary people. And Edward Weston showed us that "ordinary" vegetables can appear as quite unordinary, as erotic, in fact. For those of us who belong to the ordinary species (or at least we like to think that we do), seeing nonordinary folk, especially when they face us frontally as they do in Diane Arbus and Richard Avedon, is always a shock.

FLA: It's the content that Arbus gives testimony to that is disturbing, but this doesn't mean that she suspends her will to style and her expertise in choosing the angles, lighting, and framing. Just as Weston uses aesthetic means and a will to style while taking pictures of vegetables, so too does Arbus—it's just that her content happens to be (in these instances) much more controversial, so the critics are more likely to declaim her as immoral; this response is likely intensified by the fact that as an art, photography's essence is of a testimonial nature, one that evinces a greater or lesser testimonial trace: Weston's vegetables versus Arbus's "freaks."

HL: What you say about photography's testimonial function is central to the effects that we feel. Imagine the Vietnamese shooting—or Arbus's or Avedon's faces staring at us—in oil or acrylic. Even if these paintings were hyperrealist in style, they would lose much of their disturbing power, if only because we know they were concocted for us. And to the extent that we read photographs as testimonies of the real world around us (however much they may have been staged, or manipulated within the camera or in the dark room or on the computer), they may ultimately possess a greater potential to create discomfort than the art we know has been created by the painter's brush.

SIX | Revolting Reels

FREDERICK LUIS ALDAMA: In the last chapter, Herbie, we talked about the documentary, testimonial nature of photography that allows it to become easily disquieting—even unbearable. Keep in mind that photography is static and appears to be an actual graphic document, whether staged or not. Because of its seeming permanence (a snapshot of time and place), there's a greater sense of its existing as a graphic document. A novel shares certain traits with a photograph in the sense that you can pause on a word, sentence, paragraph, or page and read and reread as much as you'd like and for as long as you'd like. There is nothing automatically flipping the pages for the reader. On the other hand, film (as experienced in the cinema and not on a DVD player) moves forward automatically; while some film directors like Lars von Trier and Michelangelo Antonioni play with this by inserting what appears to be a pause, it is still a pause that is beyond the viewer's control. In this sense, film depicts events in more of a transient way. It's not that I would necessarily want to pause and relish in the discomforting films of a Lars von Trier, but it is important to keep in mind that in creating a filmic artifact aimed to discomfort, film directors work with a format that at once shares devices with photography and literature, but that also differs in fundamental ways.

HERBERT LINDENBERGER: To begin with, let's make a distinction between ordinary "thrillers" and truly discomforting horror films, which are the ones that concern us here. The vast majority of thrillers can be experienced much as one experiences a roller-coaster ride. You embark on the ride expecting something you know will be scary, that will make you tremble and sweat with fear, but you also know from the start that whatever discomfort you feel is strictly temporary and that everything will end safely and happily. But what if your train gets stuck in the middle and you and the other passengers have no idea if and when it will reach its destination—or even if the train behind you may crash into you? Such is the grave discomfort encountered in those rare horror films, like *The Piano Teacher, Happiness,* or *Audition,* that refuse to return you to the safety of the amusement park in which you started your roller-coaster ride.

FLA: Perhaps because of the more static nature of photographs and books that allow for long and detailed viewings and readings and that have a gestaltic impact (a photo especially), the impact on the brain is *perhaps* sharper and more direct than with films.

HL: We'd need some neuroscientific studies to determine this—if such a study were even empirically possible. How would you measure the difference in the repulsive effects created by, say, Elfriede Jelinek's novel *The Piano Teacher* and Michael Haneke's film version? There may be too many variables here to come to any precise conclusions. But to judge by my own impressions, the film hits even harder than the novel, which is cruel enough in its own right. It may not be simply the visual element but the fact that you are sitting in a dark theater sharing a film with a bunch of other people awaiting a chilling experience. But filmmakers like Haneke also know the difference between a verbal and a visual effect, and in this instance he added a subplot missing from Jelinek's novel. Much of the unpleasantness in the novel comes from her descriptions of the way that the piano teacher and her young student-lover are monkeying around with one another, and this, together with the teacher's sadomasochistic demands, leaves the reader constantly ill at ease, to say the least. Despite the ability of contemporary film to show a character's reactions to sex (the usual orgasmic sounds, which have become an insufferable cliché), the camera cannot by itself capture the intricacies of penetration or of oral sex.

FLA: Or even a hard penis—if, that is, a director wants the film to be seen by a mainstream adult filmgoing audience. Directors will even edit out scenes to get that R-rating from the MPAA instead of an NC-17, the latter of which puts a very tight straitjacket on distribution.

HL: So what does Haneke do to capture the novel's discomforting scenes but to concoct a subplot to portray the heroine's gratuitous cruelty? This demanded the creation of a new character, a pathetic young woman piano student whose hand the teacher deliberately ruins by planting pieces of broken glass in her student's coat. We see the blood and we witness the tears, and Haneke easily makes his cinematic point by means of sight and sound.

FLA: Our sound and sight perceptual system do seem to be on heightened alert, so it would make sense that Haneke's film triggers such immediate, viscerally felt reflex responses. This same sadomasochistic tendency you bring up seems to have also affected the Cannes Film Festival judges who evaluated the film. No matter that the final scene of physical abuse and then rape is an enactment of Erika's fantasy, it's deeply upsetting. Perhaps it was a masochistic streak in the Cannes Film Festival judges that led to their awarding the film the Grand Prix.

Yet the idea that film somehow packs a wallop in a more immediate way than the alphabetic arts (novels, short stories, poetry, and so on) might be more complicated than first meets the eye. We know from our own experience and also from that of children (as they become fluent readers) that we chunk sequences of words when reading novels—it could be an *Ivy and Bean* story or a novel like *The Piano Teacher* if that suits our fancy. The advances in the neurosciences show that we are just as likely to experience disgust at a series of written words that create an image in our mind as with the sight of a sequence of photographs that make up the film reel.

HL: I'm sure that inveterate readers of horror stories know how to translate these word sequences into strong emotional reactions, just as readers in the late eighteenth century knew how to read the new genre of the gothic in ways that would insure them a maximum of thrill. When we read, say, Radcliffe's *The Mysteries of Udolpho* (1794) today, it feels like a tame period piece—certainly incapable of horrifying us in the ways to which we have become accustomed by the films we view.

FLA: Yet early readers of *Udolpho* would likely have been quite horrified.

HL: There's a long history of verbally generated horror that has been with us since ancient drama, in which the fright and the lamentations of the characters and chorus are forced to find a sufficiently potent response to the offstage violence so that the audience may undergo its catharsis. I once attended a production in Italy of Seneca's *Thyestes* featuring the celebrated actor Vittorio Gassman, who, in view of the convention prohibiting violence onstage, was forced to tell his bloody story—about the banquet in which he was unknowingly served his own sons to eat—without visual aids. Whatever horror was conveyed—and there was lots of it—had to come through this fine actor's rotund voice.

The Elizabethans, in no way bound to the convention of keeping their violence offstage, could let themselves go when they wrote their own exercises in Senecan horror. Thus Shakespeare's early play *Titus Andronicus* (1589–90) contains not only ordinary murder but rape, the amputation of a tongue and hands, and, at the end, a well-planned Thyestian meal in which Queen Tamara discovers that the pie she has just eaten was composed of her two sons. And without the classical ban on onstage violence, the young Shakespeare could *really* let himself go. And this remains the stuff of horror movies centuries later.

FLA: In her film adaptation, *Titus* (1999), Julie Taymor deliberately intensifies the horror of this cannibalism scene and much more. (I think also of Peter Greenway's *Prospero's Books* and *The Cook, the Thief, the Wife & Her Lover* that ends with a cannibalistic banquet.) In a way, she makes a horror film but with a more direct allegiance to the original—and, of course, gives it an art-house intellectual spin by collapsing the time and space of ancient Rome with Mussolini's Italy.

HL: But, alas, she also departs radically from Shakespeare by creating a "feel-good" ending: Aaron and Tamar's baby carried off into the sunset. Her cavalier remark to students at Columbia that she would not have made the film without being able to add hope at the end was in many ways more discomforting to me than the film itself. To be honest, more than discomfort: I felt angry and betrayed by Taymor's tacked-on, feel-good finale. This didn't save the film from being a flop at the box office—a fate shared by *Titus Andronicus* long ago when it fell into disrepute. However, the latter has at least enjoyed a number of successful recent revivals.

FLA: I wonder, too, if the tag "Shakespeare" does make the experience of a horror film like Taymor's *Titus* somehow more palatable.

HL: Audiences' need for thrills never seems to go away, and if they can satisfy this need with *Titus Andronicus* at a Shakespeare festival, they will doubtless feel less intellectually guilty than if they are seeing, say, a Lars von Trier or a Takashi movie.

FLA: Perhaps this explains my fascination with the terribly discomforting TV show *Sons of Anarchy* (2008–14). Of course, it includes scenes of murder and rape as well as cannibalism that we witness in *Titus Andronicus*. In one episode we see a character cook, then serve up, a chili where the main ingredient is a decapitated head. Perhaps my attraction to the show is less a result of the tragi-dramatic Shakespearean plot, and more the sense that I can justify watching it because it's somehow Shakespearean.

HL: It's funny how we need to find ways to assuage our guilt about something we fear may really be trash of some sort. But at the time that *Titus* and the other revenge plays were written there wasn't a clear demarcation in the Elizabethan theater between high-minded and trash, though only a few years later these plays could be made fun of.

FLA: The aesthetic relation between the art object and the consuming subject trumps artificial demarcations. I think this is how we can best understand how some films create an aesthetic relation of discomfort in the transgression of norms whereby paradoxically pleasure (beauty, even?) is experienced in our renewed perception, thought, and feeling toward the object.

HL: I agree with you, and I think this is true of many people, especially of men. But most women I know find the films we are discussing in this section truly discomforting. Perhaps there are some empirical studies on gender and movie violence to support this. In any case, from a purely subjective point of view it seems that women object to having to witness—even in the guise of a fiction—such violent matters as rape and dismemberment, which they treat as though they were real. You can't just say to somebody objecting to these things that these are just metaphors they're watching. In fact, if they are metaphors, what precisely do they stand for?

FLA: Ah, this is when we tread that muddied water where some (theorists and media pundits) force a one-to-one correspondence between representation and reality.

HL: I can cite one instance when the line between fiction and reality seemed to be drawn in sand—and in a scary way. It was midsummer of 1960, and I was living in Riverside, California, where my academic job was at that time. One day I read in the *Riverside Press-Enterprise* that a particularly brutal murder had taken place in a ranch house much like the one I was occupying. A middle-aged couple that pursued a small business from this house had been found tied to their bed and evidently bludgeoned to death. All signs pointed to their having resisted the killers.

FLA: I can see why this brutal murder so close to home must have been terrifying.

HL: Yes, and for the next two or three nights fear took over the good citizens of Riverside, and we locked our windows, double-locked our front doors, and at every slight sound during the night we imagined an intruder with the bloodiest intentions in the house. But the local detectives soon had the answer. Three young men were arrested, one of whom had known (if only slightly) the dead couple through some business relationship he had had with them. When the men were questioned, they explained they had just been to a new movie in downtown Riverside: Alfred Hitchcock's *Psycho*. After the film, as they walked to their car they began to speculate on how they themselves could perform a deed like the horrendous one they had just witnessed on the screen. At some point they imbibed drugs to fortify themselves for their impending deed.

FLA: It is amazing how representation can generate fear in us, even when we are not direct recipients of the violence. Of course, the piece of journalism you speak of reading does by convention seek to create a one-to-one correspondence between what is represented on the page with the verifiable *facts* that exist in reality. Since the 1950s it seems that journalism, however, has become less about the representation of facts and more sensationalism aimed to trigger paranoia and fear in the general populace.

HL: In fact, the one gathering the facts was a young reporter for the *Press-Enterprise* by the name of David Halliburton. He wrote up this story over several days and eventually won a statewide award for reporting. Yet the experience of seeing the bloody bodies—and there was lots of blood, he said—was too much for him. It's one thing to watch the shower scene in *Psycho* and another thing to witness "live" dead bodies. As a direct result of this experience, Halliburton applied to graduate school and eventually began a distinguished career as my colleague at Stanford, a setting in which violent feelings are most likely to manifest themselves as mental rather than physical cruelty.

FLA: This is the same David Halliburton who taught me in the Introduction to Graduate Studies seminar when I first entered Stanford as a PhD student in 1993.

HL: And I bet he never told you or the other students about what he had seen at the murder site. The incident proved such a trauma for him that—although I had read his stories about it in the newspaper—only recently did I hear about his reaction to the sight, and it came from his wife, not from him. Unlike the three killers, one of whom landed on death row in San Quentin, he maintained a clear distinction between fiction and reality.

FLA: While we grow from birth a capacity to distinguish between fact and fiction—if it were not so, children like Corina would not know the difference between her elaborate oral storyworlds (fictional macrocosms and paracosms) where characters can do anything and her own existence within a *real* world governed by natural and social laws. Of course, there are those like the fellow that ended up on death row whose fact versus fiction discerning mechanisms are skewed. This is sometimes genetic and sometimes grown socially—and often a combination of both. In fact, for the great majority of us, the capacity (healthy) to distinguish between fact and fiction allows some of us, myself included, to especially enjoy films that breach all kinds of social rules and norms and values—precisely because we know that they are fictional. I would be appalled, upset, disgusted if I discovered a pedophile living in the house across the street. However, I'm deeply engaged by a film like Todd Solondz's *Happiness* (1998), which features a pedophile, among other unhealthy characters.

HL: That's exactly how I feel as well. These films create tantalizing "as if" situations. Some part of me always remains aware that this is a fiction and that my discomfort will leave after the film ends—or, in some cases, a day or two later once I've got over brooding about it. It's as though we need that taste of horror, with the temporary discomfort it brings on, in order to confront those rules, norms, and values.

There is, however, at least one form of discomfort that affects my body in a way that no other one does. I'm referring to disgust, which we discussed earlier on a theoretical level but which was aroused for me with special force when I saw Pasolini's great film *Salò, or 120 Days of Sodom* (1975). Although I was able to maintain a degree of composure while watching most of the atrocities depicted in the film—the repeated rapes, the murders, the dismemberments, even the forced eating of nails—what was called the Circle of Shit proved too much for me. When the Duke forced a woman victim to eat his feces, after which the whole group of victims was expected to eat a whole meal of feces, real nausea came over me, and I wished these scenes to be over with as soon as possible. Although I had felt nausea in the many scenes of Sade's original novel in which other people's excrement is swallowed, the visual portrayal in the film brought me close to vomiting (and this despite my normally iron stomach). And the horror even seemed amplified by the elegant settings of that great film designer Dante Ferretti.

FLA: The sight of the Duke taking an actual shit, then spoon-feeding it to a young woman in tears was more than my stomach (and heart?) could take. And, all these atrocious events unfold in one of those aesthetically appealing Renaissance palazzos—one that seems to invite habitation. My breaking point: seeing that all these unbearable atrocities are committed by members of the ruling class *and* by those wearing recognizably militaristic (Nazi) uniforms.

HL: This is not surprising. We know from neurobiology that the area in the brain associated with disgust, namely, the insula, and the anterior insula in particular, is more reactive to visual stimuli than to those other areas in the brain connected to the film's various horrors. To make it through that part of the film, Frederick, I kept reminding myself that the commissary at Cinecittà must have been feeding the actors some of those wonderful pork sausages I remember eating during the two years I lived in Italy.

FLA: In the case of *Salò* I'm not sure if the image of a pork sausage would have helped me, here. The fascist libertines' burning of the young men's penises, among other tortures, together with the shrieks of pain that generally fill out the film's sound channel put me off eating sausages for quite some time. It is interesting that this Pasolini film, together with Taymor's *Titus*, chooses to set the story in fascist Italy and that the fascists are decidedly marked by the increased presence of modernist objects. I recall the end scene when the two young fascist guards (civilian clothed proto-Blackshirts?) dance with one another; modernist art appears on the wall and modern music plays on the radio. This, of course, stands in sharp contrast with the older generation of libertines whose decadence is marked by classical music and baroque art. For Pasolini, whether a forward-looking modernism or a backward-looking conservatism, fascism *is* fascism.

HL: What can I say but that *Salò* is like no other movie I've seen, horror or otherwise? But let's look again at an arguably less controversial film that also contains most of the conventions of the classic horror movie: Haneke's *Funny Games* (1997). Like a goodly proportion of works in the genre, it starts tamely, even idyllically, as a thoroughly normal couple, together with their son and dog, arrive at their weekend vacation place on a lake. This sort of opening—we see it as well in *Audition* and *I Spit in Your Grave*—enables the filmmaker to introduce the unpleasant matter only gradually, with the result that viewers enter the world of horror before they are fully conscious of it. Of course, these are never really a surprise for those who have watched such films before: indeed, we learn to look for clues of strange behavior early on.

FLA: The filmgoer well versed in the genre even relishes in this gentle slide into the deep, dark pit of horror. In the 2005 *Hostel* (produced by Quentin Tarantino) nothing horrific happens in the first thirty minutes or so that sets up the story of tourists being redirected from their route from Amsterdam to Barcelona to their torture and disappearance in Slovakia; it also absents any foreboding clues of a horror to come. Had it thrown us directly into the deep end of the horror, its impact would likely have been more penetrating.

HL: We might call this convention the "tame opening." It actually goes back to gothic novels such as *The Mysteries of Udolpho*, which, similarly to *Funny Games*, opens "on the pleasant banks of the Garonne, . . . gay with luxuriant woods and vine" and a stable family "listen[ing] to the music that floated on [the river's] waves" (7). What distinguishes *Funny Games* from most other horror films is its sophistication. Haneke, unlike most practitioners of the genre, is not a horror specialist as such. Rather, he is a film director especially drawn to uncomfortable topics; we already took note of the nastiness of *The Piano Teacher*, which is also a central ingredient in his films *Caché*, *The White Ribbon*, and *Amour*—the last two use repression and dementia, respectively, as triggers of discomfort.

FLA: Haneke's work outside of horror storytelling filmmaking seems to allow him to give new shape to this genre with *Funny Games*.

HL: Indeed, he pulls our collective leg (the villains, of course, break the hero's leg) by exposing the genre's conventions. For instance, when the heroine kills one of the two villains, the other villain turns the clock back so that the film can proceed without breaking generic rules. And the "surprise" ending, in which the villains start their seemingly innocent game again at another house, reminds us that this was all a game. The latter device had become famous in Eugène Ionesco's play *The Lesson* (1950), in which a professor, after murdering a recalcitrant student, starts his game all over again when an unknowing new student arrives for her lesson. In view of the "gaminess" characterizing *Funny Games* the knowing viewer is likely to feel less discomfort here than in more "earnest" horror films—yet whatever discomfort we miss out on is more than compensated for by the masterliness with which Haneke has pulled the whole thing off.

FLA: Yes, we're distressed equally at the level of content (two of the most nasty sociopaths I've encountered in world cinema) and form (the clock hands physically turning backward in time also rewinding us in the film's chronology of events *and* the use of the direct address to expose the device of the story's artifice). Of course, there are other ways that directors can disturb audiences at the level of form and content. While there is no exposing of the device (Brecht's breaking of the fourth wall) in Alain Resnais's 1955 Holocaust documentary, *Nuit et brouillard* (*Night and Fog*), the fact that he chooses the conventions of the documentary film format intensify our horror of this repulsive chapter in world history.

HL: There's a good reason that Resnais's film, which is probably the earliest filmic depiction of the Holocaust outside of the newsreels that circulated soon after the war, is still current. It is distinguished by the fact that it is both short and honest, presenting what was left of the camps in a direct way. To bring up a term we used in distinguishing photographs from paintings, this film, unlike a fictionalization of the material, takes the form of testimonial. There have been lots of fictionalized Holocaust films over the years, and although I've witnessed only a small percentage of them, I've rarely cared for what I saw. As you know, I have a special relationship to this event, for all my aunts, uncles, and cousins who were stuck in Germany when the war began failed to survive. The severe discomfort I feel comes from what I know of the event itself—as well as from my recently writing about it, not from fictional or filmic renderings of it.

This discomfort usually takes the form of anger, not just at the Nazis but above all at the propensity of people—any people, I suspect—to be manipulated politically to perform unspeakable deeds. I think of films such as *Schindler's List* (1993), *Life Is Beautiful* (1998), and *The Pianist* (2002). However skillful the makers of these films may be, their products neither affect me nor do they excite much admiration from me, for each of them has employed what I see as slick techniques to cover up an impossible reality. Beyond *Night and Fog*, the Holocaust film I most admire is Claude Lanzmann's *Shoah* (1985), which consists of interviews with survivors and witnesses and, like the earlier film, it photographs—this time in full color—what is left of the sites. With its nearly ten hours of footage, it is long and uncompromisingly frank, and it upset me deeply—not only with anger but also just plain sadness—when I first saw it.

FLA: While we are on the topic of mimeticism that disturbs, we would be greatly remiss if we neglected to mention a protean horror film that took the mimetic shape: Tod Browning's 1932 *Freaks*. Cast with real sideshow performers with deformities such as those without arms or legs, pinheads, hermaphrodites, those with dwarfism. In its mimeticism and verisimilar gore (the end of the uncut version has the performers castrate the character known as Hercules) it certainly outweighs most horror films made today that rely 99 percent of the film time on special effects. As far as disquieting films go, this is a landmark—much more so than Salvador Dalí and Luis Buñuel's coeval twenty-one-minute *Un Chien Andalou* (1929).

HL: Yet the film seems to have faded into obscurity.

FLA: I wonder how many films we discuss here will *not* fade into obscurity, Herbie. Earlier I mentioned how a film like Haneke's *The Piano Teacher* deeply disturbs filmgoers and yet won accolades among the critics. I actively seek out films that disturb me. I'm also all for celebrating achievement. However, I do wonder if the extratextual apparatus (a film festival award, for instance) might take the discomfort out of a film. In 1990 when I first saw E. Elias Merhige's *Begotten* in Berkeley, I went because I had heard about its figuration of "God" disemboweling himself. The film was nearly too much for me: the lack of dialogue made it rather boring coupled with the repetition of extremely harsh and disturbing images (strangulation by umbilical cord, rape, and dismemberment, for instance). Yet Susan Sontag called it "one of the 10 most important films of modern times."

HL: I agree that *Begotten* is boring (Sontag, we know, was sometimes given to overenthusiasm), though I don't react strongly one way or the other to the repulsive stuff, despite the highly audible retching and the highly visible puke. Merhige is trying to redo those old fertility myths that Sir James Frazer pulled together to shock late Victorians about the savagery of their ancestors. When T. S. Eliot used Frazer in *The Waste Land*, the idea was still new. Like Eliot, Merhige stresses the Christian overtones in these myths—the buried god, his resurrection, and the like; and Merhige, unlike Eliot, also brings in the god's mother. What's new here is the visual and audial experience—but, for me at least, the discomfort level remains pretty low.

FLA: Stanley Kubrick's *A Clockwork Orange* has an incredibly strong visual and audial impact. When Kubrick depicts the very choreographed scene of Alex and his gang about to rape Mrs. Alexander (and torture and cripple the husband) he's crooning "Singing in the Rain." His gleeful (even aesthetic) dancing is punctuated with menacing gestures. Within the mise-en-scène, too, there is a beauty in the furniture and architecture. It's all beautifully filmed. Kubrick creates in us viewers a cognitive dissonance where we experience two opposing feelings and thoughts. Recall, too, that after the violent scene he returns to the social housing complex (those tenements we discussed earlier) for the deprived and destitute where he masturbates to the Ninth amid images of the night's violence. However, Kubrick puts this violence on the same disturbing level as that of the state's reforming of Alex with the Ludovico treatment (figure 38). These scenes produce spasms of cognitive dissonance in us viewers.

HL: Now that's a truly disturbing film, and, like *Funny Games*, a horror specialist did not make it, though Kubrick later also created that refined horror film *The Shining*. It's altogether thrilling, and, like most other horror films based on written texts, the images and sounds of *A*

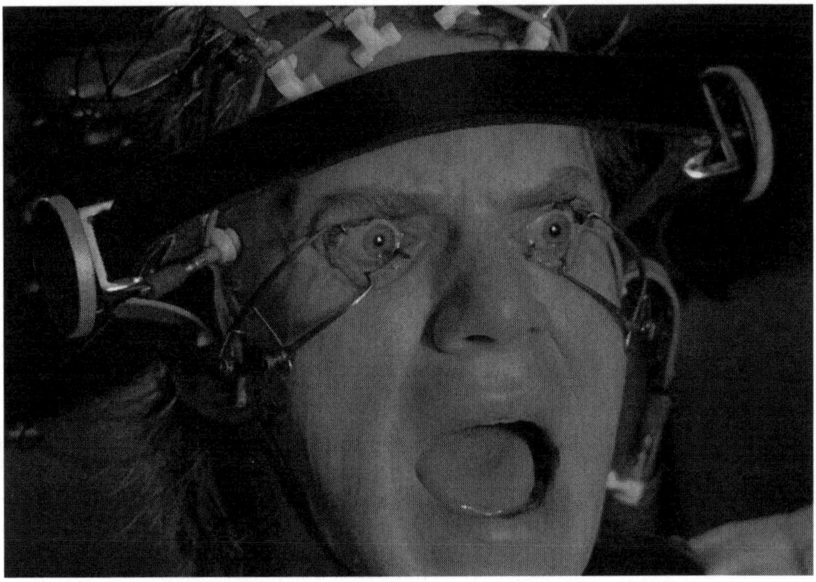

Figure 38. Alex (played by Malcolm McDowell) tortured in Stanley Kubrick's *Clockwork Orange* (1971)

Clockwork Orange can thrill more intensely than Burgess's excellent novel can do by means of words alone. Though I invoked my usual distance while viewing *Clockwork,* pleasing chills went through me—not least of all because of the way that the Beethoven's Ninth (what we earlier mentioned as a cultural icon that has served all manner of purposes) is used to accompany Alex's behavior therapy. Few directors have used music—often familiar music like "The Blue Danube" in *2001: A Space Odyssey*—as cunningly as Kubrick.

FLA: We tend to forget that sound is as important as the visuals in film. The creaking of doors, thudding of boots, and the presence of a music score that combine with the visuals (for instance, a silhouetted knife about to jab the victim repeatedly) takes us to extreme peaks of emotion. We see this careful orchestration of the sound with the visuals in horror films of all kinds, including the recent arrival of what's been identified as torture-porn in the independent film marketplace. For instance, Tom Six's *The Human Centipede* (2009) uses the sound and visual channels (in what seems to be a self-consciously clichéd way) to intensify our experience of Dr. Heiter's (sounds like Hitler?) psychopathology. The film follows several conventions of the horror film: the rainy night; the two women in a broken-down car; the action of being drugged and abducted by the demented surgeon. Yet Six takes us to a whole new level of discomfort when we become witness to Heiter's surgical procedure of joining—mouth-to-anus, no less—the two women and an Asian abductee. Postsurgery, we witness his creation: three human beings surgically welded together and forced (he cuts the ligaments in their legs) to walk on all fours as a twelve-legged creature with a single alimentary canal. A special horror hits us when we watch the Asian (the head, say, of the centipede) relieve himself into the mouth of the second (the body, say, of the centipede).

HL: While it is clearly a horror film (and you mention it as part of the torture-porn subgenre), it is also a not-so-obvious Holocaust film. In fact, it is a more satisfying Holocaust movie for me than, say, the slick *Schindler's List*. Of course the Holocaust is never mentioned as such, and that makes it all the more powerful as a statement about the Nazis. Dr. Heiter is profoundly German—and in the most stereotyped way. And we are invited implicitly to see the connection of his medical experiments on human beings with those of Nazi doctors such as Josef Mengele.

With the scene of coprophagy you mention, I feared I would suffer nausea as I had while watching the feces scene in *Salò*. It never developed here, however. Perhaps this was because I had become inured by having seen *Salò* long before. I suspect that the horrors one experiences in one movie—whether dismemberment, rape, eating feces—lessen with subsequent enactments of the same horror, though a cunning director can renew our ability to react to a particular one. But Six's images are still quite powerful: the train of bodies crawling all over the house is unforgettable.

FLA: Powerful indeed, Herbie. Heiter's disdainful kicking of the creature of his inventing was also particularly disturbing, and so was the penultimate scene when the head slits his own throat: these are all the more powerfully resonant in my mind now that you have situated the film squarely within the Holocaust genre.

HL: Indeed, the Holocaust is the key, I believe, to opening up this film.

FLA: There seems to be a long tradition of discomforting cinema in Japan. Can we say that directors grown in certain cultures might be more inclined to create discomforting films? I think of Japanese filmmakers such as the Miike Takashi and Tsukamoto Shinya.

HL: Cultural generalizations, as we know, are always tricky to sustain, especially since the Danish, Austrian, French, and American examples we are discussing are also pretty bloody.

FLA: Takashi's film *Audition* (1999) is one of the most disturbing I have seen—and, as our conversation may have indicated, I've seen a lot. His careful design (plot and characterization) as well as his use of lighting, camera lens and angle, and sound slowly builds up my sense of discomfort to the point where I have to turn away from the film.

HL: The slow buildup from the early long sections on how Aoyama is going to find a wife—like the idyllic early part of *Funny Games*—make the gradually revealed horror all the more horrifying. The villainous Asami is a new embodiment of that old archetype, the witch-lady, who starts out being sweet and compliant and, little by little, emerges as the monster she really is.

FLA: I nearly vomited at the sight (half looking through my hands that covered my eyes) of a man whose feet, tongue, ear, and fingers have been cut off and who hungrily eats vomit from a dog dish.

HL: Oddly, perhaps, I had the opposite reaction. Instead of feeling frightened or even nauseous at the sight of all the dismemberments, I found them to be more amusing than anything else.

FLA: Ah, yes, the power of humor and its physical expression in laughter. Its uninvited presence does seem to be the ultimate destroyer of genre. As discussed earlier in our conversations, no matter the degree of horror Takashi built into the film's design, all this discomfort dissolves into thin air the moment we laugh instead of shriek or cry. This was indeed my experience of Harmony Korine's feature film, *Gummo* (1997); he recently made the exceptional film *Spring Breakers* (2013), which turns Hollywood pin-up James Franco into an intensely disquieting gangster-pimp who preys on young college girls on spring break in Florida. The critics applauded Korine's ability to bring an intense sense of discomfort to everyday life in a rural Midwest. But the shooting and then selling of cats (domestic, ferule, and stray) to a butcher, the appearance of a gay dwarf and a man that pimps his Down syndrome daughter, as well as others that perform satanic rituals had me chortling more than retching.

HL: While a film's design aims to direct how we respond to it as disturbing or otherwise, this doesn't determine our reactions in an absolute way.

FLA: I wonder if this is linked to how much emotional ambiguity a director builds into his or her film. I say emotional ambiguity and not an ambiguity of thought or imagination because we have a director like Lars von Trier who creates films that are quite *open* (in Umberto Eco's sense of ambiguity) at the level of critical interpretation, but closed in the sense of its triggering a set number of emotional reactions.

HL: Yes, he has a way of concocting films that create this tension between openness and closedness. Instead of using a physical set for *Dogville* (2003) he used painted lines on a studio floor to portray an entire dilapidated American town.

FLA: And this is tame compared to the extreme tensions he creates in us with his controversial film *Antichrist* (2009). Here Von Trier chooses to identify his protagonists by the pronouns "She" (Charlotte Gainsbourg) and "He" to name the grief-stricken mother and increasingly crazed father; at the start their child had climbed on his desk and jumped out the bedroom window to his death. There's much interpretive ambiguity throughout the film, but there's not much room for emotional ambiguity. When we witness "She" pounding the penis and testicles of "He" with a log or when we see her hand-drill a hole through his leg to fix a grindstone, we certainly don't laugh. The same can be said of the images of self-disemboweling animals and so on. However, at a cognitive level, the film is wide open to interpretation. The only compass direction we have here is the film's title: *Antichrist.* Is the child meant to be such? Is the mother? Is the father? Is it meant to be read as an allegory, and if so, of what?

HL: I interpreted the "She" in *Antichrist* to be another witch-lady, like Asami in *Audition.* Von Trier first portrays her as pathetic and then, as her madness sets in, increasingly monstrous. Von Trier eschews the naturalism that many horror films cultivate but instead seeks surrealistic effects—the speaking fox ("chaos reigns"), the cawing crow, the three beggars. You feel there's an allegory here, though its meaning, if one was even intended, remains unclear. These strange effects, however, help create an image world that raises the film to some mythical level. Yet the mythical feel for me works to mitigate the discomfort generated by the more horrible moments—the clitoris self-amputation, the grindstone that "She" drills into her husband's leg. Yes, one feels the physicality of it all, even though one also feels somewhat distanced.

FLA: My goodness, yes, the clitoris self-amputation *with* seemingly rusted scissors no less. This scene and image are by far one of the most disturbing I've encountered in world cinema. I will have a tough time rubbing it from my memory. Perhaps this is because the film is not framed as a horror film; that is, we don't go into it with the expectation (the mental mind set) of watching a horror film, but rather of an art-house film. Perhaps, too, it is Von Trier's skill at directing his actors, use of lighting, camera lens and angle, and also, of course, the pacing of the story. The camera holds us captive during this moment of her clitorectomy—and we can't escape. I should also mention that unlike some of the other deeply disturbing films we've discussed like *The Piano Teacher*, *Antichrist* was not showered with accolades. At Cannes (2009) it was given the "antiaward." But I wonder if this was because of these intensely disquieting scenes at the emotional level or because of its interpretive ambiguity.

HL: I gather this antiaward was given because of the alleged misogyny, and I suspect that the jurors were correct about this. Yet the actress Gainsbourg did receive the Cannes award for best actress for her role as "She." There appears to be a disconnect between the evaluation of the film as a whole and its individual components.

FLA: Films like *Antichrist* leave lots of room for critical interpretation and yet guide our emotional responses in rather forceful ways. Solondz's *Happiness* is another film that operates somewhat like this. (This was a film where the director chose not to cut scenes for that R-rating so the MPAA gave it an NC-17.) Its openness, however, doesn't invite an allegorical reading but rather *opens* our eyes to the disturbing possibilities of human thought and behavior. With the exception possibly of the young Billy (he ends the film announcing triumphantly to his family that he "came"), with whom we might sympathize, especially after he discovers that his father's a pedophile, Solondz wants us to dislike the adults that make up a not-so-sweet suburban America: from a lonely-heart who cuts a lover into pieces to a father who sodomizes one of his son's best friends.

Unlike a film like *Antichrist* there is no room for interpretive ambiguity in *Happiness*. Not so incidentally, it was banned from independent film fests like the Sundance Film Festival. There's nothing ambiguous about pedophilia, certainly. I wonder if discomforting films with less interpretive ambiguity are more likely to be banned than others.

HL: Yes, some are definitely more acceptable than others. This movie—beautifully executed, and with memorable acting—made me squirm in a special way, and this was because of the pedophilia and the boy's masturbation. The final image, in which the latter, after many attempts, finally has his orgasm, feels embarrassing and I found myself blushing—especially after you see the semen on the balcony railing (from which the boy has worked himself up by looking down at a woman in a bikini) and, finally, the dog licking it all up.

The pedophilia had a worse effect on me: I realized I didn't want to hear about it. This may be like the reaction that women viewers often have to rape and other forms of violence. Although it was bad enough seeing a grown man cuddling his son's friend, I felt relieved that I didn't have to watch him doing things in bed with the boy. Yes, pedophilia for me—and, I suspect, for many viewers—is a less "acceptable" topic than the others around which horror films are built.

FLA: While the films we've been discussing target human beings of all ages, genders, and races, there is a strong tradition of discomforting films that focus on women. I think of those 1970s exploitation, rape-revenge shockers like *I Spit on Your Grave* (1978). The film includes one of the most disturbing scenes: a twenty-five-minute-long gang rape. Yet there's a certain satisfaction we derive from the victim's going out on a methodical killing spree; while most upsetting, don't we derive pleasure from seeing her kill them all off: she hangs one of the rapists at the moment of his sexual climax, cuts off the penis of another, kills another with an ax, and disembowels yet another with a motorboat engine.

This begs us to consider the urgent matter of gender. What do we do with these paired feelings of disgust (violence and degradation) and satisfaction (her empowerment) when there's a rape of a woman at the center of the story?

HL: Yes, there's lots of satisfaction in seeing Jennifer achieve her revenge—to the point that I didn't even squirm, as I ordinarily would have, when she sliced off Johnny's penis in the bathtub; indeed, his subsequent agonizing screams seemed most satisfying to hear. And the first revenge-murder—of the low-IQ Matthew by means of hanging after he achieves his orgasm—is equally satisfying; less so, perhaps the final murders while Jennifer manipulates the boat, for the film at this point was racing a bit frantically toward its conclusion. And I was delighted that the film ends with the murders—otherwise we would have been bored seeing Jennifer go to trial, for which she would have had to provide proof—a difficult thing without any witness alive any more—that she was avenging the rape to which her eventual victims had subjected her. But then horror movies don't need to portray the right or the wrong of it all!

FLA: I should mention that Steven Monroe's 2010 remake of *I Spit on Your*

Grave was much less discomforting. The horrors Jennifer experiences are even more graphically explicit but possibly because I was already familiar with the original it had less of an impact. A film that goes above and beyond both in shape and content is French director Gaspar Noé's *Irreversible* (2002). It unfolds in reverse chronology of twelve sequences and is set in and around a gay S-M nightclub, The Rectum, in Paris. The subsonic gut-trembling bass sounds in the film also disturb—clearly a film where the director uses the sound to intensify the horror. The sounds resist our encoding (our sense making), too, as if the electronic (deep techno) beats are being played backward as the film unfolds (backward). From beginning to end (or rather, end to beginning) the film is steeped in violent images such as the bludgeoning of a pimp to death in the opening moments to a nine-minute rape scene (with no edits and no movement of the camera) as well as a violent sound. Of all the films we've discussed, this has the most disturbing soundscape—thumping techno/electronica played in reverse. When the film ended and I walked out of the cinema, I felt thoroughly abused by the experience.

HL: When I saw *Irreversible* I was unaware that it presented itself in reverse chronology, and it was hard to make sense of it. Only at the "end," with its idyllic scene accompanied by Beethoven (the Seventh, not the iconic Ninth this time), did I begin to realize that this scene, like the openings of *Funny Games* and *I Spit on Your Grave*, was really the "beginning."

FLA: Where does our moral compass settle in films like *Irreversible* or *I Spit on Your Grave*? We are repulsed by the rape and violence against the woman but also equally taken up by the story of vengeance.

HL: Again, as in *I Spit on Your Grave*, the vengeance should give satisfaction to the viewer—but in *Irreversible* it turns out that it's not exercised on the real rapist. Still, since we experience a film like *Irreversible* in reverse, we can't even expect the satisfaction that goes with chronologically normal storytelling.

FLA: Fred Vogel's *August Underground* (2001) is even more explicit in its violence toward women (slicing of nipples, covering in feces, force-feeding of dismembered body parts, beating victims with hammers during acts of sodomy) than either of the two just mentioned. This along with so many other discomforting films seems to gravitate around the abuse of women.

HL: I'm sure this is part of the reason (though by no means the only one) that women often avoid horror films.

FLA: In a book I wrote on Robert Rodriguez I talk about how the director combines the beautiful and the repulsive in the Latina body. In my analysis of *From Dusk Till Dawn* (1996) I focus on Salma Hayek's transformation from Latina seductress into a monster, but a monster that retains her beautiful human form from the neck down. The beautiful and ugly coexist in the Latina's body that is then quickly destroyed and mutilated by the Anglo sociopath, Richie Gecko (Quentin Tarantino).

HL: I couldn't take the second, "Latino" half of *From Dusk till Dawn* as seriously as the first, "Anglo" half, and this is because the film totally shifted genres in the middle, moving from a crime-spree film to a vampire film. I much admired the way this shift worked to expose the conventions of both genres, but this also meant you experience the film primarily on an intellectual level as you think about what it says about filmic conventions.

FLA: I too had the impression of the film smelting together two distinct halves: the Tarantino, or as you put it, Anglo, half and the Rodriguez, or as you put it, Latino, half. While made by a Latino director, that second half sure is full of violence against Latinas.

HL: Along with the question of gender we have to consider how race figures in this and in other films that discomfort. Our reactions to ethnic stereotypes and slurs all depend on where we happen to come from. A Native American may well find it difficult to deal with the ways the so-called Injuns were depicted in old Westerns. A black villain in a horror film otherwise centered on whites would be insufferable, not only to black viewers but to the whole liberal white intelligentsia. A Jewish villain, in view of my own ethnicity, would likely irritate me, but it would not elicit as strong a reaction as the black villain would to blacks. This is because Jews have come to feel safe in the United States—as they do not, say, in countries like France, Hungary, and Poland. Had I seen a Jewish villain—say, a Jewish mafioso—beating up gentiles in a horror film in, say, 1939, when the American right was pro-Nazi, I would have felt far worse, and with good reason. But the modern Far Right, with its predominantly Jewish intellectual leadership from the egregious Ayn Rand (née Alisa Rosenbaum) onward, has succeeded in keeping Jews reasonably safe. Not so alas, with blacks and Latinos!

FLA: The Latino scholarly reaction to Rodriguez's *From Dusk Till Dawn* was mixed and especially negative when it came to his representation of Latinas. Recall, too, that Spike Lee refused to see Tarantino's *Django*

Unchained (2012), likely because of a white director's misrepresentation (disregard?) of black history filled with trauma, murder, and rape. As you so astutely point out, Herbie, perhaps such films would be more palatable—even come and go without much identity politics to-do—if we as Latinos (and blacks, and Asians, and Native Americans) felt more comfortable (less *uncomfortable*) as enfranchised citizens in this country.

HL: At least this has been the pattern for Jews in the United States. Given that Latinos are now the majority minority in this country it could well be that this becomes swiftly the case for you all.

FLA: Perhaps we will see the growing of more Robert Rodriguezes as a consequence. In any case, we do see that bodies that are marked as different in terms of race, ethnicity, gender—and sexuality—seem to be gravitational pulls for directors who choose to make disquieting films. While Rodriguez levels the playing field by creating Latinas and all other Latinos as monstrous aberrations, it is still the white guy (George Clooney as Seth Gecko) who saves the day and drives off into the sunset.

Of course, there are many other directors of discomforting films who choose to identify the woman as the locus of the disquietude. I think of David Lynch's *Eraserhead* (1977), which identifies the woman, Mary X, as the one who conceives (by a disturbing form of immaculate conception) a snakelike creature (with no skin, as it turns out, to hold its internal organs in place) that becomes the monstrous Eraserhead. And Lynne Ramsay's *We Need to Talk about Kevin* (2011) seems to rest the blame for all the son's sociopathic deeds (including blinding then killing his little sister) on the mother (the disquietingly near-albino white-skinned Tilda Swinton as Eva Khatchadourian).

HL: On some level, the films reflect the violence toward women and racial others that take place every day in our society. (Doubtless this violence has always been around, but the fact that it is now much talked about publicly makes it viable for filmic representation.) I suppose it is all a matter of what the director does with this material. But it's also a matter of the particular gender and ethnicity of the viewer. The long, sustained rape scenes in *I Spit on Your Grave* and *Irreversible* are likely quite painful for most women to watch. And "horrible" as these scenes are, I know they couldn't possibly have affected me in the way they affect a woman.

Let's try a little thought experiment. What if I were shown a rape scene of equivalent length in which the victim is a young man, say, a white man in prison on some minor drug charge who gets gang-raped by a bunch of hardened criminals (all white, since I want to keep race out of this experiment)? My guess is that I wouldn't be any more uncomfortable than I was in the rape scenes in the films we discussed above. And I think the reason is that a woman from early on develops a sense of horror toward rape—above all, toward the humiliation and the violence, not to speak of the fear of pregnancy—that a man simply doesn't have.

FLA: While I certainly agree that the girls and boys can be (and are) grown differently within families and society at large, our cognitive and emotive systems are more alike than not. I certainly react with incredible discomfort when watching the violent rape scenes in Edward James Olmos's *American Me* (1992), which include a victim's being raped with a knife. And I should mention that it was a female friend of mine that loaned me a copy of *Hostel*. She absolutely loved it. Of course, an obligation to knowledge leads one to suffer certain discomforts.

In the end, I suppose what we are talking about is whether or not the discomforting ingredients of a given film—and this could be the entirety of the film's design, as in *Irreversible*—aim to create something new—something that opens our minds to new ways of seeing and experiencing this reality. Some films do this better than others. Some include greater degrees of violence than others. I would only add that we might tread carefully when leaning toward a *gendering* of the experience of films. And, more globally we wouldn't want any agenda (gender, race, class, sexual orientation) to become a form of censorship that decides what's acceptable or not in terms of form and content.

HL: Yes, I would agree.

FLA: Perhaps we should end by considering what makes the difference between discomforting films with artistic merits and discomforting films that have other goals. Put simply: how do we distinguish between, say, an *Antichrist* or a *Happiness* from torture-porn or other kinds of extreme and socially taboo pornography that circulate today?

HL: When we deal with horror films, I don't think it's easy—perhaps even useful—to try to distinguish between those with what you call "artistic merits" and those with other goals, whatever these may be (cheap thrills? voyeurism?). This distinction goes back to the 1959 *Lady Chatterley's Lover* trial, in which the only way to get the book into circulation was to argue that it possessed these literary merits beyond what might be thought of as pornography.

But all the horror films we've talked about—whether skillfully executed or not—try to give the viewer a big thrill, to arouse as much fear, perhaps also disgust, as possible. When watching these films, I wasn't much concerned about how "artistic" they were. What seemed central was what they were doing to rework, sometimes even to rethink, the horror genre. Perhaps what distinguishes the best of them is not any artistically "redeeming" qualities that the lawyers for *Lady Chattterley*'s publisher claimed to find but rather the intellectual satisfactions they can offer when they game the genre in sophisticated ways.

FLA: Indeed, "redeeming" is a lawyer trick used to avoid (or release from) censorship something like *Lady Chatterley's*—the film the mainstream media damned for its promotion of adultery. There's a long history of filmmaking that used the "redeem" conceit to get around censorship codes (the Hays Code and the like). Recall the shift from a film like Gustav Machaty's *Ecstasy* (1933), which featured several frontal nude positions of Hedy Lamarr (and even a close-up of her having an orgasm), to later films packed with aquatic ballet sequences to show only a bit of flesh. We see this "redeeming" conceit really hit home in the sexploitation films of the late 1950s and early 1960s (part of the Grindhouse era of filmmaking) that showed lots more flesh (and sex) but as couched within a heavy-handed, moralistic plot.

Directors have maneuvered around censorship more recently by using a redemptive and moralistic conceit—all within an art-house style that would appeal to an art-house audience. I think of the very graphic, *unsimulated*, and very discomforting sex (orgasm by asphyxiation, for instance) in Nagisa Oshima's *In the Realm of the Senses* (1976). The film makes clear that it is a *tragedy* based on real-life events. Its moral is made clear: don't become jealous and obsessed as Sada Abe does with her lover Kichizo Ishida. If one does, one might become as crazy as Sada and cut off the penis and testicles of one's lover. But it's also redemptive in that Oshima's Sada takes us to the discomforting extremes of passion—extremes that edge up next to a kind of religious redemptivity. I suspect that it was its art-house style and exhibition along with its moralism and transcendent redemptivity that allowed Oshima's frequent (and lengthy) sequences of erect penises penetrating vaginas to be shown in nonpornographic venues.

HL: You often hear somebody argue that a work that is largely uncomfortable to experience at least has some "redeeming" qualities—like the "classical" qualities sometimes attributed to a Mapplethorpe photo that might otherwise be dismissed as "pornographic." Or you may hear a pronouncement that a particular work has absolutely no redeeming qualities whatsoever—as some people would classify most of the horror films we've just discussed. Where, one might ask, does one find anything redeeming in a pickled animal head exhibited by Damien Hirst? Or in Pasolini's *Salò,* or in the Marquis de Sade's *120 Days of Sodom,* from which the film derives? (As a side note, it's worth remarking how often we've cited Hirst, Pasolini, and Sade as makers of discomforting art.)

Yet maybe we should examine that loaded word *redeeming.* After all, it is usually associated with religion, above all, with Christianity, whose founder, distinctly more than the leaders of other cults, was above all celebrated as the Redeemer. What place does the term *redeeming* really have in serious aesthetic discourse? I can only speculate that once the aesthetic realm carved out a place for itself in the late eighteenth century, it needed a certain religious aura (especially for those who were skeptical of traditional religion) to justify itself. If you're looking for "redemptive" experiences, I suspect that you'd likely find them most efficiently by joining a church.

FLA: Many of the world's religious institutions—Jewish, Catholic, Muslim, and so on—are great fans of censorship. There is also the censorship that comes from those that put into place the Hays Code. And lastly, there's the censorship that comes from secular authorities, working under the pretext that it is protecting a population (community, state, nation) against bad habits or morals. Censorship appears in many other guises, of course. Hence the guiding principle should always be: all anarchy in art. Whether it's a *Happiness* or a *Salò,* it's all about upholding the dictum that creativity should be left alone and the decision to go see *Hostel* should be left to viewers themselves.

Epilogue: Now *That's* Disquieting!

FREDERICK LUIS ALDAMA: In the last chapter we touched on questions of evaluation. As we both agree, all art should be free of legislation. The real problem encountered is that *evaluation* when done by those in power (church or state, for instance) is simply the ascription of a negative tag to that which discomforts. I must point out that censors try to justify their censorship with the accusation of art being pornographic.

HERBERT LINDENBERGER: What is disquieting in the art that we're talking about is also what is disquieting in the real world that this art, in its own, organized way, seeks to grasp. I don't mean to say that the real world is pornographic in any way—after all, the "graphic" in the term refers to writing, and originally the term apparently meant writing about prostitutes. As the censorship of books and films declined in the course of the past century, the long unmentionable taboos—for example, incest, spousal and child abuse, pedophilia—found their way not only into art but above all into the newspapers we read and the conversations we hold. As those of my generation have discovered, the practice of these vices was far greater than we could have imagined when we were young; and some of us have even heard about such practices among our friends and relatives.

FLA: Even within what seem to be the sanctuary of our neighborhoods. A fellow who lives across the street and whom I see throwing a ball around with his two children made the front page of the *Columbus Dispatch*. He was under investigation for downloading child pornography. Needless to say, he lost his position as director of pediatric oncology at Ohio State University's medical center—and threw the community into a great panic.

HL: Unfortunately, my experience of the utterly horrific is even closer to home. My father's first cousin, the once-celebrated strikebreaker Pearl Bergoff—his name, thank God, had been changed from the original Lindenberger—was responsible, according to the obituary circulated by the Associated Press at his death in 1947, for the deaths of fifty-four men, women, and children. How many horror films can boast so overwhelming a number of corpses? In view of the prevalence of crime—whether or not violent—in our world, it's no wonder that films, novels, and also serious nonfiction have concerned themselves with this material. What a film or a book needs to do is organize all that raw material according to conventions that can communicate it to their consumers.

FLA: Some serious, extremely accomplished artists that we've discussed have created art objects that some have called pornographic. Here, however, I would ask if *pornography* itself exists. That is, there is nothing implicit that is built into the art object that makes it pornographic. Pornography is not in the object nor in the subject, it's in the relation—and, as we've established, this relation changes in time and place.

There are no pornographic objects per se. That which has been called pornographic is the result of either secular or religious censorship.

HL: The borders between material that is pornographic or not have shifted over time. *Lady Chatterley's Lover,* as we know, was once considered pornographic (the copy that I still own was printed in Japan and smuggled into the United States by a friend). It wasn't only the erotic scenes in Lawrence's book but the fact that many people admitted that they used it to arouse themselves—something I considered impossible since these scenes were so solemnly written that they made me laugh. In any case, I can't believe the book can serve an erotic purpose these days since there are now many books—all legally attainable—that do the trick far better—and, luckily, with considerably less solemnity!

FLA: There is a frequent comparison and distinction between pornography and eroticism. However, rather than placing this distinction within the art object (novel, drawing, photography), we see that it is the artist's will to style to create an object that will generate in a more immediate and in a stronger way a sexual reaction. Such art does the trick better, as you say. When the artist seeks to create a less immediately efficacious arousal, then the artist (or his critics) will call this eroticism. Both techniques can be used in a single work, too. In Peruvian author Mario Vargas Llosa's novels such as *Elogio de la madrastra / In Praise of the Stepmother* (1988) and *Los cuadernos de don Rigoberto / Notebooks of Don Rigoberto* (1997) the author uses syntax to speed up and slow down the pace, which creates an atmosphere we might call erotic, and he also includes techniques and content that create a more immediate state of sexual arousal.

HL: And the 2010 Nobel Prize in Literature went to Vargas Llosa, no less!

FLA: We now have a Latin American Nobel laureate who is not only an extraordinary novelist but also a brilliant and technically superb pornographer!

HL: Elfriede Jelinek—a specialist in the ugly side of eroticism as seen in *The Piano Teacher* and other novels—also took home the Nobel Prize some six years before Vargas Llosa! Note these sentences floating through Erika Kohut's FID as she contemplates her genitals: "Rot between her legs, an unfeeling soft mass. Decay, putrescent lumps of organic material. No spring breezes awaken anything" (197). If anybody slipped her or Vargas Llosa's books into Alfred Nobel's grave, he would likely turn over in horror.

FLA: One of your colleagues at Stanford, Sianne Ngai, ends her scholarly book *Ugly Feelings* with an afterword on disgust. She calls to task scholars who have decided to give disgust as a category an inherent negative moral characteristic. I'm certainly with Ngai here, especially when she states so clearly that disgust "is neither of the left or of the right and has the capacity to be summoned in either direction" (339).

HL: Although things have changed in recent years, the scholarly community remained inherently conservative for a long time. During the 1950s I taught at UC Riverside with a young Shakespeare specialist who submitted an article to *English Language Notes* explicating a line in *The Winter's Tale* in which Shakespeare used the word *purse* to imply *pussy* ("Your purse is not hot enough to purchase your spice"—4.3.114–15). The journal sent the article back with a letter warning the author that, although his interpretation was correct from a scholarly point of view, it would be bad for his future career if his name became associated with that particular spot on a woman's body.

FLA: How times have changed! For all its offensive semantic baggage, today *pussy* is bandied about as freely as any other term. In all my scholarly work—from Latino poetry, literature, comics like the one we discussed by Wilfred Santiago, video games to Robert Rodriguez's films and more—I have been singularly interested in understanding how each aesthetic object has been built and how it *does* what it does in the world. That is, I consider form and content to be inseparable, and so to understand, say, the story told (plot, theme, character) in a Latino comic book I have to understand how it is built—and how it might share some of its framing with the other visual and alphabetical arts, but that in the end it is its own particular beast. As you know, in a field like Latino studies, this has created some discomfort with some in the Latino scholarly community.

There's this sticky idea that somehow *form* is in and of itself ideological (Western, patriarchal, capitalist), and so any mention of *formal matters* alongside issues of style (lexicon and syntax) and content (characterization or representation, for instance) in an analysis of Latino cultural phenomena still ruffles feathers. To understand whatever slice of reality I choose to understand—and this happens to be literature, film, art, architecture (opera in your case), comic books, even video games—I need to spend the time and work acquiring a knowledge of the particular shape-giving devices used within that particular medium, for otherwise I'm not doing justice to my object of study. More importantly, this approach evaluates how *well* the object (discomforting or not) is put together and not because it comforts by being politically correct. I think it is this mind-set and approach that frees me to study whatever I want—in ways that evaluate the objects on their own terms and that lead to infinite surprises.

HL: As I look back at my long career, I find it hard to establish any unity of subject matter, for I've roamed over many periods, genres, media, and national traditions in the course of ten books. If there's anything holding them all together, it's been my desire to show how art reciprocally shapes and is shaped by the environment in which it is created. And I've always been drawn toward the darker, the pricklier aspects of art. This was especially true of my first three books, conceived and written in the 1950s and 1960s (could it be that I felt less serene than other folk in the overly optimistic America of those days?) My first book, *On Wordsworth's Prelude* (1963) examined this great long poem as a triumph over the darkness that had afflicted the poet and also the world of the French Revolution that he traversed as a young man. Although Wordsworth cheered up the Victorians more than any other poet, the good feeling that ultimately issues from his work was, I tried to show, pretty hard-earned. And after that I did two monographs on germanophone writers, the German dramatist Georg Büchner (1964) and the Austrian poet Georg Trakl (1971), whose writing was so uncompromisingly dark that it has never cheered anybody up.

FLA: Yes, you have been working formally on works that tend toward the darker and pricklier. Your recent work ventures here in an even more explicit way. I think of your book, *One Family's Shoah: Victimization, Resistance, Survival in Nazi Europe* (2013)—which focuses on a very discomforting subject: the Holocaust as woven in and through your family's painful experience of suffering and death. This must have brought up all sorts of emotions of repugnance and anger.

HL: In this respect the first part I wrote, a journal article on the death by guillotine of my first cousin, Hanni Lindenberger Meyer, proved the hardest to do. She was a member of the only Jewish resistance group in Germany, and much research has appeared in recent years on the group, called the Herbert-Baum group after its leader. One of the books on this group, by a German writer named Regina Scheer, described how the author's mother, as a medical student in Germany at the end of the war, was forced to do her anatomy carving on headless corpses, which turned out to be the preserved remains of the political prisoners whom the Nazis had guillotined. This was too much for me, and I nearly stopped writing the article. After all, I was close to Hanni's only sibling, who had immigrated to the United States in time and whom I considered virtually my own brother. But I felt this story needed to be told in a personal way that professional historians would never do, and that I needed to concentrate on the topic of whether her group's act of resistance—the firebombing of a Nazi exhibit—was heroic or foolish.

FLA: During a trip to Cuba after the revolution, Julio Cortázar told an audience of eager authors that they would need more distance (emotional and cognitive) on their subject (the revolution) in order to see the full array of devices that would give shape to their fictions. For Cortázar, they needed a lens of objectivity in order to learn about how the revolution took place—its development and consequences—to be re-created in their art.

HL: Yes, distance is the key. The only way I could deal with my family material—give shape to it—was to employ the method used by my daughter, a geriatrician who specializes in palliative care. She's learned to practice a form of compassionate care that allows her to keep a sufficient distance from her patients' distress so that she does not herself need to carry home an unbearable emotional load. This attitude worked for me so that I could finish the article and, three years later, after finishing another book, I determined to treat the fates of other relatives who had been caught in Nazi Europe. Indeed, I suspect that the distance I managed to create from the horrible material I was working on has been transferred to the way I approach the horror movies we discussed earlier.

FLA: Of course, there's much that we've left out in the arts that disquiet. We mentioned Jerome Robbins and Merce Cunningham in our earlier conversation on disquieting music. However, we haven't really touched on how bodies can be carefully choreographed to create sensations of discomfort. When I was a teenager, break dancing had become popular. I even tried my hand at a very watered-down version. In its most hardcore form it was particularly disturbing to watch as the dancers slammed their bodies onto concrete surfaces and twisted and contorted appendages to create new (monstrous, even) ways of perceiving the human physique.

Of course, there are other important aspects of dance that discomforts in need of exploration, including the neurobiological. I recall here a conversation between Mark Morris and the neuroscientist Bevil Conway that took place at the Rubin Museum of Art and that has been recorded and available to watch on YouTube (Morris and Conway). Morris shared how in the making of a music-free piece, his dancers could only move at either a fast or slow speed. Conway shared with Morris insights about how our brains encode and make meaning of only two units of movement at a time. When we watch a dance sequence, we register the movements in chunks of two movements. Our perceptual mechanisms can only process movement in these units of two, leaving that which we don't perceive to be gap-filled by our imagination that thus creates a gestalt *as if* there had been a seamless link between all the dance movements. While they don't discuss this directly, this insight seems to indicate that a choreographer who seeks to create distress and discomfort in the audience has his dancers move in ways that disallow the parsing of these chunks; that disallow our gap-filling activity; and that ultimately create discomfort by denying us the pleasure that comes with the meaning-making processes that take place as we apprehend art.

HL: There would be much to say, if we had the time and space to develop it, about the role of discomfort in ballet and dance. It works in a different way from the discomfort we have analyzed in other forms of art. Think, for example, of the precariousness we constantly experience in classical ballet. The most celebrated of these precarious moments is the Rose Adagio in *Sleeping Beauty*, in which the heroine turns a full circle on one foot as she bids farewell successively to four suitors in a handshake. The audience remains breathless for an agonizingly long period until Aurora has seen all her suitors off; if she manages the moves successfully, we feel considerable relief; and if she does not, our distress is almost as great as hers. Or, to shift to a totally different dance form, note the discomfort we are made to feel with Cunningham's group as the choreographer forces his dancers to stretch their bodies in often ungainly ways that contrast markedly with the graceful movements of classical ballet; to add even more discomfort, Cunningham, at the behest of his longtime music director, John Cage, refused to allow the music to coordinate in any way with the dancing. And it may well be that the discomfort of many Cunningham pieces, in contrast with the generally comforting work of Morris, comes from his refusing to give us what you earlier called the "gap-filling activity" that Morris practices in so compelling a way. Yes, we could go on and on to note how one choreographer after another—Balanchine, Forsythe, Morris, Wheeldon, Ratmansky—has stretched our capacity to encode new movements at the same time that he has stretched the bodies under his command. But perhaps no choreographer has been as discomforting as Pina Bausch, who had her dancers do things like spit water on one another's faces, grovel in mud, scream in pain, or have a female hit a male in his testicles.

FLA: We shall have to leave dance to the next book, Herbie. We've touched on many disquieting subjects and have drawn on several areas of research, including, of course, the advances in the cognitive and neurosciences to help increase our understanding of how disquieting subjects work in form and content. I wonder if we might keep in mind the remark on art generally that you make at the end of your essay "Arts in the Brain; or, What Might Neuroscience Tell Us?" about how neuroscience can enrich our understanding of "how we perceive, process, and enjoy art [more] than we suspected before" (34). You suggestively state that what we may learn from science might "affect the methods that we choose to exercise our interpretive and evaluative skills, and also, I might add, how we come to look at the various arts in relation to other reward-offering activities" (34).

HL: The more we learn about how our brains are processing the art we are consuming, the more conscious we become about how the arts can shape our lives. And I think that analyzing these processes helps us understand that art is not a trivial thing, a simple enjoyment that we can as well do without. And I hope that our conversation may work to encourage the more comfort-seeking consumers of art to be a bit more adventurous—among other things, to overcome their fears of discomfort. If you're always seeking comfort from art, you may well end up consuming and reconsuming the same artifacts repeatedly—to the point that ultimately you may lose the zest you once had to experience works of art. The tamer sort, when they venture out to see paintings, may limit a museum visit to Monet and his fellow impressionists while ignoring a big De Kooning show in the same building; if they attend opera, they'll opt for *La Bohème* or *Carmen* rather than take a chance on *The Abduction from the Seraglio,* let alone *Wozzeck;* when they decide to spend the afternoon with a novel, their longtime reading habits will send them back time and again to *Pride and Prejudice* and *The Great Gatsby* instead of encouraging them to take a jab at Beckett's *Molloy.*

FLA: Let's recall the Russian Formalists' concept of *ostranenie* as well as Rimbaud's and Baudelaire's declaration to *make new* in art. That is, always remaining within a comfort zone leads to a stagnation and lack of creativity. The artist's role is to create new objects in the world. But the artist and his or her work don't exist in a social void. They need the creativity of the audience (reader and viewer) with great force and urgency. Art is a relational activity: between the artist and what is fashioned anew in the world as well as between the audience and the art object. It can't exist without the creator of the art nor without the creativity of the audience. It demands on the part of the audience a certain amount of adventurousness—to take a certain distance from their comfort zone. If there is no creativity on the part of the audience, then the artist withers on the vine, so to speak. The artist needs the echo of the audience's creativity. When this relationship between the two creativities (artist and audience) is broken, there is a general stagnation in art. There's very little creativity in societies dominated by theology, for instance. There is little creativity in periods of history dominated by censorship.

HL: Artists should be free, indeed, encouraged, to create any and all kinds of art, including that which discomforts. And audiences should feel encouraged, as we have tried to do in these conversations, not to shy away from art that they fear might be upsetting.

FLA: Indeed, without such a global view of art that includes art that aims to discomfort we cripple any formulation of a general theory of aesthetics. As you suggested, perhaps this is a first step in sharing with the next generation an openness to the formal study of disquieting art.

Our sharing with the next generation should have a deliberate, clear-cut understanding of what those options carry in terms of those shape-giving devices we discussed that differently shape content, creating genres of discomfort within distinctively different aesthetic formats such as literature, film, comic books, art, music, architecture, and the like. Hence the importance of knowing the facts discovered by science, as well as *how* all sciences proceed in their explorations of reality. And the same with all the options that are included under the umbrella we call the humanities.

HL: When people are asked to defend the humanities, to argue for their supposed importance, they usually fall into platitudes that ignore the darker side of art. This was certainly true of the bland 2013 report on the humanities and social sciences, *The Heart of the Matter,* commissioned by the American Academy of Arts and Sciences to suggest a map for the future. It was done by one of those huge blue-ribbon committees motivated, I'm sure, by a need to compromise among varying constituencies together with a fear of offending the larger public. (By the time that academics reach blue-ribbon status, they usually have no more new ideas.) As I read the report, I thought of how I was chastised at the start of my career by my university chancellor for boasting that I wanted my freshmen to experience the discomfort inherent in *Othello.* To admit such things is to threaten a public that really wants to keep the humanities harmless and ultimately trivial—at best, perhaps, some form of unnecessary (though none too delicious) dessert.

FLA: Even though we have sometime disagreed in these conversations, we both felt strongly about the value of experiencing the darker sides of art.

HL: We've obviously had some disagreements along the way, even though we conceived this book as a series of conversations, not a debate.

FLA: Usually, a debate is considered to be a discussion where ideas and concepts on each side are fixed and do not move. The purpose is not to convince your interlocutor. The aim is using your best rhetorical means to disqualify the other's argument and thus to persuade and convince the audience of the greater value of your own positions.

In contrast, we see in our conversation the acknowledgment that we are two human beings with different kinds of knowledge and that in the true and honest *exchange* of ideas we seek to obtain a product that is superior, more informed in the encounter of these different ideas. I see our conversation on the aesthetics of discomfort very much as our seeking to make knowledge that is greater than the sum of its parts.

Furthermore, this exchange of ideas doesn't imply the renouncing of ideas. It doesn't imply therefore also the ironing out of disagreements. The disagreements are present, and help to enrich the final product.

HL: Frederick, you're much more of a theorist than I—a self-described Wittgensteinian—could ever aspire to be, though I find myself intrigued with your theory of the relationality in the relations between consumer and art object. Since I always want to relate any theory to some historical context, here I'd question how much your tempting theory is an expression of the intellectual ambiance within which we are now living—is this theory, for instance, a reaction to the one-sidedness we now see in reception-oriented or work-centered methods? As for some of our disagreements on individual works, have I convinced you on any of these matters, for example, our sharply differing opinions on International Style glass towers, or on the value of giving, say, Schoenberg and Cage a hearing?

FLA: Not exactly convinced, but I have certainly learned to appreciate the ways in which they discomfort. In a sense, you've helped me educate my own senses—and *sense of things*. This is to say, you've opened the possibility for my rational system to override the emotional system, allowing me to enjoy more my state of discomforts.

HL: I might as well confess that my wife shares your reaction to Schoenberg and Cage. If I listen to them, I do so alone on my earphones. But both these names, for most people, I suspect, have become icons for the most discomforting musical experiences—experiences they really don't want to have. Still, let's remember that regardless of how you or anybody react to his music, Cage still occupies a major place in the history of all the arts—I'd venture to say he was the seminal figure of the second half of the twentieth century, and in the visual arts and literature perhaps more than in music, which is the area librarians would classify him in. A few months before he died in 1992 I sponsored a week's visit of Cage to Stanford and I had ample opportunity to converse with him, or, more accurately, to listen to him converse.

It was clear that he had great ambitions to change the way we create and engage with art—and, above all, to stretch our comfort zones, or should I say, to stretch our discomfort zones? Whenever I go to museum shows of contemporary artists, particularly conceptual artists, I can see his spirit hovering over the show. His mission was always to shake things up.

FLA: Herbie, I'd like to end by celebrating both the making and consuming of discomforting art: yesterday, today—and tomorrow. I would like to invite the next generation of scholars to take up the baton and continue to deepen our understanding of this integral piece of the total aesthetic puzzle.

HL: More power to anybody willing to defy everyday pieties and look into what great art is really trying to tell us!

Works Cited

Ablinger, Peter. *Instruments and Noise* (1994–2011).

Abrams, M. H. "Structure and Style in the Greater Romantic Lyric." In *From Sensibility to Romanticism: Essays Presented to Frederick A. Pottle.* Ed. Frederick W. Hillis and Harold Bloom. New York: Oxford University Press, 1965. 527–60.

Adams, Eddie. Photo of a Vietnamese execution (1968).

Adams, John. *The Death of Klinghoffer* (1991).

Acosta, Oscar "Zeta." *The Autobiography of a Brown Buffalo.* New York: Vintage, 1989.

Adelman, Janet. *Blood Relations: Christian and Jew in "The Merchant of Venice".* Chicago: University of Chicago Press, 2008.

Adler, H. G. *The Journey.* Trans. Peter Filkins. New York: Modern Library, 2009.

Adorno, Theodor W. *Aesthetic Theory.* Trans. C. Lenhardt. London: Routledge, 1984.

Ai Weh Weh. *@Large: Ai Weh Weh on Alcatraz* (2014–15).

Aldama, Frederick Luis. *The Cinema of Robert Rodriguez.* Austin: University of Texas Press, 2014.

Aldama, Frederick Luis. *Why the Humanities Matter: A Common Sense Approach.* Austin: University of Texas Press, 2008.

Aldama, Frederick Luis. *Your Brain on Latino Comics: From Gus Arriola to Los Bros Hernandez.* Austin: University of Texas Press, 2009.

Aldama, Frederick Luis, and Patrick Colm Hogan. *Conversations on Cognitive Cultural Studies: Puzzling Out the Self.* Columbus: Ohio State University Press, 2014.

American Academy of Arts and Sciences. *The Heart of the Matter: The Humanities and Social Sciences for a Vibrant, Competitive, and Secure Nation.* Cambridge, MA: American Academy of Arts and Sciences, 2013.

Artusi, G. M., and Claudio Monteverdi. Controversy over the composer's style. In *Source Readings in Music History.* Selected and annotated by W. Oliver Strunk. New York: Norton, 1950. 393–415.

Arbus, Diane. *Identical Twins* (1967).

Arcimboldo, Giuseppe. *Vertumnus* (1590–91).

Aristotle. *Poetics.* In *Criticism: The Major Texts.* Ed. W. J. Bate. New York: Harcourt Brace. 19–39.

Associated Press. Dispatch, August 12, 1947. *Seattle Post-Intelligencer,* August 13, 1947.

Auerbach, Erich. *Mimesis: The Representation of Reality in Western Literature.* Trans. Willard R. Trask. Princeton: Princeton University Press, 1953.
Austen, Jane. *Emma* (1816).
Austen, Jane. *Pride and Prejudice* (1813).
Bacon, Francis. *Self-Portrait,* Musée Cantini (1976).
Barbusse, Henri. *Le Feu: Journal d'une Escouade* (1916).
Bascom, John. *Aesthetics; or The Science of Beauty.* New York: Putnam, 1886.
Bates, Mason. *Alternative Energy* (2012).
Baumgarten, Alexander Gottlieb. *Aesthetica* (1750).
Baumgartner, T., K. Lutz, C. F. Schmidt, and L. Jäncke, "The Emotional Power of Music: How Music Enhances the Feeling of Affective Pictures," *Brain Research* 1075, no. 1 (2006): 151–64.
Beckett, Samuel. Novel "trilogy": *Molloy* (1951); *Malone Dies* (1951); *The Unnamable* (1953).
Beethoven, Ludwig van. *Eroica* Symphony (1803).
Beethoven, Ludwig van. Ninth Symphony (1824).
Benigni, Robert, director. *Life Is Beautiful* (1997).
Berg, Alban. *Wozzeck* (1925).
Bizet, Georges. *Carmen* (1875).
Bosch, Hieronymus. *Garden of Earthly Delights* (circa 1490–1510).
Boulez, Pierre. *Le Marteau sans maître* (1953–55).
Browning, Tod, director. *Freaks* (1932).
Bruegel, Pieter. *Dulle Greet* (1562).
Bruegel, Pieter. *Triumph of Death* (circa 1562).
Bukowski, Charles. *Love Is a Dog from Hell: Poems 1974–1977.* Santa Barbara: Black Sparrow Press, 1977.
Bunge, Mario. *Philosophical Dictionary.* New York: Prometheus Books, 2003.
Buñuel, Luis, director. *Un Chien Andalou* (1929).
Buonarotti, Michelangelo. *David* (1501–4).
Burke, Edmund. *A Philosophical Enquiry into the Origin of Our Ideas of the Sublime and Beautiful.* Ed. J. T. Boulton. London: Routledge and K. Paul, 1958.
Burke, Gregory. *Black Watch* (2006).
Burnett, Victoria. "Museo Jumox Cancels a Hermann Nitsch Show." *New York Times,* February 24, 2015, Art and Design section. http://www.nytimes.com/2015/02/25/arts/design/museo-jumex-cancels-a-hermann-nitsch-show.html?_r=0
Cage, John. *Europeras* (1987).
Cage, John. *4′33″* (1952).
Cage, John. *Nocturne* (1945–50).
Cage, John. Percussion pieces (1939–43).
Cage, John. *Sonatas and Interludes for Prepared Piano* (1946–48).
Carpenter, Alexander. "Schoenberg's Vienna, Freud's Vienna: Re-examining the Connections between the Monodrama *Erwartung* and the Early History of Psychoanalysis." *Musical Quarterly* 93 (2010): 144–81.
Caterson and Clark, architects. Stanford Family Mausoleum, Palo Alto, CA (1888).
Cellini, Benvenuto. *Perseus with the Head of Medusa* (1545).

Chapman, Jake, and Dinos Chapman. *Piggyback* (2010).
Cheval, Ferdinand, architect. *Le Palais idéal,* Hauterives, France (1879–1912).
Chicago, Judy. *The Dinner Party* (1974–79).
Cimini, Giacomo, director. *Red Riding Hood* (2003).
Coleridge, Samuel Taylor. "Frost at Midnight" (1798).
Courbet, Gustave. *L'Origine du monde* (1866).
Danto, Arthur. *The Transfiguration of the Commonplace.* Cambridge, MA: Harvard University Press, 1981.
Debussy, Claude. *Pelléas et Mélisande* (1902).
Descartes, René. *The Passions of the Soul* (1649). Trans. Stephen Voss. Indianapolis: Hackett, 1989.
Diller Scofidio + Renfro, architects. McMurtry Art Building, Stanford University (2015).
Disney, Walt, producer. *Fantasia* (1940).
Dix, Otto. *The War* (1924).
Duchamp, Marcel. *Bicycle Wheel* (1913).
Eco, Umberto. *The Open Work.* Cambridge, MA: Harvard University Press, 1989.
Eichler, Joseph, developer. Eichler Homes (1950–74).
Eliot, George. *Middlemarch* (1872).
Eliot, T. S. *Four Quartets* (1943).
Eliot, T. S. *The Waste Land (1922).*
Faulkner, William. *Sanctuary* (1931).
Fitzgerald, Scott. *The Great Gatsby* (1925).
Flaubert, Gustave. *Madame Bovary* (1856).
Foucault, Michel. *The Order of Things: An Archaeology of the Human Sciences.* New York, Random House, 1970.
Frazer, Sir James. *The Golden Bough: A Study in Magic and Religion* (1890).
Freed, James Ingo, architect. U.S. Holocaust Museum, Washington, DC (1993).
García Márquez, Gabriel. *The Incredible Sad Story of Innocent Eréndira and Her Heartless Grandmother* (1972).
Gaudí, Antoni. Casa Batlló, Barcelona (1904).
Gaudí, Antoni, architect. La Sagrada Família, Barcelona (1883–).
Gehry, Frank O., architect. EMP Museum, Seattle (2000).
Gehry, Frank O., architect. Guggenheim Museum, Bilbao (1997).
Gilman, Sander. *Jewish Self-Hatred: Anti-Semitism and the Hidden Language of the Jews.* Baltimore: Johns Hopkins University Press, 1986.
Giotto. *Last Judgment* (circa 1305).
Gober, Robert. *Long-Haired Cheese* (1992–93).
Gombrich, E. H. *Art and Illusion: A Study in the Psychology of Pictorial Representation.* New York: Pantheon, 1960.
Gómez-Peña, Guillermo. *El Mexterminator* (1998).
Góngora, Luis de. *La Fábula de Polifemo y Galatea* (1613).
Goya, Francisco. "Black Paintings" (circa 1819–23).
Goya, Francisco. *Charles IV and His Family* (circa 1800)
Goya, Francisco. *Disasters of War* (1810–20).
Goya, Francisco. *Saturn Devouring His Children* (1820–23).

Greenway, Peter, director. *The Cook, the Thief, the Wife & Her Lover* (1989).
Greenway, Peter, director. *Prospero's Books* (1991).
Haneke, Michael, director. *Amour* (2012).
Haneke, Michael, director. *Caché* (2005).
Haneke, Michael, director. *Funny Games* (1997).
Haneke, Michael, director. *The Piano Teacher* (2001).
Haneke, Michael, director. *The White Ribbon* (2009).
Haydn, Joseph. *"Surprise"* Symphony (1791).
Hirst, Damien. *A Thousand Years* (1990).
Hirst, Damien, and Gordon Burn. *On the Way to Work*. [New York]: Universe, [2002].
Hitchcock, Alfred, director. *Psycho* (1960).
Hobbes, Thomas. *Leviathan* (1651).
Hoffmann, E. T. A. *Kreisleriana* (1814).
Hoover Associates, architects. Stanford Law School Residences (2007).
Howells, John Mead, and Raymond Hood, architects. Tribune Tower, Chicago (1925).
Hutcheon, Linda. *A Theory of Parody: The Teachings of Twentieth-Century Art Forms*. New York: Methuen, 1985.
Iñarritu, Alejandro Gonzalez. *Biutiful* (2010).
Ionesco, Eugène. *The Lesson* (1950).
Isaacson, Walter. *Steve Jobs*. New York: Simon and Schuster, 2011.
Jelinek, Elfriede. *The Piano Teacher*. Trans. Joachim Neugroschel. New York: Weidenfeld and Nicolson, 1988.
Jennings, Shawn, director. *"Red" Red Riding Hood* (2008).
Johnson, Philip, architect. "Glass House," New Canaan, CT (1949–95).
Joyce, James. *Finnegans Wake* (1939).
Joyce, James. *Ulysses*. Ed. Hans Walter Gabler. Harmondsworth: Penguin, 1986.
Kant, Immanuel. *Critique of Judgment*. Trans. Werner S. Pluhar. Indianapolis: Hackett, 1987.
Kim, Sue J. *On Anger: Race, Cognition, Narrative*. Austin, TX: University of Texas, 2013.
Kolnai, Aurel. "The Standard Modes of Aversion: Fear, Disgust and Hatred." *Mind* 107 (July 1998): 581–95.
Kooning, Willem de. *Woman I* (1950–52).
Korine, Harmony, director. *Gummo* (1997).
Korine, Harmony, director. *Spring Breakers* (2013).
Korsmeyer, Carolyn. *Savoring Disgust: The Foul and the Fair in Aesthetics*. New York: Oxford University Press, 2011.
Kovat, Tania. *Virgin in a Condom* (1994).
Kristeva, Julia. *Horror: An Essay in Abjection*. New York: Columbia University Press, 1980.
Kubrick, Stanley, director. *A Clockwork Orange* (1971).
Kubrick, Stanley, director. *2001: A Space Odyssey* (1968).
Kubrick, Stanley, director. *The Shining* (1980).

Kureishi, Hanif. "Tale of a Turd." In *Love in a Blue Time*. London: Faber and Faber, 1998.
Kureishi, Hanif. "The Penis." In *Midnight All Day*. London: Faber and Faber, 2000.
Lanzmann, Claude, director. *Shoah* (1985).
Lahauri, Ustad Ahmad, chief architect. Taj Mahal, Agra, India (1632–53).
Lawrence, D. H. *Lady Chatterley's Lover* (1928).
Levitin, Daniel J. *This Is Your Brain on Music: The Science of a Human Obsession*. New York: Dutton, 2006.
Libeskind, Daniel, architect. Jewish Museum, Berlin (2001).
Libeskind, Daniel, architect. World Trade Center design (2003).
Lindenberger, Herbert. "Arts in the Brain; Or, What Might Neuroscience Tell Us?" In *Toward a Theory of Narrative Acts*. Ed. Frederick Luis Aldama. Austin: University of Texas Press, 2010. 13–35.
Lindenberger, Herbert. *Georg Büchner*. Carbondale: Southern Illinois University Press, 1964.
Lindenberger, Herbert. *Georg Trakl*. New York: Twayne, 1971.
Lindenberger, Herbert. "Literature and the Other Arts." In *The Cambridge History of Criticism*, vol. 5: *Romanticism*. Ed. Marshall Brown. Cambridge: Cambridge University Press, 2000. 362–86.
Lindenberger, Herbert. *On Wordsworth's "Prelude"*. Princeton: Princeton University Press, 1963.
Lindenberger, Herbert. *One Family's Shoah: Victimization, Resistance, Survival in Nazi Europe*. New York: Palgrave, 2013.
Lindenberger, Herbert. *Opera in History: From Monteverdi to Cage*. Stanford: Stanford University Press, 1998.
Lindenberger, Herbert. *Situating Opera: Period, Genre, Reception*. Cambridge: Cambridge University Press, 2010.
Loos, Adolf, architect. Josephine Baker House (unbuilt, designed 1927).
Loos, Adolf, architect. Looshaus, Michaelerplatz, Vienna (1910).
Loos, Adolf. *Ornament and Crime: Selected Essays*. Ed. Adolf Opel. Riverside, CA: Ariadne Press, 1998.
Loos, Adolf, architect. Tribune Tower design (unbuilt, designed 1923).
Lynch, David, director. *Eraserhead* (1977).
Macedo, Miguel S., designer. Palacio de Lecumberri, Mexico City (1900).
Machaty, Gustav. *Ecstasy* (1933).
Mahler, Gustav. Ninth Symphony (1909–10).
Mann, Thomas. *Tristan* (1903).
Manzoni, Piero. *Merda d'artista* (1961).
Mapplethorpe, Robert. Exhibition of photography, Berkeley Art Museum (1989).
Massey, Irving. *The Neural Imagination: Aesthetic and Neuroscientific Approaches to the Arts*. Austin: University of Texas Press, 2009.
McGinn, Colin. *The Meaning of Disgust*. New York: Oxford University Press, 2011.
Mendes, Sam, director. *Skyfall* (2012).

Menninghaus, Winfried. *Disgust: Theory and History of a Strong Sensation*. Trans. Howard Eiland and Joel Golb. Albany: SUNY Press, 2003.
Merhige, E. Elias, director. *Begotten* (1990).
Messerschmidt, Franz Xaver. *An Intentional Jester* (after 1770).
Messiaen, Olivier. *Saint François d'Assise* (1983).
Meyer, Leonard B. *Emotion and Meaning in Music*. Chicago: University of Chicago Press, 1956.
Mies van der Rohe, Ludwig, architect. Seagram Building, New York (1959).
Miller, Susan B. *Disgust: The Gatekeeper Emotion*. Hillsdale, NJ: Analytic Press, 2004.
Miller, William. *The Anatomy of Disgust*. Cambridge, MA: Harvard University Press, 1997.
Monroe, Steven R., director. *I Spit on Your Grave* (2010).
Morris, Mark, and Bevil Conway. "Why Does Movement Move Us?" Rubin Museum of Art. February 17, 2010. https://www.youtube.com/watch?v=dVKSNLYt66w
Monteverdi, Claudio. *Lamento d'Arianna* (1608; 1614; 1640).
Mozart, W. A. *The Abduction from the Seraglio* (1782).
Munch, Edvard. *The Scream* (pastel version, 1895).
Nabokov, Vladimir. *Lolita* (1955).
Nericcio, William. *Tex[t]-Mex: Seductive Hallucinations of the "Mexican" in America*. Austin: University of Texas Press, 2007.
Ngai, Sianne. *Our Aesthetic Categories: Zany, Cute, Interesting*. Cambridge, MA: Harvard University Press, 2012.
Ngai, Sianne. *Ugly Feelings*. Cambridge, MA: Harvard University Press, 2005.
Noé, Gaspar, director. *Irreversible* (2002).
Olmos, Edward James, director. *American Me* (1992).
Orozco, Gabriel. *Asterisms* (2012–13).
Ortiz, Fernando. *Cuban Counterpoint: Tobacco and Sugar*. 1940; Durham: Duke University Press, 1995.
Oshima, Nagisa, director. *In the Realm of the Senses* (1976).
Plato. *The Republic*. In *The Dialogues of Plato*. Trans. Benjamin Jowett. 2 vols. New York: Random House, 1937. 1:591–879.
Palahniuk, Chuck. "Guts" (2004).
Pasolini, Pablo, director. *Salò, or 120 Days of Sodom* (1975).
Philipon, Charles. *La Poire* (1831).
Picasso, Pablo. *Les Demoiselles d'Avignon* (1907).
Picasso, Pablo. *Nude with Joined Hands (Fernande)* (1906).
Picasso, Pablo. *Woman with Pears (Fernande)* (1909).
Plath, Sylvia. "Daddy" (1962).
Poe, Edgar Allan. "The Raven" (1845).
Polanski, Roman, director. *The Pianist* (2002).
Polshek, James, architect. Cantor Arts Center addition, Stanford University (1999).
Povoledo, Elisabetta. "Italian Museum Removes a Sculpture by Chapmans after Children's Group Complains." *New York Times*, August 11, 2014, Arts section.

Puccini, Giacomo. *La Bohème* (1896).
Rabelais, François. *Gargantua and Pantagruel*. New York: Norton, 1990.
Radcliffe, Ann. *The Mysteries of Udolpho*. New York: Juniper Press, n.d.
Ramachandran, V. S. *A Brief Tour of Human Consciousness: From Imposter Poodles to Purple Numbers*. New York: Pi Press, 2004.
Ramsay, Lynne. *We Need to Talk about Kevin* (2011).
Reinhardt, Ad. "Black" paintings (circa 1955–67).
Remarque, Erich Maria. *All Quiet on the Western Front* (1929).
Resnais, Alain, director. *Nuit et brouillard / Night and Fog* (1955).
Riefenstahl, Leni, director. *Triumph of the Will* (1934).
Ritts, Herb. *Djimon Hounsou with Octopus, Hollywood 1989*.
Rodriguez, Robert. *From Dusk Till Dawn* (1996).
Rosenkranz, Karl. *Aesthetik des Häßlichen / The Aesthetics of Ugliness* (1853).
Rossini, Giaochino. *The Barber of Seville* (1816).
Roth, Philip. *Portnoy's Complaint*. New York: Random House, 1969.
Roth, Philip. *Sabbath's Theater* (1995).
Rousseau, Jean Jacques. *Confessions* (1765–67). Trans. J. M. Cohen. Harmondsworth: Penguin, 1971.
Rousseau, Jean Jacques. *Reveries of a Solitary Walker* (1776–78). Trans. Peter France. Harmondsworth: Penguin, 1987.
Russolo, Luigi. *Art of Noises* (1913).
Ryman, Robert. "White" paintings (1960s–).
Sacks, Oliver. *Musicophilia*. New York: Knopf, 2007.
Sade, Marquis de. *The 120 Days of Sodom*. New York: Arrow Books, 1990.
Santiago, Wilfred. *In My Darkest Hour*. Seattle: Fantagraphic Books, 2004.
Sargant, William. *Battle for the Mind*. Westport, CT: Greenwood Press, 1973.
Scheer, Regina. *Im Schatten der Sterne: Eine jüdische Widerstandsgruppe*. Berlin: Aufbau-Verlag, 2004.
Schiele, Egon. *The One Contemplated in Dreams* (1911).
Schoenberg, Arnold. *Erwartung* (1909).
Schoenberg, Arnold. *Gaze* (1910).
Schoenberg, Arnold. *Moses und Aron* (1930–32).
Schoenberg, Arnold. Piano pieces (1909–early 1920s).
Schoenberg, Arnold. *Transfigured Night* (1899).
Sejima, Kazuyu, and Ryue Nishizawa, architects. New Museum of Contemporary Art, New York (2007).
Serrano, Andres. *Piss Christ* (1987).
Shakespeare, William. *Hamlet*. 2nd ed. Ed. Cyrus Hoy. Norton Critical Ed. New York: Norton, 1992.
Shakespeare, William. *King Lear*. Ed. Kenneth Muir. Arden ed. London: Methuen, 1969.
Shakespeare, William. *Othello*. Ed. M. R. Ridley. Arden ed. London: Methuen, 1969.
Shakespeare, William. *Titus Andronicus*. Ed. J. C. Maxwell. Arden ed. London: Methuen, 1968.
Shakespeare, William. *Twelfth Night*. Ed. J. M. Lothian and T. W. Craik. Arden ed. London: Methuen, 1975.

Shakespeare, William. *The Winter's Tale.* Ed. J. H. P. Pafford. Arden ed. London: Methuen, 1968.
Shalamov, Varlam. *Kolyma Tales* (1954–73).
Shepley, Rutan and Coolidge, architects. Stanford University Quad (1887–91).
Shklovsky, Viktor. *Theory of Prose*. Trans. Benjamin Sher. Elmwood Park, IL: Dalkey Archive Press, 1990.
Six, Tom. *The Human Centipede* (2009).
Slade, David. *Hard Candy* (2005).
Solondz, Todd. *Happiness* (1998).
Spiegelman, Art. *Maus: A Survivor's Tale*. New York: Pantheon Books, 1991.
Spielberg, Steven, director. *Schindler's List* (1993).
Spitzer, Leo. *Representative Essays*. Ed. Alban K. Forcione, Herbert Lindenberger, and Madeline Sutherland. Stanford: Stanford University Press, 1988.
Stavans, Ilan, and Frederick Luis Aldama. *Laughing Matters: Conversations on Humor.* San Diego: San Diego State University Press, 2015.
Stein, Gertrude. "Susie Asado" (1912).
Stevenson, Robert Louis. *Dr. Jekyll and Mr. Hide* (1886).
Stoker, Bram. *Dracula* (1897).
Stravinsky, Igor. *Rite of Spring* (1913).
Sullivan, Louis, architect. Wainwright tomb, St. Louis, MO (1892).
Sutter, Kurt, creator. *Sons of Anarchy* (2008–14).
Suvero, Mark di. *Huru* (1984–85).
Takashi, Miike, director. *Audition* (1999).
Tarantino, Quentin, director. *Django Unchained* (2012).
Tarantino, Quentin, director. *Hostel* (2005).
Taymor, Julie, director. *Titus* (1999).
Tolamacheva, Katya. "Barbed Wire and Building" (2013).
Tolstoy, Leo. *What Is Art?* (1896).
Trakl, Georg. "Sebastian im Traum: Für Adolf Loos." In *Dichtungen und Briefe.* Ed. Walther Killy and Hans Szklenar. 2 vols. Salzburg: Otto Müller Verlag, 1969. 1:88–90.
Trier, Lars von, director. *Antichrist* (2009).
Trier, Lars von, director. *Dogville* (2003).
Tschaikovsky, Pyotr Ilyich. *Pathétique* Symphony (1893).
van Fossen, Theodore, architect. Rush Creek, Worthington, OH (begun 1956).
Varèse, Edgar. *Déserts* (1954).
Vargas Llosa, Mario. *Los cuadernos de don Rigoberto / Notebooks of Don Rigoberto* (1997).
Vargas Llosa, Mario. *Elogio de la madrastra / In Praise of the Stepmother* (1988)
Velázquez, Diego. *Las Meninas* (1656).
Velázquez, Diego. *Surrender at Breda* (1635).
Vogel, Fred. *August Underground* (2001).
Wagner, Richard. *Der fliegende Holländer* (1843).
Wagner, Richard. *Parsifal* (1882).
Wagner, Richard. *Der Ring des Nibelungen* (1851–76).
Wagner, Richard. *Tristan und Isolde* (1859).

Warhol, Andy. *Brillo-Box* (1964).
West, Benjamin. *Death of General Wolfe* (1770).
Wicker, Bruno, Christian Keysers, Jane Plailly, Jean-Pierre Royet, Vittorio Gallese, and Giacomo Rizzolatti, "Both of Us Disgusted in My Insula: The Common Neural Basis of Seeing and Feeling Disgust," *Neuron* 40.3 (October 2003): 655–64.
Wilson, Robert. *The Black Rider* (1990).
Wordsworth, William. "Tintern Abbey" (1798).
Wright, Frank Lloyd, architect. Fallingwater, Stewart Township, PA (1936).
Wright, Frank Lloyd, architect. Guggenheim Museum, New York (1959).
Wright, Frank Lloyd, architect. Hanna house, Palo Alto, CA (1937).
Wright, Frank Lloyd, architect. Taliesin West, Scottsdale, AZ (1938).
Yeats, William Butler. "Leda and the Swan" (1924).
Zappa, Frank. "Trouble Every Day" (1965).
Zarchi, Meir, director. *I Spit on Your Grave* (1978).
Zeki, Semir. *Inner Vision: An Exploration of Art and the Brain.* Oxford: Oxford University Press, 1999.

Index

Page numbers in italics indicate figures.

Ablinger, Peter: *Instruments and Noise*, 105
Abrams, M. H., 22
Acosta, Oscar "Zeta," *The Autobiography of the Brown Buffalo*, 2, 46–47
Adams, Eddie, *152*
Adams, John, 99; *The Death of Klinghoffer*, 116
Adelman, Janet, 50–51
Adès, Thomas, 111
Adler, H. G.: *The Journey*, 44–45, 55
Adorno, 105
aesthetic relation, 64, 119–20, 141, 142; Aristotle, 19; audiences, 33, 34, 140, 152; buildings, 61, 63, 65; hierarchies of value, 40–42, 136; with humans, 17, 19, 22; institutional space, 145; Kant, 21; in nature, 19, 21; with an object, 22, 65, 120, 127, 140, 159; photographs, 152, 154; Plato, 19; sonata form, 24; with subject, 9, 19
aesthetic concepts, 18
aesthetic theory, 5, 10
aesthetic shape, 10, 14, 44
Ai Weh Weh, 66
ambiguity, 168–69, 170
American Academy of Arts and Sciences: *The Heart of the Matter*, 187
anti-Western, 16
Antonioni, Michelangelo, 155
Arbus, Diane, 121, 153–54
Arcimboldo, Guiseppe, 7, 131; *Vertumnus*, 127–28
Aristotle: aesthetics, 19; theory of catharsis, 16, 23, 25
Artusi, G. M., 24, 93
atonal, 23, 105, 115
Auerbach, Erich, 16
Auschwitz, 44, 87
Austen, Jane, 44, 46; *Pride and Prejudice*, 186
Avedon, Richard, 154

Bachelard, Gaston, 72
Bacon, Francis, 3–4, 147; *Self-Portrait*, *148*
Baker, Josephine, 74
Barbusse, Henri: *Le Feu*, 55
Bates, Mason, 139; *Alternative Energy*, 115
Baumgarten, Alexander Gottlieb, 62; *Aesthetics*, 17
beauty in nature, 21
Beckett, 29, 51; *Molloy*, 186
Beethoven, Ludwig von: *Eroica Symphony*, 24; Ninth Symphony, 113
Bellefontaine, 59, 64
Benigni, Robert: *Life Is Beautiful*, 164
Berg, Alban, 105; *Wozzeck*, 186
Berlin Jewish Museum, 86, 87, *87*
Bizet, Georges: *Carmen*, 185
Borges, Jorge Luis, 9–10
Bergoff, Pearl, 179
boredom, 5, 12, 13, 29–30, 46, 51
Bosch, Hieronymus, 131; *Garden of Earthly Delights*, *132*, *133*, *134*, 153
Boulez, Pierre, 105, 108; *Le Marteau sans maître*, 104

Braque, Georges, 12
Brecht, Bertolt, 110, 163
Breuer, Josef: *Studies in Hysteria*, 108
Brothers Grimm: *Little Red Riding Hood*, 43
Browning, Tod: *Freaks*, 164
Bruegel, Peter: *Dulle Griet*, 131; *Triumph of Death*, 131
Büchner, Georg, 182
Bukowski, Charles, 52–53, 78
Bunge, Mario, 18
Buñuel, Luis: *Un Chien Andalou*, 164
Burke, Edmund, 27, 67
Burke, Gregory: *Black Watch*, 38

Cage, John, 7, 29, 41, 42, 106, 112, 115, 116, 136, 186, 188; *4′33″*, 28, 29, 105, 113; *Europeras*, 113; *Nocturne*, 113; *Sonatas and Interludes for Prepared Piano*, 113
Caterson and Clark: Stanford Family Mausoleum *60*
catharsis, 26, 157; theory of Aristotle 16, 23, 25
Cellini, Benvenuto, 26, 97
cemetery art, 59
Chapman, Dinos: *Piggyback*, 3
Chapman, Jake: *Piggyback*, 3
Cheval, Ferdiand "Le Facteur," 67, 85, *86*, 91
Chicago, Judy: *The Dinner Party*, 39
Chicago Tribune Tower, 90
Cimini, Giacomo: *Red Riding Hood*, 44
Coleridge, Samuel Taylor: "Frost at Midnight," 22
Conway, Bevil, 184
Courbet, Gustave: *L'Origine du monde*, 39, 40, 149, 150
cringing, 5, 6–7, 48, 129

Dalí, Salvador, 2, 47, 131; *Un Chien Andalou*, 164
Danto, Arthur, 34
Debussy, Claude: *Pelléas et Mélisande*, 29, 30, 51, 99
de Sade, Marquis, 65; *120 Days of Sodom*, 46, 51, 177
Descartes, René: *Passions of the Soul*, 18
Diller Scofidio + Renfro, 84
Disney, Walt: *Fantasia*, 32
Disney building, 88
displeasure, 16, 17
Dix, Otto, 150; *The War*, 142, *143*; *Wounded Man*, *143*
Duchamp, Marcel, 106, 140

Eco, Umberto, 169
Eichler, Joseph, 62, 65, 84
Eliot, George, 34
Eliot, T. S., *Four Quartets*, 98; *The Waste Land*, 165

Faulkner, William, 55; *Sanctuary*, 56
FID. *See* free indirect discourse
Fitzgerald, Scott: *The Great Gatsby*, 186
Flaubert, Gustave: *Madame Bovary*, 46
Foucault, Michel, 121, 122
Frazer, James, 165
free indirect discourse (FID), 10, 44, 45–46, 55, 181
Freud, Sigmund: *Freud Reader*, 72; *Studies in Hysteria*, 108; "Three Essays on the Theory of Sexuality," 2

García Márquez, Gabriel: The Incredible Sad Story of Innocent Eréndira and Her Heartless Grandmother, 55
Gates, Bill, 84
Gaudí, Antoni, 67, 77; Casa Batló, *78*; Sagrada Familia, 77
Gehry, Frank O., 63, 81; EMP rock museum building, 68
Gesualdo, Carlo, 10, 31
Gilman, Sander, 37
Giotto, 136; *Last Judgment*, 133, *135*
Glass House, 89, *90*
Gober, Robert, 7
Gombrich, Ernst: *Art and Illusion*, 95–96
Gómez-Peña, Guillermo: *Mexterminator*, 29

Góngora, Luis de: *Polifemo*, 10; *Soledades*, 10
Goya, Francisco: Black Paintings, 124; *Charles IV and His Family*, *122*; *Disasters of War*, 141; *Saturn Devouring His Children*, 124, *125*
Greenway, Peter: *The Cook, the Thief, the Wife & Her Lover*, 158; *Prospero's Books*, 158
Guggenheim, 75; Bilbao, 68

Haneke, Michael: *Amour*, 163; *Caché*, 163; *Funny Games*, 26, 162, 163; *The Piano Teacher*, 23, 156, 163, 164–65; *The White Ribbon*, 163
Haydn, Joseph, 101; *"Surprise" Symphony*, 24
Hays Office Code, 176, 177
Hewlett, Bill, 84
Hirst, Damien, 4, 42, 145, 177; *A Thousand Years*, 142–43, *144*
Hitchcock, Alfred: *Psycho*, 14, 67, 159, 160
Hobbes, Thomas, 51–52; *Leviathan*, 52
Hoffmann, E. T. A.: *Kreileriana*, 100
Hood, Raymond, 90
Hoover Associates, 83, *83*
horror film, 13, 14, 43, 67, 155, 156, 158, 163, 164, 165, 167, 169, 171, 172, 173, 175, 177, 180
Howells, John Mead, 90
Humanities & Cognitive Sciences High School Summer Institute, 36
hypnosis, 29, 99

Iñárritu, Alejandro González: *Biutiful*, 38
Ionesco, Eugène: *The Lesson*, 163
institutional space, 145
Iron Butterfly: "In-A-Gadda-Da-Vida," 98
Iser, Wolfgang, 17

Jelinek, Elfriede: *The Piano Teacher*, 23, 156, 181
Jennings, Shawn: *"Red" Red Riding Hood*, 44
Jobs, Steve, 84
Johnson, Philip, 89; Glass House, *90*
Johnson, Samuel, 51
Joyce, James, 9, 53; *Finnegans Wake*, 31, 32; *Ulysses*, 38, 47

Kahlo, Frida, 26, 109
Kant, Immanuel, 11, 21, 26–27, 62–63, 67; sublime, 16, 64
Kazuyo Sejima + Ryue Nishizawa: New Museum of Contemporary Art, New York, *70*
Kim, Sue J.: *On Anger*, 35
Kolnai, Aurel: "The Standard Modes of Aversion," 7–8
Kooning, Willem de: Woman, 147; *Woman I*, *149*
Korine, Harmony: *Gummo*, 168; *Spring Breakers*, 168
Korsmeyer, Carolyn, 3–4, 8
Kovat, Tania: *Virgin in a Condom*, 142
Kristeva, Julia: *Horror*, 6
Kubrick, Stanley: *2001*, 166; *A Clockwork Orange*, 165–66, *166*; *The Shining*, 165
Kunsthaus Graz, 68
Kureishi, Hanif: "The Penis," 48–49; "The Tale of the Turd," 46–47

Lanzmann, Claude: *Shoah*, 164
Lawrence, D. H.: *Lady Chatterley's Lover*, 175–76, 180
Lessing, Erich, 11, *86*, *118*
Levitin, Daniel J., 107, 112
Libeskind, Daniel, 81, 86; Jewish Museum, *87*
Lindenberger, Herbert: *One Family's Shoah*, 182; *On Wordsworth's Prelude*, 182
Loos, Adolf, 67, 74, 77, 90; Looshaus, 68, 72, 73, *73*; Tristan Tzara house, 72
Lynch, David: *Eraserhead*, 174

Machaty, Gustav: *Ecstasy*, 176
Mahler, Gustav, 42; Ninth Symphony, 25–26
making new, 5, 12, 122, 136, 142, 186
Malaparte, Curzio Merced: *Caput*, 55; *The Skin*, 55

Mann, Thomas: *Tristan*, 131
Manzoni, Piero: *Artist's Shit*, 36
Mapplethorpe, Robert, 32–33, 141, 145, 153, 154, 176
Massey, Irving: *The Neural Imagination*, 35
masturbation, 55, 165
McGinn, Colin, 5
McMurtry, Burt, 84
McMurtry, Deedee, 84
Mendes, Sam: *Skyfall*, 38
Menninghaus, Winfried, 8; *Ekel*, 11
Merhige, E. Elias: *Begotten*, 165
Messerschmidt, Franz Xaver, 117, 120; *Global Death and Destruction*, 119; *An Intentional Jester*, *118*
Messiaen, Olivier: *Saint François d'Assise*, 30
Meyer, Hanni Lindenberger, 183
Meyer, Leonard B.: *Emotion and Meaning in Music*, 96
Michelangelo, 93; David, 97
Mies van der Rohe, Ludwig 67; Seagram Building, 88, *89*
Miller, Henry, 55
Miller, Susan B., 8; *Disgust*, 3
Miller, William, 8; *The Anatomy of Disgust*, 3, 5–6
mirror-neuron system, 40
Monroe, Steven: *I Spit on Your Grave*, 171–72
Monteverdi, Claudio, 93; *Lamento d'Arianna*, 24
Morris, Mark, 184, 185
Mozart, W. A. 99, 101, 114, 186
Munch, Edvard: *The Scream*, 78, 79, 124, 127, 137
Museum of Modern Art (MoMA), 7, 28, 30, 78, 119, 129

Nabokov, Vladimir: *Lolita*, 56
Nazi death camps, 44, 86–87
negative emotions, 7, 25, 28,40, 116
New Critics, 17
New Museum of Contemporary Art on the New York Bowery, 69, *70*
Ngai, Sianne: *Ugly Feelings*, 181
Niemeyer, Oscar, 69–70
Nin, Anaïs, 55
Nishizawa, Ryue, *70*
Noé, Gaspar: *Irreversible*, 172

Olmos, Edward James: *American Me*, 175
Ortiz, Fernando: *Cuban Counterpoint*, 103
Oshima, Nagisa: *In the Realm of the Senses*, 176

Packard, Dave, 84
Palahniuk, Chuck: "Guts," 55
Pasolini, Pablo, 9; *Salò*, 4–5, 27, 46, 61, 161, 162, 177
Picasso, Pablo: *Guernica*, 13; *Les Demoiselles d'Avignon*, 10, 13, 32, 129, *130*; *Nude with Joined Palms*, *127*; *Woman with Pears* (*Fernande*), *126*
Plath, Sylvia: "Daddy," 8
Plato, 18, 19, 94
Poe, Edgar Allan, 99, 56, 99; "The Raven," 46
Polanski, Roman: *The Pianist*, 164
Polshek, James, 84
pre-Renaissance, 12
Puccini, Giacomo: *La Bohème*, 185
pyramids: Chichín-Itzá, 88; Egyptian, 59; Taj Mahal, 59

Rabelais, François, 2, 9, 16, 37, 53; *Gargantua and Pantagruel*, 14, 37, 52, 129
Radcliffe, Ann: The Mysteries of Udolpho, 157
Ramachandran, V. S., 35, 117
Ramsay, Lynne: We Need to Talk about Kevin,174
Rauschenberg, Robert: White Painting, 28, 136–37
reader-response formulations, 17
reception theory, 17
Reinhardt, Ad, 12, 13, 15
Remarque, Erich Maria: All Quiet on the Western Front, 55

repulsion, 2, 3, 65
Resnais, Alain: Nuit et brouillard/ Night and Fog, 163–64
Riefenstahl, Leni: Triumph of the Will, 121
Ritts, Herb, 153, 154; Djimon Hounsou, 153
Rodriguez, Robert, 96, 174, 181; From Dusk Till Dawn, 173
Rossini, Giaochino, 113
Roth, Philip: Portnoy's Complaint, 46, 55; Sabbath's Theatre, 55
Rousseau, Jean Jacques: Confessions, 38–39, 40; Reveries of a Solitary Walker, 22–23
Rudolf II, 128, *128*
Russolo, Luigi: Art of Noises, 106
Ryman, Robert, 13

Sacks, Oliver, 40
Sade, Marquis de, 5, 53, 161; castle, 65; *The 120 Days of Sodom*, 4, 46, 51–52, 177
Santiago, Wilfred, 181; *In My Darkest Hour*, 53, *54*
Sargant, William, 99; *Battle for the Mind*, 121
Scheer, Regina, 183
Schiele, Egon: *Die Traum Beschaute* (*The Woman Seen in a Dream*), 149–50, *151*
Schoenberg, Arnold, 26, 94, 102, 105, 115, 116, 188; *Erwartung*, 10, 23, 30, 31, 42, 108, 109, 110, 111, 112, 131, 137; *Gaze*, 137, *138*; *Moses und Aron*, 101; *Transfigured Night*, 112
Schoenberg, Mathilde, 137
Seagram building, 88, *89*
Sejima, Kazuyo, *70*
Serrano, Andres, 146; *Piss Christ*, 41, 145
Shakespeare, William: *Hamlet*, 50, 84; *King Lear*, 51; *Othello*, 49–51, 56, 57, 187; *Titus Andronicus*, 8, 157, 158; *Twelfth Night*, 112; *The Winter's Tale*, 181
Shalamov, Varlam: *Kolyma Tales*, 15, 55
Shepley, Rutan and Coolidge, *82*
Shklovsky, Victor, 8–9, 43
shock effects, 3, 14, 142
Six, Tom: *The Human Centipede*, 166–67
Slade, David: *Hard Candy*, 44
Solondz, Todd: *Happiness*, 161, 170
sonata form, 23–25, 105
Sons of Anarchy, 158
Spiegelman, Art: *Maus*, 37
Spielberg, Steven: *Schindler's List*, 164, 167
Spitzer, Leo, 44
Stanford family tomb, 59, *60*
Stanford University: Inner Quad, 81–82, *82*; Law School dormitories, *83*
Stein, Gertrude: "Susie Asado," 31
Stevenson, Robert Louis: *Dr. Jekyll and Mr. Hyde*, 99
Stoker, Bram: *Dracula*, 99
Strauss, Richard: *Salome*, 4, 10
Stravinsky, 42, 94, 108, 111, 112; *Rite of Spring*, 30
sublime, 16, 18, 20, 64, 65, 140
Sullivan, Louis, 59, 64, 91
Suvero, Mark di: *Huru*, *139*, 139–40, 141
Swift, Jonathan: "The Lady's Dressing Room," 6
systematism, 18

Taj Mahal, 59, 64, 91
Takashi, Miike, 158; *Audition*, 168
Tarantino, Quentin: *Django Unchained*, 173–74; *From Dusk Till Dawn*, 173; *Hostel*, 162
Taymor, Julie: *Titus*, 158, 162
Thomas, Michael Tilson, 25
Tolamacheva, Katya: *Barbed Wire and Building*, 66
Tolstoy, Leo, 114
tonal system, 24, 102, 104, 109
total aesthetic effect, 3
Trakl, Georg, 182; *Sebastian im Traum*, 73

Trier, Lars von, 155, 158, 168–69; *Antichrist*, 169, 170, 175; *Dogville*, 169
Trump Tower, 91
Tudor, David, 28

Uffizi, 12, 13
U.S. Holocaust Museum, 87

van Fossen, Theodore, 92
Varèse, Edgar: *Déserts*, 102
Vargas Llosa, Mario, 181; *Elogio de la madrastra*, 180; *Los cuadernos de don Rigoberto*, 180
Varo, Remedios, 131
Velazquez, Diego, 122, 124; *Las Meninas*, 121, 123; *Surrender at Breda*, 141
Vogel, Fred: *August Underground*, 172
vulgar art, 5

Wagner, Richard, 33, 94; *Der Ring des Nibelungen*, 100–101; *The Flying Dutchman*, 99; *Parsifal*, 99; his influence on *Pelléas*, 99; *Tristan und Isolde*, 131
Wainwright family, 59
Walking Dead, 14
Warhol, Andy: *Brillo-Box*, 34
West, Benjamin: *Death of General Wolfe*, 141
Whitney Museum: "Abject Art: Repulsion and Desire in American Art," 6
Wilde, Oscar: *Dorian Gray*, 99; *Salome*, 10
Wilson, Robert: *The Black Rider*, 110
Wordsworth, William, 182; "Tintern Abbey," 22
World Trade Center, 86
Wright, Frank Lloyd, 62, 74, 88, 91; Fallingwater house, 67, 75; Guggenheim, 75; Hanna house (Honeycomb house), 75, 76, 83; leaky roofs, 71; Oak Park houses, 75; his influence on "Rush Creek," 92; Taliesin West, 75; Usonian style, 92

Yang, Jerry, 84
Yeats, William Butler, 34; "Leda and the Swan," 56

Zappa, Frank, 110–11
Zarchi, Meir: *I Spit on Your Grave*, 171, 172, 174
Zeiki, Semir, 35
zoos, 66–67